Praise for *Walk Away to Win*

From my time in college football to my work in television with colleagues on a shared goal, what stands out is the imperative to build one another up, to be good teammates. In *Walk Away to Win*, Megan Carle promotes a positive culture that gives a workforce its best chance at being a successful team, beginning with a shared respect for one another.

— **Kenny Mayne**, broadcaster and founder of runfreely.org

In *Walk Away to Win*, Megan Carle offers first and foremost unique and user-friendly strategies for recognizing and managing workplace bullying. She lays out practical, actionable ways to deal with this toxic behavior, whether the reader is the target, a colleague who witnesses it, or a leader at the company where it occurs. Great recommended reading for anyone encountering bullying behavior that is negatively impacting their career.

— **Deanna Oppenheimer**, Chair, IHG Hotels & Resorts

In *Walk Away to Win*, Megan Carle shares just how costly bullying is to people, teams, and organizations. Full of engaging stories, this is a great book to coach people on bullying, inclusion, and belonging.

— **Christine Porath, PhD**, author of *Mastering Community* and *Mastering Civility* and coauthor of *The Cost of Bad Behavior*

The fact that someone as honorable, intelligent, and hardworking as Megan Carle has written a book about workplace bullying got my attention. In *Walk Away to Win*, Carle tells her story, offering emotional and professional validation for countless others who haven't had the strength to talk about their own experiences. Her ability to nurture, protect, and mentor is evident on every page. A coach's daughter (and total badass) who thrived in a man's world, she is the perfect person to tell this tale. *Walk Away to Win* is the ultimate look at how to overcome adversity; I can't recommend it enough.

— **Matthew Del Negro**, actor and author of *10,000 NOs*

With this mighty little book, Megan Carle demonstrates what being brave looks like, and why it doesn't mean being without fear as the word "fearless" suggests. *Walk Away to Win* reminds readers that having the courage to do what scares us, while remaining human in the process—no matter how many times work may try to knock the human out of us—is the key to not only surviving, but thriving, in the workplace and in life. I have a single tattoo on my left wrist that reads *I got you*. Carle's book is confirmation that these three words must be tattooed, not necessarily on our bodies in ink, but certainly in our brains and in our hearts. Get this book.

— **Jennifer Pastiloff**, bestselling author of *On Being Human*

As someone who has personally experienced, explored, and written about the Hollywood version of workplace bullying, I was drawn to the insights in Megan Carle's book. What I quickly discovered was that Megan knows of what she writes. Even more importantly, she redefines the concept of "winning" in such a situation as reclaiming oneself. *Walk Away to Win* is a timely and important book that should be required reading across industries.

    —**Naomi McDougall Jones**, award-winning filmmaker and author of *The Wrong Kind of Women: Inside Our Revolution to Dismantle the Gods of Hollywood*

There is nothing more defeating to employees than to see a true leader mistreated by their organization. Megan Carle is one of the greatest managers and coworkers with whom you could have the great fortune to intersect. While she was publicly mistreated at the brand she devoted her life to, *Walk Away to Win* is the perfect illustration of Megan's style: taking the tough steps to better the rest of us. Anyone who wants to learn how to be a better leader, starting today, needs to read this book.

    —**Phil Cook**, Chief Marketing Officer, Women's National Basketball Association

My sister tells this story about me protecting her from some neighborhood tough guys when we were kids. She says I stepped in front of her, and told the juvenile delinquents, "Don't mess with my sister." They listened. I wasn't there to protect my sister when she got bullied for real in the workplace. She alluded to it, but I never truly listened. She had accomplished so much in life, and she had already taken its biggest punch. She was my Superwoman. She still is, but now for reasons you will all understand when you read *Walk Away to Win.*

    —**Neil Everett**, coanchor, ESPN SportsCenter

Megan Carle's book, *Walk Away to Win*, is *the* catalyst for an eye-opening conversation; not only about the marginalization of women in big business but also about the majesty of a woman's grit when it comes to navigating, surviving, and thriving amid the predatory challenges of workplace bullying. As an expert in narcissism, I am keenly aware of the damaging impact on those dealing with pathological bullying and toxic environments. Megan brings illuminating experience to this must-read playbook, capturing the bully construct so clearly and creatively. She escorts her reader through a rich and robust conceptual framework of workplace bullying with clarity, guiding you toward hope, reclaiming your voice, and resuscitating your right to sanity and success. For anyone dealing with, or recovering from, the chaos, self-doubts, and subjugation generated by the toxicity of workplace bullying, this book is an essential resource for your personal library.

    —**Wendy Behary**, LCSW/psychotherapist and author of *Disarming the Narcissist*

With her book, *Walk Away to Win*, Megan Carle has crafted a masterpiece about workplace bullying, including the specific choices targets and witnesses can make to take back their zest for work and life. Until all organizations have processes in place that ensure competent, equitable, mature, and decent managers and leaders are vetted, selected, and evaluated—in order to assure thriving workplace cultures are built and maintained—Megan's book will be a required, slam-dunk tool to help readers navigate and transcend toxic workplace cultures.

    —**Matt Paknis**, author of *Successful Leaders Aren't Bullies*

WALK AWAY TO WIN

A PLAYBOOK TO COMBAT WORKPLACE BULLYING

MEGAN CARLE

Mc
Graw
Hill

NEW YORK   CHICAGO   SAN FRANCISCO   ATHENS   LONDON
MADRID   MEXICO CITY   MILAN   NEW DELHI
SINGAPORE   SYDNEY   TORONTO

1 2 3 4 5 6 7 8 9   LCR   28 27 26 25 24 23

ISBN   978-1-264-94963-2
MHID   1-264-94963-4

e-ISBN   978-1-264-95012-6
e-MHID   1-264-95012-8

Library of Congress Cataloging-in-Publication Data

Names: Carle, Megan, author.
Title: Walk away to win : a playbook to combat workplace bullying / Megan Carle.
Description: New York : McGraw Hill, 2023. | Includes bibliographical references and index.
Identifiers: LCCN 2022059890 (print) | LCCN 2022059891 (ebook) | ISBN 9781264949632 (hardback) | ISBN 9781264950126 (ebook)
Subjects: LCSH: Bullying in the workplace. | Conflict management. | Violence in the workplace. | Organizational sociology.
Classification: LCC HF5549.5.B84 C37 2023 (print) | LCC HF5549.5.B84 (ebook) | DDC 658.3/8—dc23/eng/20230109
LC record available at https://lccn.loc.gov/2022059890
LC ebook record available at https://lccn.loc.gov/2022059891

McGraw Hill books are available at special quantity discounts to use as premiums and sales promotions or for use in corporate training programs. To contact a representative, please visit the Contact Us pages at www.mhprofessional.com.

McGraw Hill is committed to making our products accessible to all learners. To learn more about the available support and accommodations we offer, please contact us at accessibility@mheducation.com. We also participate in the Access Text Network (www.accesstext.org), and ATN members may submit requests through ATN.

To Jackie and Spencer,
who told me to stand up for myself,
and to keep standing up for myself.

To Mom,
who taught me how.

And, to Chris,
who helped me find the words.

Contents

Part III: STUDY
The Xs and Os of Workplace Bullying

Part IV: IDENTIFY
Bullying in the Wild

Part V: NAVIGATE
The Bully Culture

Let Me Prey

The Workplace Bully's Manifesto

You've never read anything like this because I've never written anything
   like this.
I operate quietly, on a "no need to know" basis.
Silence is my ally; you know, "Leave no trace."
I'm the backpacker of belittling.
The Navy SEAL of making people in the office feel inferior.
Get in, get out, get the job done under the cover of darkness,
The darkness of gender, of power, of "the way it's always been."
The darkness of numbers, which always favors me.
The darkness of "Don't tell or you'll be seen as weak."
The darkness of "If you do tell, nobody will believe you,"
In part because the higher-up you'll seek justice from is—surprise!—me.
A regular-looking/dressing/talking hipster who controls the narrative.
I'm like plain M&Ms left in the sun: tough on the outside, a chocolate
   mess of insecurity on the inside.
Deep down, I know I'm in over my head.
I know I got this far not because of what I know but who I know.
Who I tee it up, guest-suite it up, and strip-club it up with.
I know you're smarter, more imaginative, and more courageous than me.
And deep down, that's what fuels my quiet rage:
I know I'm a Lie and you're the Truth.

So in my desperation, I create chaos to hide my ineffectiveness.
I start the fire, report it to the authorities, and show up on Twitter
With a headline that says, "Look at me, I saved the forest."
I talk teamwork but prefer a three-on-one fast break—
With you as the "one."
When it comes to targets, I am an equal opportunity bully.
Fast, slow, big, small, women, men, they, and them.
I exploit you all.
Power and fear are my oxygen.
Black, Brown, White, and all shades in between.
I make you feel small. So small, you disappear.
Heck, I can't even be bothered to get your name or your pronoun right.
From Fortune 500 companies to six-person startups—
Makes no difference to me because the bottom line is me.
Seeing you succeed amplifies my feelings of failure.
Seeing you happy reminds me of my own misery.
So I blow up whatever bridges I can see you're about to cross.
I believe in the magic of demeaning, devaluing, and dehumanizing.
I believe in screaming, a smack on the ass, and a creepy whisper.
I believe in scare tactics, paralyzing humiliation, and shock value.
I believe in manipulation, exploitation, and Machiavelli.
In short, I believe empathy and vulnerability are for losers.
I jerk you around. I yank your chain. I reschedule the meeting. Over
    and over.
I care more about the order of your PowerPoint slides than the message
    you're delivering.
I get others to talk behind your back
So you'll start to feel the target on your back.
Deceit is my face paint.
I believe bullying is a professional sport.
I believe bullying is therapy.
I believe bullying is a noble means to a me-me-me end.
I believe your pain is my gain.

I believe in threatening and rethreatening, but always under the cover of
  darkness.
Remember? Leave no trace.
I believe in the hunt.

I am a workplace bully.

So bow your head and let me prey.

Author's Note

I n October 2016, I bid farewell to Nike with a one-on-one goodbye to cofounder Phil Knight, at which I thanked him profusely and tiptoed around the real reason I was leaving. Eighteen months later, a former colleague invited me to lunch.

The invitation came soon after the *New York Times* had published its bombshell front-page story headlined "At Nike, Revolt Led by Women Leads to Exodus of Male Executives." At least six men, several of whom had been involved in the mishandling of my situation, had been removed from the company or were said to be leaving.

Said the *Times*:

> Women were made to feel marginalized in meetings and were passed over for promotions. They were largely excluded from crucial divisions like basketball. When they complained to human resources, they said, they saw little or no evidence that bad behavior was being penalized.
>
> Finally, fed up, a group of women inside Nike's Beaverton, Ore., headquarters started a small revolt.
>
> Covertly, they surveyed their female peers, inquiring whether they had been the victim of sexual harassment and gender discrimination. Their findings set off an upheaval in the executive ranks of the world's largest sports footwear and apparel company.*

---

*Julie Creswell, Kevin Draper, and Rachel Abrams, "At Nike, Revolt Led by Women Leads to Exodus of Male Executives," *New York Times*, April 28, 2018.

The lunch was at Nike's sprawling world headquarters 20 minutes from where I lived. As we took our seats at one of the many cafes on the plush campus, my friend apologized for hosting me there, concerned for my comfort level. I told her I wouldn't have agreed to the location if I wasn't OK with it.

"What happened here?" I asked gingerly over salmon salads in the Deschutes Café.

"Well, Meegs, you left," she said. "And we knew that it wasn't to go 'take care of your kids.'"

My salad was suddenly lodged in my throat.

"You know the 'dissident female group' that you've read about in the paper?" she said. "That's me."

Geezus, I thought, I'm sitting across from Deep Throat.

I raised my eyebrows at her, having had no idea she was part of the group that developed a survey, fed it to dozens of female colleagues, and took the findings—rampant sexual harassment, sexism, and bullying—to Nike's CEO.

"Megan, your leaving had a ripple effect on the organization, and then a bunch of other women left, and those of us who remained sort of looked at each other and said, 'What the fuck do we do now?' So we took matters into our own hands, crafted our own simple questionnaire, and the result is what you're reading about in the paper."

I looked at her, stunned. But *seen*.

"I want to thank you for inviting me here and telling me your story," I said. "Most of all, I want to thank you for what you did. You showed such courage."

"Meegs, it didn't feel courageous at the time, just necessary. I wanted you to know that your leaving was not in vain. We did not forget you. We organized, in part, because of you. So I invited you here today to thank you. You were the match that lit the fuse that blew up the toxic executive leadership here."

That may have been an overstatement or oversimplification, but for someone who'd been made to feel so small and insignificant in the final days of a nearly 30-year career at a place I had loved and given my all to, the words were salve to my wound. Perhaps I would finally be able to find meaning in all of it—the workplace bullying I experienced, the betrayal of the company I'd served with undying allegiance, the executives I thought I could trust, who turned their backs when I asked for help.

By the time I'd said goodbye to Nike, the key people I reported to didn't see me at all. And frankly, I no longer saw myself. When I looked in the mirror, it was blank.

Nothing. Invisible.

What happened?

Who am I?

Where am I?

And what can I be?

Over the subsequent months, I wrote this book to be a catalyst for a conversation. I want targets of bullying, leaders, HR professionals, allies, and even workplace bullies themselves to gain not only a new understanding of bullying in the workplace, but also, and perhaps more important, an appreciation for the ingredients that make up a healthy workplace culture.

There may be stories in this book that sound familiar to you because you are going through something similar. While all the stories in this book are based on true events, some of the stories are composites of experiences, and to protect people's identities, some company and individual names have been changed. Additionally, in describing my own experience as a Nike employee, I did not intend, nor should it be construed, to disparage, defame, and/or malign Nike's products or services. To the contrary: I always took great pride in knowing that I was part of a team that produced world-class products and provided first-class services. I continue to believe Nike's products and services are some of the best in the market. My observations are limited to what can happen to workplace culture when it becomes unhealthy. Finally, to the extent there is dialogue in this book, no conversations were recorded. My experiences and conversations left an indelible impression on me, and in sharing my memory of them, I am confident they will be of help to you as well.

I hope that my story and the story of others shared with me through interviews provide you with guidance, whether you are being bullied, witnessing others being bullied, or leading an organization in which work-place culture and, specifically, workplace bullying are seen as important subjects to discuss. This book is only the beginning of an ever-evolving conversation about how we can do better and, ultimately, be better.

Music is such an important part of our lives. It has the power to help us process powerful feelings. For me, before I had written one word, I made a *Walk Away to Win* playlist. I thought of it as my own pregame hype music I guess, but more than that, I knew if I could feel what I had experienced through music, I might have a shot at healing. If you too need motivation, permission, or an invitation to work through what we collectively have experienced or are experiencing in the workplace, go ahead and press play.

https://open.spotify.com/playlist/WATW

Prologue

The meeting in Paris was to begin in five minutes.

As Nike's new vice president/general manager in charge of basketball for North America, I was about to be introduced by my new boss to my new global teammates. I was like an athlete pumped up for a game, less nervous than focused.

With this role, anything and everything having to do with basketball in North America—Nike basketball's largest revenue generator—would be the responsibility of my team and me: sales, merchandising, retail, brand, operations. The whole enchilada.

I was in my element; basketball was in my DNA. As a coach's kid, I ate, drank, and slept basketball growing up, so this felt like coming home.

The global basketball team had tied this gathering to an event called "Quai 54"—a world streetball tournament held at the Trocadero in Paris, with the Eiffel Tower looming overhead. More than 20,000 fans screamed, clapped, and cheered on as a "salad bowl" of talent—ten nations—competed in five-on-five basketball games under the banner that read, "Bring Your Game, Not Your Name." Special guests Scottie Pippen and Carmelo Anthony judged the slam-dunk contest, and hip-hop artist French Montana closed out the evening.

I was in heaven as I watched what the players and the fans—*consumers*—were wearing, reacting to, and experiencing.

Afterward, I and the other executives convened to a conference room in our nearby hotel for our corporate strategic review sessions.

No meeting was more important than the first one. My new boss, whose previous position I was filling, had become global vice president of basketball. He welcomed everyone. I breathed in deeply, ready for him to introduce me to the team I'd be joining.

Only he didn't.

Bosses and "Ballers"

There's God. There's Phil Knight. And rounding out the trifecta, there's Bruce Springsteen, whom I'd never refer to as "The Boss." That title belongs to Mr. Knight. Never "Phil." But "Mr. Knight," out of respect.

I mention Mr. Knight at the outset because I am deeply grateful for his trailblazing spirit that led to the founding of the company that saved my life. For his drive that wouldn't let him quit even when the company, in its early years, was struggling to survive. And for my getting to be a part of it all.

All in all, I spent nearly 30 years as a Nike executive, ascending to leadership positions in Europe and North America no woman had held before. Mr. Knight had provided the opportunity, and my family had provided the toughness I'd needed not only to survive in a male-dominated company, but to thrive, to lead. Growing up in a household full of boys, led by a strong, principled male and a steady, loving female, I had learned how to hang with the boys and not complain. I also had always been expected to have a voice at the table and elsewhere. As a tomboy, that included rough-and-tumble basketball games in our driveway, the will to fight through the toughest screen, and the confidence to stand up for myself.

My stepfather, Dave Robertson, was a high school basketball coach—among the state of Washington's best—and I was raised in the game. Basketball wasn't just something we played. Basketball was our life. It was who we were. As for who I would become, it was my mom who taught me that no dream was too big, a written inspiration to me from one of our favorite books, *The Little Prince*: "You alone will have stars as no one else has them."

For most of my Nike career, that toughness and tenacity served me well.

And yet, over the course of my last several years as one of the top executives at Nike, I was the target of workplace bullying. I eventually decided to leave the company because of the emotional and physical effects inflicted by bullying behaviors.

In Paris, I was ready to contribute. I was ready to implement my team-first approach to this part of the business. This role was everything to me; I was being recognized. All the work I'd put into the company, including my previous role as the vice president/general manager of the Western European running division, was being acknowledged. My philosophy of "head down, bust your butt, and the work will speak for itself" had paid off. So, yes, I was feeling grateful—as if I had arrived.

My new boss stood up. He greeted my colleagues from around the world. The moment had come for him to introduce me. But he moved on without even saying my name. No name. No nod. No nothing.

Because I'd been at Nike for more than a quarter of a century, I knew many of the people in the room, but still it bothered me. *Strange way to start a relationship.* I would never not introduce the new person, whether the setting was in a meeting room, around a conference table, or at any other gathering. Introductions are important. I learned this early on when my dad taught me that offering a firm handshake, making eye contact, and clearly stating one's name can be the most important ingredients of any business meeting.

Introductions connect us to each other. They imply an endorsement of sorts. In this case, an introduction would have said: "I respect and trust this person. I'm confident you will too."

On the other hand, it seemed like a minor thing, right? A lot was going on. We were in a foreign city, and we were processing a variety of new information; in short, there were a lot of moving parts. So I told myself: "Don't overthink the oversight; just move on." Perhaps my new boss was taking the "bring your game, not your name" theme literally.

In the years since, I've learned a great deal about workplace bullying. Like the fact that not introducing a new team member may be a red flag to a subtle bullying tactic that is often misdiagnosed as a lack of manners.

I've talked to many of the few experts on the topic. I've read, watched, and listened to deep analysis of the subject.

I've also met and spoken to countless targets of bullying from multiple companies, at various levels and positions. These people were strong, successful, powerful, creative, and great at their jobs, but nonetheless were targeted by workplace bullies. Through my work, these employees have sought me out to tell their stories, hoping to learn how to stop the bullying and how to process the trauma they've suffered.

I've come to understand what to do about workplace bullying. I've learned its causes, the devastating consequences for both targets and organizations, and most important the most effective responses and courses of action for targets, allies, and leaders.

This book is about workplace bullying, as seen through the eyes of myriad targets. It is divided into these parts:

- Part I is devoted to *recognizing* workplace bullying. Think of it as the fundamentals of workplace bullying.
- Part II is dedicated to *understanding* the cultural context in which workplace bullying thrives. The big picture that will help you better understand bullying.
- Part III is an opportunity to study different scenarios of workplace bullying *using a game film approach*.
- Part IV focuses on *identifying* bullying in the wild through real-life workplace bullying examples. The different ways bullying shows up.
- Part V will help targets in *navigating* and moving on from workplace bullying, whether that means staying in your role or walking away.
- An Appendix at the end of the book provides a comprehensive *playbook* for targets as an at-a-glance reference.

Think of this book as the what, the why, the where, the when, and the how of workplace bullying so it doesn't ruin you, a colleague, a comrade, or a company.

If you, too, are a target, my story, along with those of others, will help you understand what is happening to you and what you can do about it. It will give you the words and language to use rather than suffer in silence. When you are the target of workplace bullying, you begin to doubt yourself. You start to question your own values and eventually your own sanity. The emotional, physical, and professional consequences are real and can be severe. This book will help you realize that you are not alone. It will help you process what has happened and then take action to end the bullying and to recover.

If you have witnessed workplace bullying, this book will help you understand the significance of what you've experienced and how to be an effective ally.

If you are a leader at any level of a company or organization, this book will help you grasp the ways that bullying happens, the toll it takes on your people and your bottom line, and the actions you should take.

Finally, if you are the bully, this book will help you understand why what you're doing is detrimental not only to the target and to the company, but to you. In other words, the life you save may be your own. (Meanwhile, bravo for having the courage to read this!)

When I left Nike, I thought that workplace bullying was something that had happened just to me. Since then, I've come to understand that workplace bullying happens frequently, that it happens in certain kinds of workplace cultures, and that there are specific strategies and tactics that targets, allies, and leaders can and should use.

It's my fervent hope that this book will help in that effort—and that together we can put an end to workplace bullying.

That night in Paris, as I stared out my hotel window at the Eiffel Tower, it was as if my world had shifted. As if, on this workplace river-rafting trip, the challenge wasn't the water-in-your-face rapids that were all part of the journey for the whole team. Instead, it was as if, downriver, I could hear the pounding of a waterfall.

Try as I might not to, at times I would end up flailing over that water-fall. It would mean questioning my values and doubting myself, not just as an employee, but as a human being on the edge of madness, some might say over the edge—and at my lowest point, putting my family at risk.

And yet it would be my family that would see me through.

PART I

RECOGNIZE

The Fundamentals of Workplace Bullying

When you're raised by a coach, winning puts food on your table.

Winning was the air my brothers and I breathed, the fifth food group. It was winning through effort, hard work, and perseverance. It wasn't winning in a cage-match, sweep-the-knee way. No, we played fair while we beat each other's brains out. And when obstacles appeared, as they did, we worked through them. Like a pick set in basketball, you adjust and fight your way around it.

I still remember the high school basketball game when an opposing player set a pick on me. As I fought around her screen, she shot her knee out directly into my unsuspecting, unprepared quad. It dropped me.

Coach called a time-out. We wrapped up my leg, and although I was struggling, I got back in and played.

At Nike, a muscling-through, working-hard, all-out effort approach boded well for me for a long time. I rose in the ranks. I played, and I won. And then I ran into a pick I couldn't work around. No matter how I adjusted, the knee to the quad got me every time.

That's what workplace bullying feels like.

It drops you.

While behaving like a bully is unthinkable to most people, it's fair to say that bullying is far more common than is generally acknowledged. That's one of the reasons I wrote this book.

In Part I, we'll discuss what bullying looks like—how bullies behave and how to distinguish between bullying and bad behavior. From there, we'll introduce the pros and cons of a number of response options: ignore, resist, comply, and enlist.

Through information and practice, not only will we gain a better understanding of the bullies in our lives, but we will regain control over our own experience.

Let's find our way around the pick.

1

From the Playground to the Boardroom

Bullies [are] scared people hiding inside scary people.

—MICHELLE OBAMA

M y first memory of being bullied was when I was 10.

It was December 1975, a typical winter day in Spokane. Grandpa Mike and I had made the two-block trek to Cannon Hill Park, where I would hit the ice and skate my heart out in my annual performance for my audience of one. On the days I performed for Grandpa Mike, I channeled Peggy Fleming, Dorothy Hamill, and every other great skater I never knew.

I was putting on my best performance ever when suddenly I stopped mid-pirouette. Five girls from my school had surrounded me.

"Is that her?" asked one, pointing at me. "Is that the stuck-up one?"

I turned toward the voice. It was the older sister of a girl I hardly knew. The rest of the girls laughed. "Yes, that's her!"

They giggled before skating off to the far side of the ice.

I was horrified.

It had been such a great day. I had been fearless, attacking the ice, feeling so special and safe. Then, in a blink, my feelings of joy and triumph were undercut. Why would I have even cared about what some girls thought of me? Except I did. Of course, I did. I was 10.

My walk home with Grandpa Mike was quiet.

"What's wrong, Megan Ann?" he asked.

I mumbled something about eating too much candy, being too cold, having sore feet. But he knew. The pond wasn't big enough for him not to have seen and heard what happened.

At school the following week, graffiti littered a once-pristine playground wall. Huge letters shouted out, "MEGAN MORFITT IS STUCK UP." One of the only times in my life that my name had been spelled correctly.

It was in such a location that passing cars could see it as they drove by the playground, only adding to my embarrassment and shame. It took the school janitor almost a week to erase it, first drawing a lame black line through it, as if that would somehow nullify its intent. I was diminished and let down by the place that had been like a second home to me.

Bullying Happens Everywhere

Bullying not only happens at neighborhood ice skating ponds, school playgrounds, and parks—it happens in workplaces as well. It's confusing. It trips us up. It blindsides us. It makes us unsteady on our skates.

When bullied as a child, I fled to the safety of my grandpa. When bullied at work, Dr. Ruth Namie didn't flee. Instead, in 1997, she and her husband, Dr. Gary Namie, founded the Workplace Bullying Institute (WBI).

In the nearly three decades since, workplace bullying has been studied more deeply, but little has been written from the perspective of targets, those who are preyed upon. This book will change that precedent, but first we need to understand the fundamentals of the game.

For starters, just what is bullying? It's not simple rudeness or incivility. It's not healthy debate, creative tension, or a difference of opinion. It's not about being challenged or pushed or having a bad day. And it's not about conflict.

Bullying is about one person dominating another. It's about dehumanizing, degrading, and devaluing targets. It's about power and control.

It's so important to understand that bullying is real, has a name, has perpetrators and targets. Why? Because unless you name it, you can't deal with it. Of the dozens of interviews I did for this book, one was with a 40-something woman who recalled the moment a therapist connected her boss's behavior to bullying. Note the impact it had on the woman after she shared another soul-crushing encounter with a boss who'd gone from ally to enemy:

> When I recounted the just-ended meeting to my counselor, and how it made me feel, I remember she turned and looked at me. "You know that's bullying, right?"
>
> I was shocked. What? No, I didn't know that. Bullying was what we talked to our elementary school children about. It happens when kids don't understand how their words hurt others, and cover up their own insecurities about being a big kid, or having no friends, by attacking those they perceive as weak and vulnerable. That doesn't happen in the workplace, certainly not our workplace, where we are all professional adults.
>
> We talked further about it. What I remember from that conversation was the relief I felt hearing her name the behavior, name what was happening to me, and recognize it as professional opinion. That it wasn't just me not being able to handle a difficult, diminishing boss. I didn't feel better then; I just felt validated, and maybe a little less crazy, a little bit relieved. I gained a tiny bit of control, in a time in which I felt I had zero agency over my own experience, by giving this a name. Bullying.

The WBI defines workplace bullying as "repeated, health-harming mistreatment by one or more employees of an employee: abusive conduct that takes the form of verbal abuse; or behaviors perceived as threatening, intimidating, or humiliating; work sabotage; or some combination of the above."

Some experts say it goes even further.

"Workplace bullying is psychological violence," says Lynne Curry, author of *Beating the Workplace Bully: A Tactical Guide to Taking Charge.* "A bully is someone who repeatedly and intentionally goes after a target."

And often causes honorable people to feel small. One first-rate leader told me that months after her first "dark meeting" with her once-friendly boss, "I would suddenly feel my entire body stiffen, and feel like I was slowly suffocating under a great weight on my chest. My usual ease when I was on stage presenting to large groups disappeared; I became very nervous, my voice and hands shook. I began to shorten presentations and limited my stage time whenever I could."

Workplace bullying has affected almost 80 million US workers, according to a WBI survey in 2021. To provide some context, that means one out of every two workers has been affected by workplace bullying. *One out of two.* The survey goes on to highlight that 67 percent of workplace bullies are men, and their preferred targets are women. The preferred targets of female bullies are also women. Although one in three employees reports workplace bullying, workplace bullying remains "the undiscussable," says the WBI.

So let's discuss it.

Let's discuss this thing that can be so subtle, like the frog in the kettle that doesn't know it's being boiled to death.

Workplace bullying is about the beatdown that happens in a thousand large and small moments.

It can come straight at you and hit you between the eyes, and it can be so nuanced—a strategic approach by bullies whose sole purpose is to cause the target to feel self-doubt in a slow and steady build. As Dr. Gary Namie said, "Workplace bullying is a systematic laser-focused campaign of interpersonal destruction."

It is predatory, meaning bullies get a thrill out of doing it. Like an animal on the hunt, bullies enjoy causing damage to others, because they can. Bullies are sneaky, opportunistic, and controlling.

Workplace bullying changes lives. It instills doubt in people who are confident and competent. It freezes clear-minded, goal-oriented, visionary leaders in a fog of self-doubt, unable to move forward, backward, or sideways.

Bullying can be subtle. And bullying can be dramatic.

"I got a one-sided, vitriolic spew," one target told me, saying she then went to her car in a fog. "I was sitting in the driver's seat. I could drive away. But turning on the car and driving would mean I would have to focus on driving, and right then, I couldn't focus on anything. I wanted to cry, but tears didn't come. Instead, I felt a crushing weight all around me. I couldn't breathe well. I didn't move. Time stopped."

Bullying leads to the loss of talent. Because the targets of bullying can be at literally any level of the organization, this loss of talent occurs across the entire breadth of any company that tolerates or enables bullying. Bullying forces targets to leave organizations in which they're still contributing at a high level with plenty of runway ahead.

It brings their immediate earning power and their confidence to an abrupt halt. Not only that; it affects the organization as a whole by harming morale for bystanders, witnesses, and allies. All while the status-seeking bully stays and thrives.

Bullying manifests itself in myriad ways. The targets are usually, but not always, women. The tactics are often, but not always, laced with intimidation. The settings are often, but not always, supervisors finding ways to gaslight people under their supervision. No two stories are alike—and if you're reading this because you believe you've been targeted by a bully or helplessly watched others being bullied, I'm betting you'll relate to one or more of the following real-life stories we'll discuss:

- The 6'4" woman who always wore heels—"I can do locker room, and I'm always going to compete"—and yet was reduced to a mere shadow of her former self after years of belittling and humiliation by a colleague. "Why," she asked, "did I shrink?"

- The employee who was berated in front of others at a meeting and was headed into the bathroom to splash water on her face when she felt it: her bully, with a creepy smile on his face, had slapped her across the ass.
- The confident, up-and-coming young man whose boss began bullying him over a single glitch in a spreadsheet and was joined by other managers in what's called "mobbing." "The bully set my reputation before I even had a chance to," he said. "I lost all sense of who I was."
- The bully's right-hand person who wasn't even the target, but a witness to the person being targeted, who suffered so much anxiety over the repeated offenses that she stopped sleeping, lost weight, and began to throw up before work each day.
- The manager who watched her boss turn from ally to enemy, castigating her in one-on-one meetings so viciously that it led her to seriously consider which highway barrier she could hit to ensure certain death while not hurting anyone else.
- And a top executive who, after decades of all-for-one camaraderie, found herself targeted by an all-new toxicity that went well beyond the no-intro, hung-out-to-dry experience at her first basketball meeting in Paris. That's me, of course.

The stories go on and on, each substantiating a growing problem in workplaces across America. A problem that we can no longer ignore. A problem we need to stare down like the monsters under our beds.

Bullying Is Not Simple

First, however, it's important to distinguish between sexual harassment and bullying in the workplace. The Equal Employment Opportunity Commission defines sexual harassment as "unwelcome sexual advances, request for sexual favors, and other verbal and physical conduct of a physical nature." It takes on many different forms, including sexual assault; unwanted sexual looks, letters, or materials; whistling; or telling sexual jokes. "Unwelcome" is defined by the target.

While there can be a sexual or physical component to workplace bullying, often there is not. Instead, the definition is somewhat vague: "persistent health-harming mistreatment." It is a form of abuse that is not readily defined as taboo. In fact, many companies and organizations consider it a normal business practice.

As if workplace bullying isn't "slippery" enough, it—unlike sexual harassment—is not illegal. But if not actionable in court, there is nothing preventing employers from instituting policies prohibiting workplace bullying conduct.

By now, you're probably starting to understand why workplace bullying isn't talked about more: in part, because it's *not simple.*

So let's try to simplify the complex.

Bullying is either public or private. It is either overt or covert. (See Figure 1.1.)

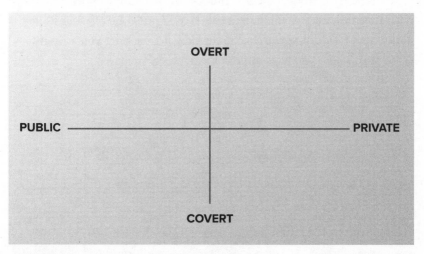

FIGURE 1.1 Bullying can be overt or covert and public or private.

Overt bullying behavior is obvious. It's yelling, banging on a table, aggressive, threatening behavior.

Covert bullying behavior is hidden, nuanced, subtle. It's quiet and confusing, at times delivered in one-on-one meetings like one that leveled one woman I interviewed.

She told me: "On stage, or in front of a large group, my manager was jovial, casual, curious. In larger meetings when more senior leaders were on stage, he was always the first to raise his hand to ask a question."

But in private, he ripped her so badly, she said, that "I felt my face turn hot, I felt like my body was slowly melting off my bones, and my bones would not hold me if I tried to stand up. At some point I heard him change the subject and say that he expected more from me at staff meetings, and that I was clearly disengaged and disrespectful; I should not be looking at my iPad during the meetings. He dismissed my now probably tiny voice reminding him that that's how I take my notes; I don't use paper."

Public bullying is witnessed by others.

Private bullying is witnessed by only the bully and the target.

In Part III, "Study: The Xs and Os of Workplace Bullying," I will deep-dive into each of the bully types (see Figure 1.2), offering strategies and scripts for dealing with each. For now, let me offer you a thumbnail sketch by type so you have some context.

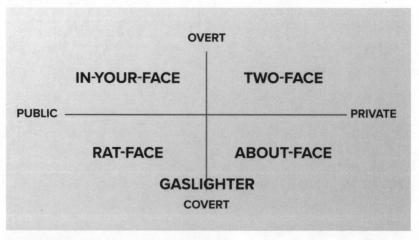

FIGURE 1.2 The five bullying types.

The In-Your-Face (IYF)

The public/overt bully's sole purpose is to denigrate someone in a public setting. The IYF bullies want witnesses. They want everyone to know that they're in power; they're in charge; they're untouchable. In the horror movie, they're the axe-wielding monsters we see coming at the target. Think *Texas Chainsaw Massacre* or *Nightmare on Elm Street*. In the workplace, they're the managers who yell, bang the table, point the finger.

The Rat-Face (RF)

The public/covert bully lives to trip you up. This bully's name is taken from an American slang term that I first heard when I was 11 and my mom took me to the movie *All the President's Men*. I learned that "rat-f*#king" was a way to create confusion. In the workplace, RF bullies play dirty, sabotage your work, and can be easy to spot because they're the ones who like to laugh at other people's expense. Like the IYFs, they want you to know they're in power; they're in charge and can be particularly gnarly in attaining and keeping that power. Unlike the IYFs, though, they're sly and sneaky; they want to keep targets and everyone else guessing. Their favorite move is to set their target up for a fall. In the horror movie, they're not wielding the axe; they're just tossing it up and down, like a baseball, while staring at the target. The Joker (from *Batman*) comes to mind. In the workplace, RFs are the managers who intentionally mispronounce your name, plant their operatives on your team, and look at their phone and laugh while glancing at you.

The Two-Face (TF)

The private/overt bully is first-team "all you" in public but humiliates and diminishes you in private. Like the IYF and RF bullies, TF bullies want you to know they're in power; they're in charge, but their beatdown will happen in private, after singing the target's praises in public. In the horror movie, they are the literal backstabbers—all smiles and accolades to the target's face, while standing at the ready to strike in private. Think *Scream.* (*Spoiler alert:* The smiley friend did it.) In the workplace, they're the managers who tell anyone and everyone what a great job you're doing and, in private, cut you down with biting, demeaning language.

The About-Face (AF)

The private/covert bully is a special breed of bully, so named because just when the AF seems to be heading one way, this brand of bully will abruptly pull a 180. Tough to put your finger on, the passive-aggressiveness of the AF is nuanced, subtle, hidden in the shadows. AF bullies are particularly gifted at making you believe they are your friend when they're simply using you and the information you share with them to direct their desired narrative, while advancing their own agenda and interests. They want you to *think* they have no power, bullying from the sidelines, often with what they don't say and don't do. In the horror movie, they show you the axe and say, "I wonder whose axe that is," as you notice their initials branded into the handle. Think *Get Out* for a brilliantly creepy example of the AF. In the workplace, AFs are the passive-aggressive managers who change the time and/or location of the meeting without letting you know, feigning innocence or pretending not to hear you when you ask them about it. They ask you about your meeting when they've already been updated about it from their precisely placed operatives.

Gaslighters—the Fifth Type

Within the covert bullying family is a particularly disturbing kind of bully, the Gaslighter, that lands somewhere between the Rat-Face and the About-Face. Gaslighters, whose name comes from the 1944 film *Gaslight*, starring Ingrid Bergman as the target, overachieve in their ability to trick and deceive targets. Gaslighters are the ultimate at head games. In the movie, Bergman's husband/bully hides things from her and then makes her believe she has lost them. He turns what she knows as fact into fiction, plants false gossip and, in doing so, defines her reality. He creates an audible assault by stomping around in the forbidden upstairs of the house, making her think she is losing her mind.

Gaslighters want you to know they're in power; they're in charge by keeping you guessing and off balance. In the horror movie, they show you the safe place they've put the axe and then ponder aloud, "I wonder where that axe is?" When you open the cupboard in which they put it, it's gone. They then blame you for it being gone even though you know you've never touched the axe. Dare I remind you of *Single White Female* or *The Hand That Rocks the Cradle* for spot-on, scary examples of gaslighting? In the workplace, gaslighting is done by the managers who sabotage your work, ask you for information you've already given them, move meetings, and then ask, "Where have you been?"

One target I interviewed said she knew the chain of command had turned into this particularly toxic form of bullying when:

> You're required to provide weekly reporting with high-value news, results, challenges. The chain of command harasses and badgers managers for submissions which you file on time, complete, consistently. In turn, your submission receives no comment, feedback, or inquiry. Almost as if no one ever read it. Further, you are not deemed senior enough to receive the completed, aggregated report so that you can see if you were edited, nor can you see what your peers submit. You are literally being hounded and treated like you're an irresponsible fourth grader who can't turn your homework in on time, when in fact you're actually a 30+-year executive, in a vice presidential role, running a $2 billion business.

Fun fact? Workplace bullies can be one type, several types, or all types. In other words, one day a target might be contending with an In-Your-Face, and the next day or, better yet, later in the same day, that same bully shows up as a Rat-Face. The common theme? Power and control. Either real or imagined.

Targets are left unsteady, unsafe, and uncertain about which technique is going to come at them next. The cumulative effect of the constant bullying assault is debilitating, paralyzing, and frightening, making the targets feel as if they are disappearing. Targets end up feeling confused, crazy, and responsible for their own deterioration. Because of bullying, I've seen once-confident people start to doubt their capabilities—one in particular stared back at me in the mirror.

At the park that day in Spokane so long ago, I experienced In-Your-Face bullying in a very typical way—name-calling. In today's culture, being called "stuck up" would be like leaving someone open on Snapchat, not following someone back on Instagram, or negatively referring to someone as a "bitch." Graffiti on the school playground? Classic Rat-Face at work. It was a public display meant to trip me up.

And it did—even if the grown-up version I'd later face would make it pale by comparison.

DRILLS

- To recognize workplace bullying, start observing what is going on at work. What is going on with you, to you, and around you?
- Is there an overall climate of fear and intimidation?
- Are the values of the organization you joined being bent to accommodate misbehavior or overlooked completely?
- Does everything run through a singular filter—the bully?
- How are others feeling? Most important—how are *you* feeling?
- Have others validated your observations of bullying behavior?

- Gain an understanding of the different types of bullying behavior in the workplace. Have you experienced or witnessed any of the types of bullying described? Spend some time thinking about it. Write down what happened. Identify the bullying behavior you experienced. How did it make you feel?
- What does this mean to your overall health and wellness—psychologically/emotionally—to be able to assess and evaluate what is happening to you? Think about the impact your ability to put language to what is happening to you has on you.

2

What Bullying Isn't

I'm very gentle and really sweet,
and if you f*ck with me, I'll mop the floor with you.

—CHER

"CRRRRUNCH."

I heard the sound, but I didn't know where it was coming from. I continued. I was in the zone.

"CRRRRRUNCH."

There it was again. I was doing my best to make eye contact with the six sets of eyes staring at me from around the large conference table, as I balanced a running shoe on my left hand, which I had formed into a kind of tripod.

To have gotten to this point, I had graduated from the University of Oregon, landed and promptly quit a "marketing" job handing out kielbasa at a supermarket, worked for a year as a customer service rep at Nike's distribution center in Wilsonville, Oregon, and beaten out hundreds of applicants to get to the finals for what's called the "EKIN" job. *Everyone* wanted the Portland EKIN job in 1988.

I had already crushed some softball questions about why I'd be the best choice for this coveted technical rep position with its backward spelling of Nike, exclaiming to all that Nike's tech reps, EKINS, know Nike forward and back. I was working my way from the outsole of the shoe, highlighting Bill Bowerman's waffle iron story, how the former University of Oregon track and field coach—and Nike cofounder—had used wife Barbara's breakfast skillet to invent a new rubberized shoe sole. I was killing it as I concisely and confidently made my way beyond the dual-material midsole to the upper. I was the sneaker, and the sneaker was me. And then it happened yet again.

"CRRRRRUNCH!"

I was mid-sentence—" . . . mesh has the added advantage of breathability . . ."—when I finally realized the source: a woman at the head of the table, staring at me as she methodically placed one corn nut after another into her mouth, never taking her eyes off me.

Not just any woman—the biggest business card in the room—*the* decision maker on whether I landed this job was eating Corn Nuts, the noisiest snack ever invented.

I was nearing the end, but she could see that I'd spotted her. She intended for me to see her, to hear her. I paused, held her gaze.

"Hey, um, can we maybe get you a quieter snack? Maybe a yogurt or a Life-Saver?"

Silence. Had I just blown any chance for this coveted position?

All eyes were now on the Corn Nuts cruncher for what seemed like forever.

It started in her eyes. I could see it as it extended to form crinkles that began at the corners, then moved to take over her entire face as she erupted into a full-blown giggle-fested staccato laugh that reminded me of my Grandma Regis. The rest of her table cohorts followed suit, and the whole room was filled with laughter as I blessedly brought my interview "clinic" to a close.

As I left the conference room, I saw the next candidate waiting in the lobby, sitting in the chair I had previously vacated. I gave her a cocksure smile as I swaggered by, noticing that she was wearing an uncomfortable-looking blue interview suit instead of the colorful Nike tracksuit I had chosen that screamed, "I am *the* Portland EKIN!"

I beat out the suits, secured the job, and learned a valuable lesson about the brand I had joined. You had to be on your toes. There would always be a Corn Nuts cruncher in the audience.

Corn Nuts Wasn't the Bully

Would I define crunch-gate as workplace bullying of the Rat-Face persuasion? Nope. But it's important to know what bullying *isn't*, lest you set your bully-o-meter too sensitively and mix up acceptable workplace distractions with the real thing.

Bullying is about a pattern of health-harming mistreatment. There's a persistence to it. Prior to the interview, I had met with Corn Nuts (the name I've dubbed her for this anecdote) for an informational interview about the job for which I had applied. Perhaps it was a good thing that I didn't know who she was. I took everything at face value, starting with her office. Spacious with windows, but what really caught my eye were the archival Nike posters, framed and hung throughout. Stuff I had never seen. She invited me to sit, and her first question was, "So what did you think of France?"

She had taken the time to read the résumé I had sent over prior to our meeting and had taken note of my study abroad. We spent the next several minutes talking about all the things we liked—and the few things we didn't like—about the country. Corn Nuts was gracious and spent an hour talking to me, providing me with tips about the role for which I was interviewing. In other words, Corn Nuts created a safe space for me. She had credits with me, and I believed, I with her. We had built a rapport. Trust points.

With the crunching, Corn Nuts was not threatening me, humiliating me, or harming me. She was testing me. She was introducing me to her Nike. Not dissimilar to the household in which I was raised. "King of the stairs" actually meant "king of the stairs"; everyone else got thrown down the stairs. "Throwing elbows" meant "throwing elbows," or you didn't get the ball. "Playing football" meant "playing football," and sometimes I was the ball!

"On my toes" was part of my childhood makeup.

It's important to be able to spot bullies in the wild. But just because managers challenge you to be better, to be more, to be ready for anything, doesn't mean you're being bullied.

Let's take the same scene but change Corn Nuts's reaction. We'll take it from:

> "Hey, um, can we maybe get you a quieter snack? Maybe a yogurt or a Life-Saver?"
>
> Silence.
>
> All eyes were now on Corn Nuts cruncher for what seemed like forever.
>
> "You think you're all that, do you?" the longest-tenured, most powerful woman in the company snapped at the young woman who was about to go back to handing out kielbasa sausage samples at the local market.
>
> "I don't need your help with my snack selection. Who are you? What makes you think you're so special? What are you, the snack sheriff? You can see yourself out. Don't wait for our call—because it won't come."

The candidate who received the laugh and levity in the first example—yours truly—would go on to have a long, successful career. The interaction with Corn Nuts set a precedent for how I would approach similar situations throughout my career, and Corn Nuts would turn out to be a sponsor and advocate for me.

On the other hand, the candidate who was publicly berated (in the preceding hypothetical example) would never attempt to counter something coming at her in that way again. In fact, she would slowly lose her ability to take any sort of off-script risk or show much of her personality at all. Instead she would constantly second-guess herself, her instincts. Because of that, she would lose a little piece of who she was, how she had been raised, and who she would become. Other leaders would keep her at a distance and let her know that she was firmly on her own, fending for herself.

Unbeknown to me, when I used humor to deflect the disruption that Corn Nuts was causing, I was stress-testing the interaction, attempting to continue to control the room, as the presenter. She responded in kind, giving me the same energy back. She not only laughed; she went on to become one of my biggest champions during my early years at Nike.

Bullying Versus Nonbullying Behavior

Here are five ways to help you differentiate bullying and nonbullying behavior:

- **Bullying elevates one person at the expense of the other.**
  Nonbullying puts people first. For example, "The CEO says" or
  "Get your sh*t together" is not language that puts people first.
- **Bullying singles out a target.** Nonbullying considers that
  everyone is on the same team in a safe space. Instead of embracing
  diversity, ridiculing someone for a difference of opinion, taste, or
  approach does not foster a safe environment.
- **Bullying is relentless attacking.** Nonbullying will challenge,
  push, and partner. When nothing you do pleases the bully, there
  is no collaboration, no partnership; it's all about making sure that
  the bully is happy and that you stay in good favor.
- **Bullying is work sabotage.** Nonbullying is work elevating and
  celebrates the team. Blocking people from work that is clearly

theirs to do and/or taking credit for work done by the team is not
work elevating and does not celebrate the team.

- **Bullying is repeated health-harming mistreatment.**
Nonbullying is healthy competition filled with support and
motivation. Berating an employee for sport on a daily basis is not
an environment of healthy competition filled with support and
motivation. It's stressful and health harming.

At many companies, stress is like air. Like breathing, it's a given and
a part of every day. Employees are peppered with challenges like welter-
weight prizefighters taking punches. Corn Nuts taught me early on that I
had to be on my game at all times—not only for my business, but for my
teammates. They were counting on me, and I had to keep up and deliver.
I was fueled by the responsibility I had toward a cause bigger than myself.

I thrived on all of it—the organized chaos, the constant challenge of
the work, the healthy debate. When I was promoted to lead all of Nike
Women's Merchandising, my new manager challenged me in front of my
teammates, asking difficult questions about the product, assortments,
and financials. Once he left, someone who had witnessed the interaction
asked, "How can you stand that; him peppering you like that?"

"Hey, his questions will make me better. I'd rather have him asking
me those questions than our customers, external to the family."

And that's exactly how I thought of Nike. We were family. No different from the one that raised me. We were there for each other during
good and challenging times; we pushed each other; we teased each other;
we supported each other no matter what.

For me, the results I was helping drive were motivation enough to
not only manage through, but almost welcome the stress that came with
it. Sales goals were surpassed; product was industry defining; market-
places were transformed. I was all in, all the time. And just as I always felt
about my own family growing up, I was grateful to be part of the Nike
family. Few brands were as aspirational in pushing their employees each
and every day. No dream was too big for us, and we proudly carried the

swagger that went along with that. Nike was full of people who wanted the ball when it counted.

Long hours, competitive personalities, and work that can always be better are the norm at many companies. "Better, Bigger, Faster" is the mantra today. For many, it's aligned with their competitive wiring. The stakes are high, and the talent within organizations matches the demands. Imagine an all-star team made up of the cream of the crop, the most competitive people that can be found, all working together. The result is an alpha pack of teammates who have reappropriated their competitive drive from varying levels of sports, military, education, and other experiences and deliver it in a daily siege to attack the business at hand.

It's intoxicating and addictive, and it's one of the most common descriptions that targets of bullying use to explain why they continue to work for an organization in which workplace bullying is taking place. But a highly charged, competitive environment is not *necessarily* a bullying environment. There are crunchers of Corn Nuts and crunchers of people.

They are not one and the same.

DRILLS

- Think about an interaction you've had that, in the hands of a workplace bully, might have turned out very differently. What would it have meant to you? How could it have affected your trajectory?
- What are some reasons you're telling yourself for staying at a workplace in which you are being bullied or witnessing others being bullied?

3

Your Response Options

When someone shows you who they are,
believe them the first time.

—MAYA ANGELOU

What most of us who were targets of bullying have in common is that we didn't know what was happening to us, so we didn't know how to talk about it, much less how to combat it. We didn't recognize what was happening to us as bullying behavior.

When you don't know how to put language to something, it's tough to determine what to do about it. In the absence of language, workplace bullying often doesn't get called out for what it is and therefore remains "the undiscussable."

Not knowing how to describe what is happening to us—and fearing punishment even if we are able to talk about it—often leads us to hide. We play small. Some of us sleep, eat, drink, and pull the covers up over our heads. Some of us get sick. Some of us work harder. Some of us start to believe we're the problem; we *are* incompetent. Some of us fight back. Some of us ask for help. Most don't. Most of us suffer in silence.

Some of us obsess about our bully every minute of every day. We try different approaches to appease the bully, thinking, "Maybe this will work" and "Maybe that will work." Maybe disappearing will work. We think we need to change. Maybe something we, as targets, can do will stop the bullying. After all, we're allowing this to happen to us, right?

Hold up. What was that?

If you take just one thing from this book, it is this:

Being a target of workplace bullying doesn't have anything to do with you.

Shall I say it again for those in the nosebleed seats?

Being a target of workplace bullying doesn't have anything to do with you!

Of course, you're involved, but it's not your fault. You're not *allowing* anything. You didn't *do* anything. You didn't somehow *make* bullying you necessary. No, the bully has found you and targeted you. Once you realize this, accept it, and embrace it, you'll stop trying to figure out how you can disallow the bullying. Why? Because there's no controlling the uncontrollable. No reasoning with the unreasonable. And there's no disallowing something that doesn't have anything to do with you allowing it to happen in the first place. Because you didn't allow it! You became collateral damage when you got in the path of a bully. You're as much to blame as a house is to blame for being ripped away by a tornado.

But if you start to recognize what is happening to you, your own rational thinking can help prepare you for when the bully does what bullies do.

You now know how to recognize bullying—what it is and isn't—and you have a simple framework to spot which type or types of bullying you're experiencing or witnessing (IYF, RF, TF, AF, Gaslighting). So now, what do you do about it? Or do you just try and ignore it? (Short answer: no.)

Equine Therapy to the Rescue

To help you understand your response options, I'm borrowing a framework from a seemingly odd place, a trauma-informed model of equine therapy called Natural Lifemanship (NL) that prioritizes connected relationships and the idea that "a sound principle is a sound principle regardless of where it is applied."

In terms of workplace bullying, as targets, we must stay connected to ourselves and aware of what's coming at us, so we have a shot at applying a sound principle to the experience we're having. This would assume that we have sound principles in our toolbox to apply to a workplace bullying situation once we recognize we've been targeted. Apply sound principles. Sounds easy, right?

It's not. When my bullying came to a head, I didn't have any tools, much less a toolbox. I had a whole lot of angst and shame and confusion. No sound principles in the mix, and I was already so far back on my heels that I had no shot at any sort of response.

Equine therapy is about relationship principles—human to horse—and in our case—bully to target. Bear in mind, I am taking a complex, long-studied neuroscience psychotherapy and simplifying it into four options to add to our "sound principles toolbox" for when a bully strikes. The four options are: ignore, resist, comply, and enlist. Let's walk through them one at a time:

- **IGNORE.** Refuse to engage or take notice, detach, walk away. Instead, stay connected to yourself and self-aware. As a target, your goal is to work the bullying behavior into extinction. If a target ignores a bully, the bully might increase their pressure, but there is a good chance that the bully, tiring of the effort required to hook the target, will move on.
- **RESIST.** Hold your ground; set boundaries; withstand the action; exert force in opposition; counteract. Chances are, if a target resists a bully, the bully may remain at the same level of bullying. When that doesn't work, the bully will up the energy.

It is important for targets to remember to stay connected to themselves, aware, and regulated when resisting a bully. When emotionally dysregulated, the human brain loses its ability to think clearly and logically. Meditation, mindfulness, and movement are some of the ways to build resilience around emotional regulation. A target who is resisting may increase the energy in response, remembering that staying connected and emotionally regulated will yield better results.

- **COMPLY.** Do as you're told. Chances are, if a target complies, the bully will ease up. For the time being. But compliance takes a toll. If we acquiesce to the bully's demands, we become discordant. Simply put, our feelings and desires don't match our behaviors. This creates an incredible amount of stress that can be internalized and thereby unhealthy. We may even see or feel physical symptoms of stress such as rapid breathing, eyes that may widen and tear up, a jaw that tightens, and, for some, anxiety and/or panic attacks. In order to avoid this discomfort, targets may collapse, give up, or dissociate. Though compliance may seem easier in the short term, it can have a lasting and devastating impact on the nervous system.

- **ENLIST.** Mobilize your allies in the workplace to help you. Not only will this provide you with much-needed support, but allies may become witnesses to the bullying behavior.

Now, back to our equine friends and a note about submission. Once a horse is controlled into submission, the horse has been broken. Similarly, once the workplace bully controls a target into submission, the target has been broken.

How does a bully gain such control? Pick your poison:

- Demeaning a target and the target's work
- Forbidding others to talk to or work with the target
- Blocking the target's ability to do his/her/their job
- Excluding the target
- Interfering with, and sabotaging, the target's work

Remember, bullying is about control. The most extreme symbol of this control with a horse is the whip. When the bully increases the bullying behavior and uses a whip on a horse, the horse will do whatever the bully demands. A horse can walk through a whip, but it must understand and believe that its weight, strength, and power can withstand it. If the horse knows that, it will walk through. But at what cost?

You know that saying, "Control what you can control?" Well, here it comes again, because once a bully has targeted you, you've been targeted. Your strength is in knowing what you can control. In knowing you've been targeted, you put yourself on the offense, and you understand the play that is being run at you. You walk through. You *recognize* it. And if possible, you enlist others to help you fight the fight.

You might find yourself thinking: "Something is happening to me at work that is not right. This is bullying behavior. I'm working with an IYF, RF, TF, AF, Gaslighting bully. I'm going to apply my own sound principles (*ignore, resist, comply*) as my guide, and I need help. I also must *enlist* support from others.

Choosing Your Best Response

In basketball, being off balance—on your heels—can ruin you because you end up out of control. Like choosing a principle from our sound principles toolbox, on the court we need to pick our move. Establish and implement our strategy. Imagine, for a minute, that ignore, resist, comply, and enlist are four different basketball moves: say, a skyhook, a three-point shot, a pressing defense, and the deadly zone defense. There's a time and a place for each of these, a time and a place where each will help you and your team advance your cause—i.e., score points and keep the other team from scoring points. Inherent in that, of course, is the idea that none of the concepts is going to work every time or in every situation, but each one holds the possibility of changing the momentum of the game.

The success of each is based on circumstances, among them:

- **TIMING.** If you're in possession of the ball, then it's not pressing defense that you're looking to play at that moment, right? Likewise, in the workplace environment, you must know where you are in the game. Are you on offense? Are you on defense? Is it early in the game? Late in the game? If it's early, your style of play might be *ignore* because you need to test the apparent bully and see if that's really what's happening. Does the person have social credits with you and vice versa? Could the bully be like Corn Nuts cruncher, not pranking you but testing you because she believes in you and wants to sharpen you? If it's late in the game, if you're down big, it's not a time to play conservatively; you may need to fire more three-pointers than you might normally attempt to even things up. Play riskier. Similarly, in the workplace, you may need to *resist*, which can feel risky.

- **YOUR STRENGTHS.** As a young basketball player, I practiced a skyhook. Why? Because I loved it. I loved the ball floating high in the air; it was a graceful shot. Plus, it was Kareem's signature move and looked cool. But come game time, it wasn't a move for someone short like me. My game was to drive and dish or look for a nice mid-range jumper. Likewise, in a bullying environment, you need to play to your strengths. Some people's nature is suited more to *comply*; some are more naturally suited to *resist*. Play to your strength if you believe it can help you get to where you need to be.

- **YOUR OPPONENT'S STRENGTHS.** Is the opposing team a fast-break, run-and-gun type, or does it want to slow down the tempo? If the opposing team's got a player in the middle who can also bring the ball down and shoot from the outside, chances are you're going to want to shut her down. Similarly, if you know you've got a workplace bully on your hands and she has shown she enjoys belittling you, get yourself ready to respond. Pick your move. Playing a zone, for example, might be your best bet. When you *enlist* allies, you have four other teammates positioned at strategic places on the floor, there to thwart the enemy and, in so doing, remind you that you're not alone in all this. Others are defending with you—and, if you're fortunate, *for* you.

Reacting to a bully is not like mathematics or science where there's a nice, neat formula: whenever you add 2 + 2, it always equals 4. Whenever you drop a ball from your hand, gravity will take it downward. We may wish it were that simple, but it's not. Because it involves unpredictable human beings. It's dynamic—like a basketball game. Ever-changing.

Just as every game is going to be different, every workplace culture is going to look different. And it involves change. What might be a healthy workplace at one point might, after a handful of ill-advised hires, be a toxic environment at another point.

So you test the waters. You see what works. What doesn't. The key is understanding the game that is being played:

You're being bullied.

It's not your fault.

You need to respond—and remember, not responding is a response.

DRILLS

- Do you recognize workplace bullying happening to you or around you? Write about it. Can you identify any patterns? What response are you ready to try?
- If you've been the target of workplace bullying, assess where you are. Is it an ongoing situation or in the past? If ongoing, how would you describe your responses to this point—ignore, resist, comply, or enlist?
- Finally, in terms of context, compare your workplace environment with what it was 5 or 10 years ago. Has something changed? If so, why might it have changed? Has "all for one and one for all" turned into an environment of "king of the mountain," more likely to breed bullies? Don't assume that because a workplace hasn't shown itself to be a place of bullying that it can't become such.

4

Know Thy Bully

Not my circus, not my monkeys.

—RED, IN *ORANGE IS THE NEW BLACK*

There's a reason that teams watch game film as part of their preparation. They want to *see* what their opponents are going to throw at them. They want to *know* their opponents as best they can so they can be prepared. Here's what we, as targets of workplace bullying, know. Our self-evident truths, if you will:

We know if a workplace bully comes at us and we ignore them, they will most likely double down.

We know if a workplace bully is coming at us and we resist, the bullying will continue and probably escalate, tinged with revenge.

We know if a workplace bully is coming at us and we comply, they will pause until they feel like bullying us again.

We know if a workplace bully is coming at us and we enlist help from an ally, the bully may be confused, become off balance, and then find a new, more covert route to bullying.

That's what we're dealing with. It's that simple and that complex.

It's Not You—It's the Bully

Because we are getting to know our bullies and we are learning our bullies' plays, we understand that every time we engage with a bully, there is a significant chance that the bully will bully us, whether publicly or privately, overtly or covertly. Once the pattern of bullying has been set, the chances of breaking it are slim—unless management understands what's really happening and has the courage to intervene. Bullies will test targets, and the minute they get a foothold, the pattern is established.

I know what you're wondering right now, what you're asking yourself: "Why me? Why am I—or was I—being targeted? Why?"

The reasons are endless. Maybe the bully is threatened by your talent. Maybe the bully is so insecure, they feel as if they have to bring someone else down and you're it. Maybe you represent something the bully wants to be but is not capable of being.

Perhaps it's your outlook on life. Your personality. Your wins. Your ability to learn from losses. Perhaps you're an independent thinker. You're competent. You're well liked. Perhaps you're ethical and honest. You're a self-starter. You're emotionally intelligent and someone with whom others like to work. Perhaps you're a great team player.

And all this threatens the hell out of the bully because they aren't any of these things—and deep down, they know it.

You want some other ideas about why bullies bully?

- Bullies are scared and insecure.
- Bullies know their workplace culture subtly supports their behavior because the company looks the other way and allows the bullying to continue.

- Bullies think bullying makes them look large and in charge—at least to any equally warped colleagues.
- Bullies were abused, and subconsciously, they think that justifies their abuse of others.
- Bullies believe that bullying is an important business practice to increase productivity.
- Bullies have one thing on their minds: their own professional trajectory.
- Bullies are unhappy, and they want to make others unhappy.
- Bullies don't know any other way to be.
- Bullies don't know that what they're doing is considered bullying behavior.

A reminder: I offer this insight just to give you some contextual nuance, not because I believe it's your job to super-sleuth your way through to determine whatever triggers or motivates a bully. As Red in *Orange Is the New Black* says, "Not my circus, not my monkeys." It's not your job to try and figure out what makes a person a bully. The fact of the matter is, we show up to work expecting to be treated professionally and respectfully. Is that too much to ask?

In some workplaces, it might be. Does everyone know what a professional and respectful workplace environment is where you work? Has your company made it clear? If not, it's anyone's guess how each employee will show up for work. We come with our own influences, based upon our upbringing, our family, and our culture, which makes it critically important for companies to be clear about what's expected of their employees.

It's your job to do your job, and when you run into bullying, it will be helpful to be ready with an approach. So even though you can't stop something over which you have no control, you can be at the ready with your own "sound principles." Your own moves to make.

Preparing for bullying is a bit like training for CPR. You practice it over and over and get certified—with hopes, of course, of never having to use it. But if you do, it's almost automatic. It doesn't have to be perfect. It's meant to stabilize the patient, not assess or treat. There is no 911 for workplace bullying—there should be—but there are steps you can take to arm yourself when in the midst of bullying behavior:

Bullying "CPR" Steps

- Know that any interaction you have with a workplace bully may result in bullying behavior toward you.
- Regulate your heart rate through a simple breathing technique. A deep inhale through the nose for four counts, followed by a long eight-count exhalation. If it helps, cross your arms so that you can take a full belly breath and show your bully through your body language that you're not open for business. This not only allows you to manage yourself physically; it gives you time to think about how you're going to respond to the bully.
- Recognize what is happening to you. You are not making this up. You are being bullied.
- Make your move—ignore, resist, comply, or enlist.
- Always use your bully's name when addressing your bully. Bullying is about the bully, so make it so by using the person's name.

I know. I know. You're saying: "You want me to do belly breathing as a technique to combat workplace bullying? Have you lost your mind?"

I get it, but hear me out: as targets, we need everything in our arsenal to help us stand our ground. Hold our space. Regulate our brain. Allow in what we want in and keep out what doesn't belong. The calmer we stay as targets, the better we can anticipate the bully's next move. When we manage our breathing, keep our heart rate at an acceptable level, and steady our nervous system, we're better thinkers. We stay calm. We stay upright.

Bullies want us to be on our heels and off balance. They're still going to be bullies, but we're going to start controlling what we can control.

A final note: The "on-paper" plan may seem easy compared with the "boots-on-the-ground" reality. There is no doubt that you will face a far more complicated situation than you might have expected. In part, that's because other people's biases might preclude them from seeing the same reality you do.

Here's how one woman I interviewed talked about her coworker's reaction to her concern that she was being bullied:

A trusted friend pulled me aside and asked me to meet with her, right then. My friend turned to me and quickly asked, "What's wrong with you? What's going on?"

I didn't have time to answer. The friend went on to say that a few of our shared teammates had expressed concern about my "attitude." That I seemed short-tempered, negative, even disrespectful at times in small groups. That I wasn't acting like a positive contributor and teammate, as she'd always known me to be, and I wasn't building a great reputation in my new role.

I walked away from that meeting with my friend jolted. Well, actually, *she* walked away. I just sat there. The negative change in me wasn't just my own perception, I now knew. And as I remember it, I walked from that meeting directly to my car, parked just a few yards away near my office building. I felt helpless and empty.

Later that month, I reached back out to this same friend. I told her what had been happening with my manager, whom she knew, too. I don't think my friend believed me; that did not describe the guy she knew, and I don't think she thought he was capable of treating anyone like that, especially a former teammate. Yet she was concerned. "I'll call him myself. That just doesn't seem like him."

A few days later, I was at JFK Airport when my phone rang.

"I'm so sorry," my friend blurted out. She went on to explain how she had called him with the idea of just finding out more about what I, and a couple of others, had told her. She said as soon as she began to ask questions, he became belligerent. He had never spoken to her like that; she had never heard him talk about others like that. His tone and condescension were a shock to my friend.

Now she was calling to say that she was sorry for doubting me, and she was also sorry that this had been happening to me. Beyond that, however, although we didn't discuss it, we both knew there was nothing she could do about it. It just didn't work that way in our corporate world.

Bullies are complicated. Workplaces are complicated. Guess what? In most cases, you can't control either one. But you can control your own actions and responses—and it helps to understand your bully's moves as you plan yours.

DRILLS

- Consider again what types of bullying behavior you're witnessing. The next time this happens, does it make sense to ignore, to resist, to comply, or to enlist? What is the likely outcome of each of these options?
- Articulate to yourself what is happening: if you are the target of bullying, frame the behavior for yourself; if you are a witness watching a target being bullied, consider what is happening and the options available to you.
- If you determine you are either a target of or a witness to workplace bullying, practice your belly breathing and find other techniques, such as tapping and walking, to help you stay calm and regulated through your day. When you're in a meeting with your bully and other people, practice your belly breathing. It may be a new muscle for you and will take practice. Do you notice a difference?

5

There's No Reasoning with the Unreasonable

You should just be grateful . . .
we heard that all the time . . .
it was one thing after another,
and the little things then became big things.

—JULIE FOUDY

When it comes to being bullied, don't let gratitude get in your way. That's right. There's such a thing as too much gratitude.

I was so grateful to be at this phenomenal company doing all these exceptional things that my gratitude blurred my ability to see how I was being mistreated. Not only does the bully establish a foothold, but targets do as well. We become accustomed to being mistreated, so being mistreated becomes our norm.

I didn't have time to spend analyzing and evaluating the culture. I was busy. I punched through, plowed ahead, and spent zero time reflecting on the company for which I worked or the effect that workplace bullying was starting to have on me. In fact, if introspection crept in, I swatted it away. No time. I had been selected to be on the ultimate varsity squad; there would be no more tryouts. I had made it.

I was one of very few women on the corporate leadership team, and I was going to keep working hard, keep grinding through, and show no weakness—or at least what I perceived to be weakness. And I never stopped feeling a sense of gratitude—that those in power picked me, that they put me in the game, and that they *let* me keep playing. I now realize that my sense of gratitude may have kept me from recognizing exactly what was happening to me.

Now back to the "Do as I say, not as I did" mantra: I approached my bullies like I was in that movie *50 First Dates*. You know the one? Drew Barrymore has no short-term memory, so Adam Sandler must woo her every single day. Like Drew's character, it was as if I had no memory of the bullying behavior from a well-established workplace bully. I expected something different every time I interacted with the bully. I anticipated the best because that's who I am. When the worst would come at me, as it most assuredly would, I wasn't remotely ready. I was in a state of constant confusion, and because of that, I spent a lot of time with my feet tangled up, turning the ball over, and getting flattened.

It's like when I was a kid and I would leave the dinner table, only to return to find most of my food having been eaten by one of my many brothers. Fool me once, shame on you. Fool me twice, shame on me. I recognized the play—dinner plate left unattended results in food disappearing. So I chose my own play. I started to lick my food—all of it (especially the roll)—before leaving the table. Food disappearing stopped.

I was quick to wise up with my brothers at the dinner table. I was unable to take the same approach with the workplace bullying to which I was subjected. Why?

Trust.

My brothers, my family were safe places for me. We were connected to each other. We had each other's backs and lived in a household culture that was built on trust.

When a workplace bully goes on the prowl, that's the opposite of trust. In fact, the bully wants to do us harm.

When we're being bullied, we're so fixated on what the bully did to us, we lose sight of our own value systems.

Why You Can't Change a Bully

The thing that targets must keep in mind is this: the bully's value system does not match our value system. It's easy to assume otherwise, that once the bully is called on the carpet, the bully will, well, repent. Not the case. Because what you accept as normal behavior and what the bully accepts as normal behavior are night and day. Right from the jump, there's misalignment. Ironically, that is one of the most oft-shared reasons that targets stay at a company in which they are being bullied instead of leaving.

We think we can change the bully.

No. You can change lots of things, notably yourself. But you can't change the bully.

Remember that "yelling" I did in Chapter 3 about how being a target of workplace bullying doesn't have anything to do with you? Well, here's another high-decibel lesson that's worth repeating:

You can't change the bully!

And it's not your job to do so.

This one is so tough because it's tangled up in that whole "I'm allowing myself to be bullied" narrative that we've embedded in that part of our brain where things go to stay embedded, never to be unembedded. Author Jennifer Pastiloff refers to those as our "bullshit stories."

But, honestly, that's one reason so many targets endure being bullied rather than report it or quit. They have unrealistic expectations about the ability of the bully to change.

One man I interviewed shared a story about being bullied out of a job at a successful automobile company, but later was invited back to an even better position—and said yes. Why? Maybe the man believed that his bully shared a similar value system to his and the bully had come to see the error of his ways. Maybe the man needed the job and had forgotten the toll that workplace bullying had taken on him and his family. Maybe he believed that once back in the saddle, he could magically make the bully change into the kind of person with whom he wanted to work. He quickly discovered that the workplace culture hadn't changed, and the bullying simply started back up without missing a beat.

Other Reasons We Accept Bullying

But believing we can change the bully is not the only reason targets put up with bullying and, in many cases, return to the bully. Here are some more:

- We don't know any better. Perhaps being mistreated is the norm for us.
- We believe in the structure of the organization and have concluded that mistreatment is just part of the deal.
- The bully must know what they're doing.
- We're new to the company, so we don't know any better and we have no support system in place.
- We've seen others raise their hand to report mistreatment, and they are no longer "valued members" of the organization.
- Doing the right thing doesn't garner results in the form of recognition or raises or promotion. Keeping our mouths shut seems to.
- Internal competition breeds bullying. In other words, bullying is part of the winning culture.
- We don't feel we have any power.
- The culture doesn't discourage bullying.

- The company either doesn't have or doesn't enforce an anti-bullying policy.
- The bully has threatened us directly.
- Raising our hand for help will negatively affect our career.
- We're embarrassed and ashamed because we've been singled out so we must have done something wrong or shown some sort of weakness to justify that.
- We need this job, so if bullying is part of it, so be it.
- Reasoning with the bully hasn't worked so we'll keep trying.
- We suffer from impostor syndrome, so we don't think we deserve the role we're in.
- Sometimes the bully is really nice.
- We fear retribution.

Let's drill down into a few of these.

Many targets I've interviewed have shared that their respect for a hierarchical structure actually *worked against them*. I would include myself in this mix. Our healthy respect for "those in charge" blurs the lines between treatment and mistreatment. Respect is mutual. We bought into this because we believe in a mutually respectful relationship. We enter into the agreement with that belief, and when bullying occurs, we are so shocked by what unfolds, it's like we've been hit with a stun gun. We end up back on our heels, confused, and embarrassed.

I personally can relate to most, nearly all, of these reasons, but let's take a look at the bottom of the list.

Targets feel embarrassed and ashamed for having been targeted. It must have something to do with us, right? Wrong. We keep our mouths shut because we think we can handle it. We think we've done something to be the target; we deserved it. And—are you ready for this one? We think we are the only one. That's right. We think we're somehow special in our "target-ness." We have no idea others are experiencing the same thing. In fact, at some companies, lots of others are. Our shame silences us and perpetuates the culture of workplace bullying. In other words, we become culpable in our own mistreatment.

We need this job. It pays well. There are great benefits. All our friends work here. We still feel grateful for some or even a lot of the job, for the chance to work at a certain place or do a certain kind of work. We may even love what we do when we get to do it without a bully tripping us up. In fact, several people shared with me, "They need me." That's right, the company *needs* us. Even if that were true, the question I hope you'd ask yourself is, "At what cost?" What's your "rock bottom"? It's not a rhetorical question. What's your rock bottom? How low will you go to maintain your job?

If we can just reason with the bully, the bully will stop bullying us, right? Wrong. There is no reasoning with someone who is unreasonable. This is critical to get through your head. There's no "But I'm right, and the bully's wrong." If you want to be part of the Justice League, go get yourself a superhero costume and find something else to do. The workplace bully is not interested in your definition of right and wrong. There's no, "If I say it this way, the bully will change." This is not a foreign language class, although it feels like you're speaking two different languages. This is much deeper than language. This is about values, the stuff that's baked into our DNA.

In fact, if we could get outside ourselves as targets and spend some time evaluating our bully, we would save ourselves a lot of time and anxiety. We are so fixated on the latest bullying maneuver, mistreatment, aggression, that we lose sight of what is really going on. Yet we keep trying the same thing over and over again, thinking we will get different results.

And you and I both know what that's the definition of.

Insanity.

Your bully has declared who they are. Now it's time for you to declare who you are.

DRILLS

- Get outside yourself and evaluate the bully who has targeted you or whom you've witnessed bullying someone else. Ask yourself these questions: "Is the bully a good person?" "Do the bully's values match your values?"
- Create a picture of your bully. Describe how the bully treats others. How does that compare with how others deserve to be treated?
- If you or someone you know accepts being bullied, try to identify and understand the reasons for the acceptance—perhaps drawing on the list of reasons described earlier in this chapter.

PART II

UNDERSTAND

The Cultural Context of Workplace Bullying

It was 1974 when I got called up to The Bigs.

I was nine.

Summer basketball camp in Spokane, Washington, where 49 fifth grade boys and 1 fifth grade girl would learn the fundamentals of the game—passing, dribbling, defensive stance—sweating through drill after drill until the sound of the whistle called us to split in half and line up on each end of the court to shoot a final free throw before jumping on bikes and enjoying the rest of a Spokane summer day.

The free throw.

If you made it, you were done for the day. If you missed it, you were running a set of lines—to the free throw line and back, to half court and back, and so on.

After everyone shot—swishes, bricks, and all points in between— my stepdad, Big Dave—always referred to as "Coach" when camp was in session—blew his whistle and yelled, "Get on the line!" Kyle Klevenger and Johnny Merka always made their free throw, and yet there they were, sprinter stance, ready to run.

It didn't take long for me to figure out what was going on. Whether you made your shot or missed your shot, you ran. We all toed the line together. We all ran together. We all finished the day together. We were a team, and that was our team culture.

Every team and every organization has a culture. Some cultures are healthy and encourage people to support one another and to do their best. Others are unhealthy and divisive.

In Part II, "Understand: The Cultural Context of Workplace Bullying," you'll gain an appreciation for what contributes to both a healthy and an unhealthy workplace culture, including two of the most potent ingredients: sexism and scarcity. Through shared stories of healthy and unhealthy workplace culture, you'll learn what to be on the lookout for so that workplace bullying doesn't take hold.

6

Culture

Culture eats strategy for breakfast.

—PETER DRUCKER

P art I highlighted the basics of bullying—what characterizes bullies and bullying behavior, how to recognize and articulate what is happening, how we might respond to bullying—to provide you with a framework to recognize workplace bullying.

Now to help you understand how bullying begins and how it thrives in some workplaces, we turn to a broader topic: culture. Specifically, leadership within the workplace culture. And not simply the report-up, press-release, keep-the-shareholders-happy leadership. That's important. But here's a well-known but grossly underexecuted fact: Leadership that brings out the best in its people—from top to bottom, side to side—will attract, engage, and retain a happy and productive workforce that creates and nurtures a healthy workplace. Full stop.

Sounds simple. So why is this book about workplace bullying even necessary?

Because when leaders lose sight of their most important resource and start treating people as a commodity, things go downhill. And by "things," I'm talking about the culture of the company. And the descent is quick. When workplace culture is solely tethered to the bottom line, it deteriorates to a point of being unbearable, and employees exit. The algorithm such employees have established for themselves and their households no longer adds up. Their values don't align to those of the company, which now resembles a bad apocalyptic zombie movie.

It stands to reason that leadership and a positive, nonbullying workplace culture are inextricably linked. Leadership and a negative, toxic, bully-enabling workplace culture are also inextricably linked. In other words, *how* a company gets to that bottom line matters.

There are lots of books on leadership. This isn't one of them, but to fully understand workplace culture, and thus workplace bullying, it helps to ground ourselves in the key ingredient of culture: leadership, or lack thereof.

Emotional Intelligence

Leadership goes beyond influencing, creating a vision, and driving functional excellence—"core competencies" as those are known in some circles. As Daniel Goleman wrote in his seminal book *Emotional Intelligence: Why It Can Matter More Than IQ*, core competencies are "threshold capabilities." They are the price of entry. But as Goleman points out, what sets successful leaders apart from everyone else is emotional intelligence (EQ)—"a person's ability to manage his feelings so that those feelings are expressed appropriately and effectively."

In fact, Goleman discovered that "the most effective leaders are alike in one crucial way: they all have a high degree of . . . EQ. Emotional intelligence is the sine qua non of leadership." Goleman asserts that EQ is "the largest single predictor of success in the workplace." He breaks down EQ into five components: self-awareness, self-regulation, motivation, empathy, and social skills.

Leaders who can balance their own self-confidence, drive, and persuasiveness with an openness to learn, optimism even in the face of failure, accountability for themselves and others, and a heavy dose of self-deprecating humor are more likely to outperform those who don't. These leaders are experts not only in building and leading teams, but in retaining talent.

Leaders with high EQ instill confidence in others, meaning employees are more likely to show up as leaders every day. Employees know they have a voice in the process, and because leaders are modeling a high EQ, employees will do the same and pay it forward. The more time we take in developing people, the more time they will take in developing their people. The result? A more respectful work environment where even a hint of bullying won't be tolerated.

If you build your employees up, they will build up others, not tear them down. Such an atmosphere shows them they are valued and leads to a healthy workplace culture.

Leaders who want to hear from their employees about anything and everything make it obvious through an invitation to do so. They make it obvious through open and inclusive interactions. They make it obvious through an understanding that the ability of their employees to do the job for which they were hired is only part of the equation. Not only do such leaders have high EQ, but they know that the health of the organization relies on everyone being able to show up and lead up.

Organizations whose leaders fall short on the EQ scale will be unable to cultivate a healthy workplace culture and will tear down whatever healthy culture exists. It takes a long time to build up a healthy workplace culture. It takes no time to tear it down.

What Culture Should Be

So what, specifically, is "workplace culture?"

It's the way we treat each other; it's us on our best day; it's a set of norms that we follow.

It's the way founders, owners, and leaders behave. What's allowed. What's not allowed. What, technically, isn't allowed but actually *is*.

It's thinking before you speak. It's knowing the effect you have on others on your best day and on your worst day. It's passion for the work and that being the motivation. It's the ability to find common ground and to build rapport. It's the see-something, say-something, do-something approach.

It's seeing the woman balancing three bags arrive at the office and instead of saying, "Wow, it's the bag lady," and waltzing past, stopping and offering to help carry the bags and open the door. It's the person who says in a meeting, "I don't think so-and-so was done speaking; please continue."

It's realizing in a meeting when someone's voice has been absent and asking the person if they have anything to add. It's celebrating the small wins, often and well. It's external slogans matching internal realities about how employees are treated. It's checking on the friend who seems to be drifting away. It's setting positive intent each day with each and every interaction. It's agreeing to behavioral intentions before a meeting and sticking to them. More important, when those intentions are not followed, it's having the guts to stand up and say something. And to leave no one behind who needs help.

In August 2014, I was invited to attend my first signature athlete meetings, which brought me face-to-face with basketball great LeBron James. LeBron had been drafted straight out of high school and became part of the Nike family in 2003 when we collectively marveled at this "man-child" and his superhuman strength, speed, and court sense. In our meetings, it was obvious that LeBron loved the ideation process and that he was clear about whatever he touched having staying power. As we finished up, I was one of the last to leave the building; I would have to walk quite a distance back to the main campus for the next portion of our meeting.

"Hey! You need a ride?" he said while sitting on the back of an idling golf cart.

I hurried over and hopped on next to LeBron. As we bounced along, he told me how excited he was to welcome his third child, a girl, in a handful of weeks.

Later, when I shared the news of my day with my kids, they responded in unison, "You got to meet LeBron, Mama?"

Yeah, I got to, and guess what, the guy who paid tribute to Michael Jordan by sporting No. 23 noticed the people around him, reached out to make their way easier, and made sure the last person to leave the meeting had a ride.

———

I used to think of workplace culture in simple terms—it's the air that oxygenates the workplace. But as I've learned, there's nothing simple about it. Yes, it starts at the top; teams tend to emulate the behavior of their coaches. But if you're only looking to those at the top to nurture the culture, you're missing the point. It's important that those at the top model the type of behavior that fuels a healthy culture, but make no mistake, healthy workplace culture comes from within the ranks as a shared system of values, beliefs, and behavioral norms. It shows up most obviously in how we treat each other—or mistreat each other.

Leaders and Culture

If workplace culture starts and stops with how employees treat each other, the "what" plays second fiddle to the "how," which brings me to what I consider to be the most powerful definition of workplace culture: "The culture of any organization is shaped by the worst behavior the leader is willing to tolerate," according to Gruenert and Whitaker, in their 2015 book, *School Culture Rewired*.

In one powerful sentence, Gruenert and Whitaker get at the heart of workplace culture. It's not only the way employees treat each other, but the rules that are followed or not followed, and the referees who either enforce such rules or look the other way.

The workplace culture in which I thrived was comparable to that of my upbringing. I knew the rules of engagement and worked with people who had a similar work ethic, similar desire to win, similar approach—a combination of keeping your head down, doing good work, and maintaining a sense of levity.

In my experience, the unspoken rules were these:

- **I trust you're not gonna screw this up, but I'm here to support you if you do.** When you miss your free throw, we're all going to run with you.
- **Being independent is allowed for; heck, it's encouraged.** When your team has your back, you call for the ball.
- **Risk taking is applauded because when there's trust and support, *you* take the shot.** You drive the lane. You take the charge. You stay loose. You play to win.

And we're going to need some levity to get us through it, no matter the outcome. Perhaps that's an ideal that has long since vanished in your work environment. Still, do you remember that feeling? When you were walking tall with the faith and confidence that others have in your abilities. Like you're valued? It's not that you can do no wrong. It's that when you do screw up, you're going to have help picking up the pieces and moving forward.

So how do you know? What questions should you be asking to evaluate the culture of a workplace, organization, or team? Here are four inspired by Peter Senge's *The Fifth Discipline*, as shared with me by Matt Paknis, author of *Successful Leaders Aren't Bullies*, to get you started.

Where Do You See the Brand in Five Years?

Yes, this is a big question, and it's an important one in understanding culture. It provides the team with a shared orientation from which to move forward. If the answer is unclear and internally focused solely on a bottom line, rather than clear and externally aspiring toward a bigger purpose, the result is an already competitive, everyone-for-themself environment pushed to being solely profit-oriented instead of mission-oriented. The result is uncertainty and a trail of casualties. Conversely, a healthy workplace culture is one that not only has a clear purpose, but lives it each day with everyone in lockstep, supporting and motivating each other to hit well-understood goals.

How Does the Organization Solve Problems?

If the answer starts with a one-way, top-down turf war, rather than a two-way, shared relationship, it's no longer an environment of collaboration. Conversely, when the person at the top says, "C'mon, I don't have all the answers," that's an invitation to be part of a healthy organization that welcomes new ideas and perspectives. The structure of a brand must allow for collaborative ideas that challenge the problems to be solved instead of constantly questioning the people trying to solve them. A healthy workplace culture feels like a relationship with clear expectations, objectives, and boundaries. An unhealthy workplace culture breeds fear, mistrust, and an aversion to speaking up.

How Do Employees Know They're Valued?

If the answer is something about an annual performance review, rather than an understanding and belief that, regardless of title or level, you can be part of making something better, the result is a feeling of unworthiness on the part of the employee versus a feeling of commitment. Leaders must serve their employees every day. To do this well, an understanding of what motivates their employees is job one so that all shareholders feel valued. In other words, leaders must take the time to know their teams in order to value their teams. Additionally, a key ingredient in valuing employees is to value their ideas and to allow those ideas to build to a crescendo in an energetic, collaborative environment. Leaders who tailor their style to meet the needs of their employees are well on their way to creating a healthy workplace culture.

What Behaviors Are Rewarded?

If the answer solely revolves around results, core competencies, and compliance, and does not include behaviors that build commitment and trust, then employees will not feel supported to do their best, which includes taking accountable risks. In a healthy workplace culture, core competencies serve a purpose, but only when they are supported by valued behaviors. If we double-click into Goleman's EQ, we find it chock full of the behaviors that the most successful leaders share—empathy, optimism, and transparency—to name a few. Camaraderie, self-reflection, gratitude, and accountability are also included. As important as it is for companies to be clear about which behaviors are rewarded, it's just as important for them to be clear about which behaviors are not rewarded. Unhealthy workplace cultures are teeming with apathy, pessimism, and secrecy and have no shot at building commitment and trust.

Healthy and Unhealthy Markers

When healthy markers stack up—externally serving, future thinking, shared responsibilities, partnerships, commitment—employees will experience the benefits of working in a healthy workplace culture. One in which they feel included, valued, and seen. Employees know why they're showing up every day to work.

When unhealthy markers stack up—myopic behavior, current thinking, hero leader, autocratic structure, compliance—employees will feel the negative effects of an unhealthy workplace culture. One in which toxicity, hostility, and bullying are the norm.

It's important for leaders to start honestly discussing these questions. The shift from original expectations to misaligned directions can be subtle, so recognizing the waywardness is the first step in returning to a healthy workplace culture.

Leaders must think of change in a workplace culture in terms of six steps:

- **AWARENESS.** Recognizing where you are as a workplace
- **VISION.** Recognizing where you need to get—or get back *to*
- **STRATEGY.** Recognizing the steps you need to take to do so
- **OBSTACLES.** Recognizing the impediments that could prevent you from getting where you need to be

- **VALUES.** Recognizing that *what* gets done is secondary to *how* it gets done
- **COURAGE.** Having the guts to start the process

Each of these steps back to health is important, but no workplace will change if the people with the power to effect change don't, at first, notice that something's wrong. When unhealthy markers stack up—top-down turf, risk aversion—small transgressions are overlooked, and what starts as a message that toxic behavior will be tolerated leads gradually to hostility and, finally, to overt bullying. Over time, those exhibiting inappropriate behaviors are rewarded and promoted, creating a self-perpetuating environment where no amount of HR intervention or employee committees will make a dent.

An unhealthy workplace culture is the result of many factors. Among them is a cutthroat culture that's been established so:

- Teammates are encouraged to compete against each other to the point of obliteration.
- Employees exploit others for their own benefit.
- Employees are not properly vetted before hiring.
- Employees who exhibit bullying behavior are rewarded either explicitly with promotions or implicitly with good standing and favoritism.
- Bullying behavior is seen as taking the initiative.
- Those at the top model bullying.
- Profits are placed above people.

Leaders must create a workplace environment in which trust and connection form the number one goal. When teammates feel valued, empowered, and confident, there is no limit to what will be accomplished. In the workplace, when there's no EQ-inspired approach holding the entire team accountable, bad behavior goes unchecked. It's permitted, even encouraged by virtue of it being ignored.

The result? A team that is no longer a team, but instead a group of individuals with their own agendas, no longer tethered to each other or to the vision of the organization. A team acutely susceptible to the rise of bullying.

DRILLS

- What is your first/best memory of culture, personally and professionally? How did one inform the other?
- What is your first/best memory of leadership? What made it so? *Who* made it so?
- What is the worst behavior your organization is currently tolerating?
- When organizations become solely focused on winning, bullies flourish. Great results no longer paint the full picture. What are your organization's wins covering up?

7

Sexism Plus Scarcity Equals Shame

You pull up as many folding chairs
as you need or build a bigger table.

—BROOKE BALDWIN

A section about workplace culture wouldn't be complete without the inclusion of two of its most potent ingredients: sexism and scarcity.

Sexism is a key ingredient in an unhealthy workplace culture. Whether consciously or unconsciously, sexist assumptions perpetuate hierarchical thinking, which is limiting and detrimental to employees' well-being, performance, and job satisfaction.

An effective marketing tool, creating scarcity is a slam dunk for accelerating demand. It encourages consumers to buy sooner and perhaps *more* because supply is limited. When implemented in the workplace environment, scarcity can be a dangerous enabler of an unhealthy workplace culture.

As a business practice, scarcity is leveraged to pit those who are underrepresented against each other. It works like this: companies place a single minority (let's say a woman) on their executive team, which signals that there is a single spot for her, or anyone that identifies as *her*, at that table. It literally says, "This one spot is *the* one spot we have for a woman."

It's not surprising that, just like consumers competing for that coveted product, those in the minority try to box each other out when that one spot is vacated. The perceived scarcity of a product creates a larger demand for that product. The obvious scarcity of female representation in the C-suite equates to infighting—conflict that wouldn't exist as intensely if more spots were available. If *all* spots were available.

In its own eyes, the company checked its "diversity box," and the few women who made it around the table frequently found themselves sitting in a male-dominated, often-hostile environment that made it difficult for them to succeed. The result was a self-fulfilling prophecy where those minorities who were placed in elevated roles were not set up for—and failed to achieve—success, further proving to those in the majority that if you wanted something done right, you'd better hire *them* to do it.

When that one woman made it through, she often operated in such a dictatorial way that she was not of any help to other women. She didn't want to be. After all, she hadn't gotten any help, so why should she help pull other women up? Instead, the thinking was, "I had to scratch and claw. So, too, will you." The perfect petri dish for workplace bullying to germinate.

When we don't see those who look like, sound like, or behave like us progressing or playing, chances are that's a culture in which scarcity is hard at work and workplace bullying isn't the exception, but the norm.

Why? Because false scarcity encourages internal competition in which those who are in the minority think they're all going for the same spot. A culture of bullying, backstabbing, grandstanding—you get the idea—thrives.

How is the scarcity game played? Subtly, yes, particularly by those in the majority, but as assuredly as Oregon rain. Remember the men who run together, golf together, and party together after work hours? Those are the guys making the decisions. They mostly all look the same, approach ideas in the same way, and bounce out those who don't follow along. They make up a homogenized group with homogenized ideas.

Enter the outlier. In this example, that would be someone who identifies as "she" or "they," BIPOC, or LGBTQ. Essentially, anyone who doesn't look, sound, identify, or act like the group in control. When those in the "scarcity group" want to join those in the in-charge group, but don't see anyone with whom they identify, the *illusion* of scarcity is alive and well. For example, if I see one woman on the leadership team I aspire to be part of, the illusion suggests only one spot is available. Therefore, internal competition for that spot intensifies. Supporting those who belong to one's same group diminishes.

One of the key takeaways of not falling for the scarcity model is to understand it is an illusion. One person's success is not at the expense of another. In other words, you getting ahead does not come at the cost of another. This goes against the image and story being served to us. When we deny this illusion, we understand that for one of us to succeed, we all must succeed. And for all of us to succeed, we must be willing to *represent* each other and hold each other up.

As a leader within your organization, get the table extensions out and make a bigger table. Optimize all your talent and make room. Your employee's experience will be enhanced, your business will prosper, and you'll be contributing to a healthy workplace culture in which people will be less likely to bully and to be bullied.

As you can see, sexism and scarcity are inextricably linked in sort of a "game within a game" that's easily missed if you're not paying attention. At a celebratory going-away event in Milan, I completely missed it.

Let me set it up so you understand the context:

As a leadership team, we traveled, amoeba-like into various cities, studied the retail landscape, immersed ourselves in a cultural experience of some sort—ran with a local run club, cycled throughout the city, attended a football match, experienced a basketball clinic—though tougher to find in football-obsessed Europe.

In August 2014, we arrived in Milan for what would be the site of my final "city tour" before I was to repatriate to Oregon. Nearly 30 of us loaded into five Sprinter vans, winding our way through the city of fashion, food, and fete and stopping to visit various places along the way.

At one stop, I heard the gasps and exclamations before I saw the reason for them: a painting that I had studied in an Intro to Art History class covered the wall at the far end of what otherwise was used as a dining hall. We were being treated to a private viewing of one of the most iconic paintings ever created. There, in all its glory in this tiny stuccoed chapel, was Leonardo da Vinci's "The Last Supper."

Later, at what was essentially my own last supper, I was seated next to Marco Belinelli from the recently anointed NBA champion San Antonio Spurs. As the first Italian to ever win an NBA championship, he was now resting and celebrating in Milan and graciously joined us for dinner. Between the earlier art viewing, the beautiful meal, and the dinner conversation, it was unfolding into a memorable evening.

There were two of us, both women, repatriating in a few short weeks—me, to North America Basketball and the other to Global Football.

Beautiful toasts were made to each of us with the clinking of glasses marking the moment. And then the quizzes began.

The group—all men—proceeded to quiz Kate on her knowledge of soccer. Of course she crushed it.

When it was my turn, instead of quizzing me on basketball—it was shared that no one knew enough about hoops—I was quizzed on my knowledge of French in a sort of rapid-fire Google translate, which resulted in rounds of laughter and applause. Amid the changing environment, I detected glimpses of the company I joined.

From dinner, we made our way over to a long, thick, wooden bar where shots of tequila were set up for Kate and me. We bellied up and shot 'em down. Others joined in, and we had a wonderfully raucous going-away party. Later, after I'd gathered my oversized orange wooden shoe with scrawled Sharpie well-wishes from all my teammates, Kate suddenly shook her head in disgust.

She shared with me how humiliated she felt being quizzed on soccer. She had played soccer; she had refereed soccer; she was about to take a leadership role in Global Football, also known as—soccer. But two things were clear to her: that not one man on the team had gotten to know her well enough to understand that about her. And more galling, that no man would ever have been tested in quite the same way.

I felt complicit in Kate's pain. Not only did I not *represent* my female colleague; I hadn't given a moment's thought to the double standard of the quiz or the spectacle in which we were starring. On the contrary, I was enjoying the moment, looking to the future, and excited to be repatriating. But had I truly been representing Kate, my success and enjoyment during that evening would not have come at her expense. Empathy, it's been said, begins when you get into the shoes of someone else and try to feel what that person might be feeling.

Although sexist in nature, the pop quiz didn't qualify as workplace bullying. Stupid, yes. Bullying, no. Underestimating Kate's knowledge of the game because she didn't fit the description that the men had of a soccer player was discriminatory and sexist and contributed to an unhealthy workplace culture.

Slander and Shaming

Kellan's introduction to sexism came early on in her career.

She had just been hired as an apparel sales rep, and her boss, Laura, was coming to travel her Minnesota territory with her. This would be their first time meeting each other. Kellan was excited, nervous, and thankful that Laura would show her the ropes in such a hands-on way.

At their first dinner, they were enjoying a glass of wine and recapping their day of sales calls when Laura suddenly said, "Hey, this is a bit delicate, but you're going to need to be more discreet about your relationship with Alex. People around the office are starting to talk."

Midbite, Kellan looked at her, perplexed. "My relationship with Alex? You mean 'Fairway?'" Alex's last name, Driver, translated to "Fairway" at their nickname-happy company. "I don't have a relationship with Fairway, other than the fact he's one of my best friends. We were in the same onboarding class."

"Really," Laura said, looking confused, "Well, he's telling the guys in the office that the two of you are hot and heavy—providing details. John asked me to talk to you."

"*John*—the head of our company? *John*—*your* boss?"

Kellan was stunned. Here she was, being accused of some X-rated tryst with one of her coworkers within "John's" organization that she had just recently joined. She was horrified.

"Laura," Kellan said, "there is absolutely nothing going on between Fairway and me. I thought we were friends, but I guess not. I'm sickened by this. Oh my God, what people must think of me." Her reputation had been slandered before she had a chance to accurately establish it herself.

"Don't worry, Kel. I will make things right in the office. Meanwhile, you should talk to Fairway. He's spreading rumors about how, and I quote, 'great Kel is in bed.'"

"Laura," Kellan said, "I don't want to talk to him. I want him fired."

Now Laura was the one who looked stunned, but Kellan wasn't backing off.

"You can't allow a coworker to spread unfounded rumors about me, a brand-new member of the team, that *your* boss actually gives credence to. How does that make me look? How am I supposed to establish my value with the team when these lies are being spread about me within the first couple of weeks on the job? How is that right?"

"OK, OK, settle down, Kel," Laura said, trying to placate her as the "house special," venison stew, congealed in front of them. "We can resolve this. Let me talk to Jimmy, and we'll figure out what to do."

"*Jimmy?*" Kellan said, her voice rising. "Jimmy is in on this too?" Jimmy was Fairway's boss, Laura's counterpart.

"Kel, I know this is hard, but, yes, all the guys know about it."

There was steam coming off Kellan as they left the restaurant, and not just because of the frigid January weather. She could not believe what she had just heard. Laura asked her to let Jimmy "handle Fairway," allowing them to run a disciplinary process. Kellan agreed and waited for word from Jimmy.

He called her the next day. Jim O'Halaran was a charismatic, dark-haired Irishman and looked exactly like his name.

"Hey, Kel, Jimmy O here. How ya doin'?" His Minnesota accent reminded Kellan she was a long way from home.

"Well, not great, Jimmy. As you know, Laura shocked me with some news last night at dinner that I'm still trying to make sense of."

"Yeah, Kel. I'm really sorry about that. I've had a chance to talk to Alex. You know, this is a locker-room-talk type thing that I think got away from him. Clearly, there's some maturing that still needs to happen."

"But what are you going to do about it?"

"Well, Kel, as I said, I've talked to Alex. He's really sorry and embarrassed that he did this. Um, what do *you* think we should do about it?"

"It's not my job to tell you how to discipline your employee, Jim, but if it were my job, I would fire him."

"Oh, wow, Kel. So that's how you feel?"

"Yes, that's how I feel. This guy has disparaged me, not even allowing me to establish myself with my new teammates. I moved to Minnesota, sight unseen. I don't know anyone here—except for the guy that I thought was my friend. And now he's done this? Yeah, Jim, he needs to go."

"OK, Kel. Let me get back to you. I need to talk to John."

The next day, as promised, Jimmy got back to Kellan to let her know that "Fairway is on probation."

"So he gets his hand slapped."

"Well, it's more than that, Kel. We'll have him on a short leash, and his first step is to apologize to you. So he will reach out to do so. I'm really sorry about this. Just know that we are all still so excited for you to be part of the team."

And so with that, Kellan was introduced to the "boy's club," in which a woman could be shamed and then placated with a "nothing punishment" of her accuser. It wouldn't be the last.

She took the apology call from Fairway. "I'm so sorry, Kel. I don't know why I said those things."

"Yeah, me neither. You were my one friend out here, and now I can't even stand the sound of your voice. Thanks for nothing." She hung up.

On the surface, Kellan was learning the apparel business, traveling her territory, and winning national sales contests. She was excelling, but an unsteadiness started to establish itself along with a realization of what it meant to have joined a male-dominated company.

Kellan responded to the hurt and embarrassment of being the subject of a shame-inducing campaign by doubling down on work, running, and—she was ashamed to admit—negative self-talk. After all, Kellan thought, she must have done something to allow herself to be treated this way. Right?

Wrong. Kellan did nothing to invite Fairway to spin lies about her, and the three most senior leaders within the company did next to nothing to protect her. When they should have been seeking advice from their HR business partner, they were busy gossiping and perpetuating a story they took as fact. Yes, they discussed what had happened and then put Fairway on probation. But by chalking it up to "locker-room talk," Fairway was able to go about his business while Kellan suffered.

Slander and Shaming 2.0

Elin was working for a talented and energetic leader.

Sean was happily married and had three children, one of whom was Ellen, pronounced like everyone thought Elin's name was pronounced. Most people get Elin's name wrong—it starts with the long E sound, not something they're used to. Her rule of thumb—if you're someone she's going to have a relationship with, she'll correct you; if not, she won't. Elin correcting you is an invitation for the two of you to have a connection. And if you become tight, you'll end up calling her "Lin."

Sean called her "Lin."

During a meeting Elin was holding with a few of her colleagues, a woman made an offhanded comment implying that Sean and Elin had more than a working relationship between them. It wasn't an overt statement, but Elin caught a vibe she didn't like. It was enough to prompt her to ask the woman to stay after the meeting.

"It seems like you were implying something earlier about me. Can you clarify? Something about Sean and me?"

Elin noticed red splotches springing up on the woman's neck, a sure sign she was nervous about something.

"Um, well, um, some people are just saying that the reason you have risen so quickly is because you and Sean are sleeping together."

"Huh? Are you kidding me? Sean? What is it with this place? Who? Who started that rumor?" Elin was now putting the figurative squeeze on the woman, who was in no way considered to be a pushover. In fact, she had been a collegiate hammer thrower, but Elin could see by the woman's flaming red neck that she had the woman up against the ropes.

"Um, Tammi," the woman replied.

"Who?" Elin asked. "I have no idea who that is."

"She's an associate product line manager," she said.

"Wow. There's some young woman spreading rumors about me, and I don't even know her, and she's an *associate* product line manager?" Elin was sideways.

"Thanks," Elin said. "Meanwhile, do me a favor, and stop spreading rumors about me. And, how 'bout this. How 'bout when you hear someone else spreading that nonsense, you step in and stop it? How 'bout you be a leader? It's not even remotely factual, and it's really hurtful, especially for Sean, who is happily married."

Embarassed, the woman apologized and quickly left. Elin made her way to Sean's office.

"Hey, do you have a minute?"

"Sure, what's up, Lin?"

Elin proceeded to share what she had just learned. Sean's face, always so animated and just plain happy, turned somber and introspective.

"Huh. I don't really know what to say. I mean, thanks for telling me."

"I'm doing more than that. I'm going to meet with Tammi and let her know this is unacceptable. I just wanted to let you know so you're not surprised by this—*ever*."

"OK. I appreciate that, Lin."

True to her word, Elin located young, naïve Tammi and asked her to join Elin in her office. Once Tammi was settled into her seat at the small round table, Elin shut the door and joined her.

"So I hear you're perpetuating a rumor about Sean and me." It wasn't a question.

Tammi was stunned and not prepared for Elin.

She stammered, and Elin jumped in.

"You know what—Tammi, is it? First, that is untrue, and second, there aren't enough women in this place to even begin to make a dent, and you think you need to come after one of them? We're supposed to support each other, and I gotta deal with you, someone that before today, I've never even heard of. Are you *kidding* me?"

Tammi was crying. Quiet tears, unsatisfying to Elin, who wanted to see some full-on remorseful bawling.

"I've been scratching and clawing my way through this place for years so people like you, *women*, coming up behind me have an easier time of it, and you think it's a good idea to spread a lousy, false rumor about me? Not to mention the damage this does to Sean, who is happily married with a family."

By the time Tammi left Elin's office, Elin had offered her some tissues and let Tammi know that she hoped she'd learned something, sending her on her way with a final, "We've gotta be in this together, not trying to tear each other down."

Tammi nodded and sniffled her way through her apology, assuring Elin she understood. Elin had put up with this nonsense before, but this time it felt worse. It was a woman coming at her. A woman making stuff up about her. It was a woman expending energy to talk trash about Elin and a guy because she assumed that was the only way Elin could be promoted. Elin went to bat on this one for herself, for other women, and for her teammate Sean.

Although different from bullying, sexism contributes mightily to the unhealthy workplace culture that fuels bullying. It can come from those you least expect, and it can express itself in both obvious and discreet ways.

Obvious in the you-slept-your-way-to-the-top version, and obvious in being excluded from the pickup basketball game, the run, the golf outing, or whatever else.

Obvious in the gender pay gap that exists, but discreet in the fact you don't know about it.

Obvious in commenting on a woman's appearance, speaking over her in meetings, and thinking she shouldn't get the same housing allowance that her male counterpart did when she relocates to Singapore.

Expat . . . on the Cheap

In 2010, Niamh was asked to consider a newly formed role based in Singapore. She didn't have to think about it for long. She and her family were going.

After a whirlwind house hunting trip, Niamh and her husband settled on a school and nearby home. Both the school and the neighborhood had come highly recommended to them by an outgoing director, Darren, a gentleman at the same level as Niamh. Once Niamh and her husband returned from their trip, Niamh received a call from the HR person assigned to her.

"Hi, *Nee-ah*. I'm just reviewing the property you've selected. We don't have the budget for that, so if that's the house you want to rent, you'll need to pay the difference."

"Hi, my name is pronounced *Nee-ev*. I'm not following. We found a house on the same street as Darren; in fact, ours is next door and costs less than his. I'm confused."

"Well, we don't have the same budget for your housing costs, so if that's the house you want, you'll just need to cover that."

"Umm, just so you know, we're not going to *pay* to move into a job I was asked to take."

"Well, I hate to tell you, but if you want that house, you will need to cover the gap."

"OK. So let me get this straight. The guy who just repatriated, Darren, who's at the same level as me—that guy just vacated a house on the same block—wait, next door—with a higher rent, and his housing cost was covered without any out-of-pocket expense, and mine isn't? You might be wondering how I know that. Darren's a friend, so I asked. So just to be clear, we are not going to be out of pocket, taking this expat assignment. If that's what's needed, you should tell your boss, the guy who just hired me, that he needs to keep looking. And my name is pronounced *Nee-ev*."

There was a long pause. "I'll call you tomorrow, *Nee-ah*."

The next day, Niamh received confirmation. She had been approved for the house.

The Trifecta of Hell

You're receiving a crash course on the relationship between sexism and scarcity with workplace bullying. It makes sense, right? A culture that ignores the obvious signs of scarcity and sexism prompts those who are targeted to experience denial and secrecy. The trifecta of hell that robs us of our joy and convinces us to isolate ourselves in all that awfulness. Don't do it. It only feeds the shame.

A pop quiz, gossip about pretend sexual encounters, and different rules for different genders—all these things draw attention to, and perpetuate the idea of, "otherness": "Of course, I can't know as much about soccer as you because I don't look like you." "Of course, you can talk about me because I'm new, and you've now just alienated me." "Of course, you think you can give me a lower moving budget because you assume I'll take it, no questions asked." And of course, all these decisions happen under someone's watch, which, without a word, gives permission to other someones to do the same. Soon the entire culture is made up of the "us" versus "those who aren't us." The "thems." The "others."

DRILLS

- How are you showing up for others? What are you doing to forward another person's agenda/need?
- What are the steps you are taking to drive abundance versus falling into the scarcity trap?
- If you're a woman, have you been treated differently? If you're a person of color or gay or older or from a country outside the United States, have you been treated differently? How did you respond? How might you respond in the future?

8

The Three Types of Valuable Relationships

Allies, Sponsors, and Mentors

I run in order to acquire a void.

—HARUKI MURAKAMI

The previous two chapters highlighted the relationship between leadership and culture as well as sexism and scarcity, and how all these are contributing factors to the type of workplace culture that is established. Healthy, positive leadership equates to healthy workplace markers stacking up. Unhealthy, negative leadership equates to unhealthy workplace markers winning the day—and all too often, bullying begins and is tolerated in unhealthy workplaces.

This chapter and the three that follow drill down into real-life examples of workplace environments across various companies to illustrate both healthy and unhealthy workplace cultures. You'll know which is which, and you'll start to get a feel for those that breed commitment and trust and those that breed conflict and fear.

This chapter describes a healthy workplace environment and illustrates the three kinds of invaluable relationships you likely have with your own colleagues.

My First Marathon

I don't remember life without running. Starting way back when I was a little girl, my brother, Neil, would send me home from the Corbett's house to "go get the stuff to play."

"If you make it back in time, you can play with us."

Never waiting around for the definition of "back in time," I would sprint the three blocks back to our house, speedily rummage through our sports gear, and sprint back, arms full, to the sound of Neil's voice, " . . . 96, 97, 98 . . . ," having no idea if it meant I was on time or not.

"Close call this time," he'd say. Whew. But I was always chosen early in the first round to play with the boys.

I was a sprinter and jumper for the Kiwanis AAU Track Club growing up. As a high school athlete, I incorporated longer-distance running into my fitness program to ensure I had enough gas in the tank for game day. As an adult, I ran to stay in shape. Beyond that, running released me from the stress of life, the stress of work, the stress of loss—having experienced the sudden death of my beloved mother when she was 45 and I was 18. Running was my forward motion. Running allowed me to see myself as an athlete, and as an athlete, I knew I could do anything.

In 1999, when I was invited to join Nike Running for the first time in my career, little did I know what was in store for me. Nike was born from running; running was born from Nike. Every story about Nike begins with "a handshake between a track coach and a runner." The first shoes

Nike sold were running shoes; and they were sold out of the back of a car owned by a runner at running events. Oregon track and field coach Bill Bowerman's waffle iron outsole experiment is the stuff of legends.

Everywhere you look on the Nike campus, there are running references, from the moment you drive onto campus and spot the Michael Johnson track, Prefontaine Hall, and the bark-chip trails surrounding the property. And so it was with both excitement and trepidation that I found myself working in Nike Running, for although I ran, I didn't consider myself a "runner." I was a woman in her thirties who ran to stay in shape, and I was about to be surrounded by the running geeks of Nike. I was proud and honored to join Nike Running.

Here's what I learned very quickly about the people on the running team, those who worked on Nike's biggest business of running footwear—they were a tribe with their own common language and customs. Many of them ran competitively in college; some went on to compete in the Olympics, Olympic Trials, or other high-level running competitions. They ran together at lunch *and* after work. That's right; they ran at least twice a day.

One guy ran to work in the morning—from the east side of Portland, and I'm not talking about just-over-the-Willamette River east side; I'm talking about deep-into-Irvington—including many hills and a nasty right turn at Skyline to make sure it's a full 20-mile training run to Nike's campus in Beaverton—east side. He'd add some sprint work at lunch for "something easy." Years later, he would become the most decorated member of his Club Masters squad, holding world championship titles in multiple events. By day, he was the footwear product director for Nike Running and would quickly become my friend, mentor, and confidante.

"Hey, it's been a while since I've studied our running footwear," I told him. "Would you be able to teach me the line and talk me through what's coming out of the Innovation Kitchen?"

Kelvin had a crooked smile, a face that looked like it was cut from rock, and a voice by way of Georgia that sounded like sandpaper rubbed smooth. He smiled big at me and said, "Meegs, I'd be honored to do that with you."

I entered his office and was immediately surrounded by "running."

"You've created quite a cool cave for yourself here."

"Yeah, the crazy thing, Meegs, is from the outside looking in, you can't tell that we've tricked it out. It's an optical illusion of some sort so I'm staying ahead of the office sheriff that makes her rounds to ensure we haven't hung anything on the walls or changed the 'inspiring' blank spaces in any way. Anyhow, let's talk componentry first."

He proceeded to wax on for several hours about the beautiful parts that made up Nike running footwear, shifting from current models and finishing with what was coming next, ideas born from the most imaginative minds of those charged with keeping Nike at the forefront of innovation. By the time Kelvin finished, it had been four hours, and I felt as if I'd gone through a baptism. Part pastor, part conductor, part poet, all of it blending to evangelize the beauty of Nike Running to me, his new shadow.

Later, I would come to see Kelvin as an ally and as a colleague with whom I was aligned in our core values. These are exactly the kinds of informal allies who can help you simply to see yourself. While they may not be able to prevent bullying, these allies remind us of the things we sometimes forget when we are the target of bullying—that we are engaged in useful work, that there is a common mission with which the entire team is aligned, and that we are not alone.

It was during this time that I decided to run my first marathon. I knew it would be the best way for me to test footwear, ours and that of the competition. So I visited a Portland running specialty store as a "secret shopper" and was properly fitted without any reference to the fact I was a Nike employee. The store clerk asked me about my running and my goals and used a Brannock Device to measure my feet. After disappearing into the stockroom, he returned with four options—one from Nike and three others from, respectively, Asics, Brooks, and New Balance. After trying them on and running a bit in each one, I left the store with all four models and rotated among them as I trained throughout the streets and trails of Portland. With Kelvin's help, I had a weekly running schedule, tips for sleep and nutrition and, leading up to the event, a heavy dose of encouragement. I had told only Kelvin and one other coworker what I was doing, worried that I would back out on race day.

On the morning of the race, I forgot all the tips my coconspirator had provided and went out too fast. By mile 20, I was struggling, and my husband, Chris, jumped in to propel me to the finish line. Like a cycling peloton, I tucked in behind him and made my way through the tape.

"Boy, I wasn't sure I was going to finish that," I said while swaddled in my complementary foil blanket, chugging a blue drink that tasted salty.

Without missing a beat, the voice that carried me through the last six miles simply replied, "I knew you would."

At work the next day, everyone on the Nike Running team knew I had run. People knew my time, my splits, which water stations I used, and how many handfuls of gummy bears I shoved into my mouth. I was pleasantly surprised to be met with high fives and congratulations. After all, these were the people on the Nike Running team. These were *actual* runners—attired in split shorts, carrying a second pair of sneakers, running as transportation. Many of them had also run the marathon, with some winning and setting records in their particular age group. Running was what they did. For those who didn't run, they showed up and watched. Some counted swooshes that went by, while others counted competing marks to get a feel for how our brand fared.

At one point, Kelvin called everyone together. There was a cake and a gift to mark my first-ever marathon. In a large frame, a poster entitled "A Message from Nike Running" was presented to me. I was touched by this gesture from a culture that was familiar to me in the way it both supported and stretched me. I hadn't known it as I prepared for the marathon, but staring at this sacred gift that only a select few possessed, I realized that running the Portland Marathon had been my initiation into the Nike Running group. Running that marathon reminded me not only that I could do anything I set my mind to, but also that the connection in the workplace mattered to me a whole lot.

It was the relationships and camaraderie that propelled me forward. Kelvin taking the time to train me on footwear componentry would be invaluable to my ability to speak about product throughout my career.

He and the rest of the running team represented *Animal House* meets the Fieldhouse, and together we fueled a multibillion-dollar business with industry-defining innovation that blew the competition away, all while contending with the pressures that came with working in Nike Running.

The guys kept things loose by following Nike's Maxims, values that the company lived by, and adding a handful of tongue-in-cheek knockoffs of their own: "Always take credit for other people's work," "Work hard. Play harder," and "When in doubt, blame someone else."

Each day at exactly 5 p.m. the screeching sound of a vuvuzela was heard throughout the floor, signifying that it was time to put our work down, pause, and celebrate a good day's work. Pavlovian, the sound immediately prompted a collective release and a certain "fellowship" at the church of Nike Running. Mondays might mean "Mullet-Wig-Monday." Thursdays were always an optional "Thirst-Thursday" culminating in the chucking of empty PBR and soda cans—and an occasional bottle—up to a bin on the open floor above, drastically off target (they're runners, not ballers); and my personal favorite, the Friday dumpster races, whereby each team of two grabbed a dumpster, one person jumping in while the other provided a dramatic shove for a race down the long, wide hallway to an agreed-upon finish line in front of a cheering crowd. Prizes consisted of sweaty headbands, half-eaten doughnuts, and ripe singlets.

Afterward, it was back to work until the next day and more "reindeer games" that we all enjoyed. Together. As teammates. A team of mates. The kind of atmosphere that supported the unwritten message, at least in hindsight, that "No way could bullying happen here."

Allies, Sponsors, and Mentors

Not only did my experience in Nike Running provide me with memorable experiences and friendships I hold dear to this day, but within that group I had three kinds of colleagues who were invaluable to my workplace experience: allies, sponsors, and mentors. In other words, had I run into obstacles, and I did, I had people I could turn to for support.

You, too, have relationships across your organization that fall into these three categories. You may not have articulated these relationships in quite this way before, or understood the power of each, but all of us do have allies, sponsors, and/or mentors.

First, the classic ally.

I was introduced to the word "allies" from my mom, a history teacher. At dinner, discussions at the kitchen table included the Tet Offensive, D-Day, and all points in between. Once cleared, that same kitchen table became the backdrop for highly combative rounds of the board game Risk, ending with my brother Neil annihilating the rest of us. The definition of "allies" was simple. It meant "you're on my side."

It still means that, and so much more. No longer is it enough to tell me or show me that you're on my side when it's easy for you or when my cause is aligned with yours. Now, more than ever, "allies" holds some real gravitas, some real commitment. It takes my simple definition and doubles down. Today's allies speak on others' behalf, even when it's not the popular thing to do. Scratch that—*especially* when it's not the popular thing to do. Allies can be peers, subordinates, or superiors. As long as they address your interests, they are allies. They are the see-something, say-something, do-something crew. And they understand they can use their voice to help and support people and groups that are underprivileged, underserved, and just plain under.

Allies are advocates, and we all need them. Who are your allies? Who are the colleagues who seem to share your same outlook and understanding of both their own role and the mission of the organization? Remember, your allies do not have to be closely proximate to you, either physically or on the org chart. These are colleagues you trust, who see you, and who align with your interests.

Next, let's distinguish allies from sponsors.

Sponsors are those that put their name on you in a way that says, "I support this person for that role, experience, promotion." The alliance between you and your sponsor can be a powerful one. Your sponsor makes connections for you. Sponsors influence decisions about your career. I benefited from having sponsors during my time at Nike. There were sponsors who supported me for roles that I didn't think I was ready for; yet their confidence in me sparked my confidence. In other words, I had sponsors who expanded my perception well beyond what I thought I could do. And there were sponsors who were conditional sponsors. If you perform well, I'll continue to support you. If you don't, get lost. There were sponsors that I'm sure I don't even know about, who probably changed the course of my career—for good and ultimately for out.

Do you have colleagues you would consider to be sponsors? You don't need an explicit agreement, nor is it necessary for sponsors to perceive they are helping you personally rather than simply doing what helps the organization. What matters are the actions this person has taken in the past to support you and express confidence in your abilities.

And finally, mentors.

Mentors are those that advise, perhaps teach us. Kelvin was a mentor, not only when he helped me get ready to run, but when he taught me about footwear componentry. The time he took doing that made me a better employee.

Mentors provide guidance across a wide array of subjects: "Can you take a look at my résumé?" "I've got this interview coming up. Can you help me prep?" "My supervisor asked me to do something that I don't agree with. What should I do?"

I had people who supported me, were thought partners with me, and showed up for me. Some organizations have official mentoring programs. As a mentee, I found that I had the most success with my mentors when I drove the process. It wasn't about quantity, but quality. I reached out, set up check-ins, and always had work product to discuss as opposed to an unprepared, spontaneous approach.

Do you have a mentor, whether formally or informally? Are there people in the organization you look to for guidance, people you hope to learn from and who seem eager (or at least willing) to provide you with that knowledge? Consider these relationships, and add them to your list alongside your allies and sponsors.

Nike Running was a clique, but not the kind of clique that was closed to new members. Instead, it was one I was welcomed into by allies, sponsors, and mentors with open arms, an open road, and open minds. Taking it all in, I knew that, just like all the best teams, this was one in which the team was always bigger, stronger, and more talented than any one individual. We understood and committed to the vision. We solved problems together, respectfully. We felt valued because our ideas were valued. And we rewarded and celebrated each other along the way.

Within the Nike Running team, we had codified and operationalized a healthy workplace culture into our business practices. In other words, "workplace culture" wasn't something separate and distinct from the work we were doing. The processes we put in place across all functions— including the lighthearted games; the breaks to run, exercise, and move; the willingness to teach a new teammate and to learn from her as well; and the shared accountability—cultivated a healthy workplace culture and produced beyond the results we expected.

When you're surrounded at work by people who not only have your back, but will go out of their way to help make you better, you know you've landed in a healthy workplace environment. You know it because you feel safe, heard, encouraged, and seen. You look around, and you're certain these people would break down and through walls on your behalf.

Within my Nike Running environment there were allies, sponsors, and mentors. In a healthy workplace culture, your allies, sponsors, and mentors help you achieve, contribute to the common goals of the team and the organization, and grow. In an unhealthy workplace, these relationships might help you navigate bullying behaviors, toxic conditions, and unaligned teams.

Either way, it will be useful for you to consider and categorize the relationships you maintain in your organization—and later in this book, I'll help you understand when and how each can be helpful.

DRILLS

- How are you contributing to a healthy culture in your workplace or organization?
- Who are your allies, sponsors, and mentors?
- Do you serve these roles for anyone else? If so, how?
- If the workplace culture feels healthy, are you optimistic that it will always remain so? Is it good or bad to trust that bullying could never seep into your workplace? What role can you play to maintain a healthy culture?

9

There's No "I" in "Team"

What about your friends?

—TLC

The previous chapter highlighted the relationship between leadership and an environment rich with allies, sponsors, and mentors, all contributing to a healthy workplace culture. A team performing at its best, delivering wins, and nurturing a healthy culture is easier to spot than one that may be delivering results and wins but is contributing to an unhealthy environment. In this chapter, you'll gain a further understanding of the latter.

Nobody is harder on Ashley than Ashley. Her own inner drive to succeed is higher than what anyone else, including her retired Air Force general father, could ever ask of her. She approached her job in global finance with the same high expectations. She was disciplined, prepared, and always willing to put in the work.

Then it happened. Bullying in a way she had never experienced. A 15-year veteran, she found herself struggling for a glimpse of the company that had inspired her for so long, had challenged her in the healthiest, most motivating ways, had always put the team first, had valued her, had allowed her to see the world, had led her to work with the best people, and had surrounded her in what had always been her passion—economics.

Yet she was blindsided when she did something she had always done and always done well—coached a member of her team.

Ashley's team embraced her "open-door" policy, and she discovered that many of her team, particularly the women, were looking for advice on how best to navigate a global company and how to emerge as leaders within the organization. This part of Ashley's job was the most gratifying, and she soon earned a reputation for being someone who would help others with career planning at a moment's notice.

Although she was an advocate for both men and women, when she was assigned to a high-level position in London, it was the younger women who gravitated to her office. These "emerging leaders" were from all over the world. They were starving for attention from someone who had worked at headquarters and who could coach and consult with them. As women, they wanted to know what steps they needed to take to navigate a male-dominated company within a male-dominated industry. By word of mouth, they started lining up at Ashley's door.

The Hierarchy

After working in London for two years with an incredible team of people, Ashley was promoted to senior vice president. The job was based in Germany, and she, along with her family, was excited about the move.

At work, Ashley's new team also consisted of people from around the globe. For Ashley, having grown up a self-proclaimed "military brat," and having lived in Japan, Germany, and the United States, she embraced the opportunity to work with multiple cultures. Although, she kept hearing about one person on her team, Helen, in a "good luck working with *her*" sort of way, she was looking forward to getting to know each member of the team.

Ashley had never met Helen, and she knew that she would give her the same respect and chance she gave everyone else. It wasn't that she didn't care what other people's experiences had been with Helen, but she'd long had the freedom and encouragement to form her own opinions about her teammates—especially females—whom she wanted to support in any way she could in their male-dominated environment.

When Ashley met Helen, it was her handshake that she first noticed. It nearly dropped her to her knees. Helen had a grip of steel, eyes of determination, and a directness that Ashley immediately liked.

However, it wasn't long before she saw hints, and then head-on collisions, of what people had warned her about. Helen could level people with just a few well-aimed words.

"Tell me something helpful," Helen spat out at an associate, who looked to Ashley for guidance and decided not to verbally strike back.

"That does me no good," she hissed to another colleague, who looked to Ashley for support.

And to another, "Is that the best you've got?"

These were her teammates, all working toward a common goal and all looking at Ashley with pleading eyes until, finally, after a particularly damaging meeting, one of her most senior leaders came to her with a simple question: "We are all walking on eggshells; how much carnage do you think we can withstand from Hurricane Helen?"

Ashley didn't need a second question. These were tenured leaders of the company who had all been disrespected by Helen. Not only that, but the team's work started to suffer. People were so busy trying to placate Helen—*don't set her off*—that their own processes, protocols, and potential were diminished.

Ashley's first step was to go to Helen's direct manager, a male peer of Ashley's. Elias and Ashley had always had an easy rapport, although this was their first opportunity to work directly together.

Ashley entered his office, took a seat, and outlined the situation for him.

She began, "I'd like to sit down with Helen and give her some constructive coaching to ensure that her interpersonal skills support her in what I know will continue to be a long runway here. She's a real powerhouse talent, and I want to make sure that's what people are seeing and feeling."

"Ah, that's just Helen," Elias replied. "I tell you what you do: use this approach with her. In fact, here's a great quote from a book I'm reading. It will really work on her."

Ashley waited patiently as he flipped through a leadership book sitting on his desk.

"Ah, here it is: 'Remain calm. Be kind. Have a vision. Be demanding.' It's so great how the author talks about being demanding while being kind. This will be the perfect angle with Helen."

Although the advice was a bit condescending, Ashley appreciated Elias's support. She left his office, confident the two of them were on the same page with regard to coaching Helen. A few days later, Ashley sat down with Helen in her office.

"Helen, I'm so glad you're on my team," Ashley said. "I can see why you were handpicked for this role. You are already doing such a great job."

"Well, thank you," she answered, smiling.

"Yes, the work you and your team are putting together will be industry-defining. I'm really pleased with how you're tracking. I do need to talk to you about what I'm observing with the team, just to make you aware. You have such a long runway here, and I'd like to support you with that. I just want to ensure that your approach with people, especially your teammates, is going to contribute to the collaborative environment that I'm establishing." Ashley went on to share some of the specific observations she had seen.

Helen sat up a bit straighter, a look of concern crossing her face.

"I've never heard this type of feedback. I don't understand."

"You are great at what you do, and I'd like to support you in ensuring that you're interacting with your teammates in a way that will encourage collaboration and teamwork so that everyone is operating at their best."

Ashley reached for the book quote. "I know you can find the balance between being demanding of the team while being kind. Please take my feedback in the spirit in which it is given—as feedback. And know that I support you."

Helen abruptly rose from her chair.

"Thank you," she said, bristling, and walked out of Ashley's office.

Twenty minutes later there was a soft knock on Ashley's open door. Helen had returned.

"I was a bit caught off guard earlier. I want to thank you for your feedback, and I also want you to know that you will never have to have that kind of conversation with me again."

"That's a great goal, Helen. I want to reiterate how excited I am to have you on my team. I'm here for you, and I'm really looking forward to continuing to work with you. I appreciate you coming back to tell me that."

Despite the rocky end to their first meeting, Ashley was pleased with how the conversation had gone. As she made her way to Elias's office to close the loop with him, she was confident that she and Helen were on the same page.

"Hey, just wanted to let you know, I spoke with Helen. I used the approach you recommended, the book quote, the whole deal, and I think it went well. At first, she was a bit taken aback, but she came back to my office to thank me and to let me know she's on it."

"Ah, that's great. I knew she would take it well."

Leave It Alone

Several days later, Ashley got a call from the executive to whom she dotted-line reported. He was based at the company's US headquarters. Amid catching each other up on a few things, he surprised her by asking if she had talked to Helen recently.

"Yes, I had a coaching conversation with her," Ashley answered, thumbing through her notebook to find where she had documented the conversation.

"What about?"

Ashley got him up to speed, using her notes as a guide.

"I need you to leave that one alone," he said.

"What do you mean 'leave it alone'?"

"I'm just gonna have to ask you to leave that one alone. Word of your conversation got back to the managing director, and he's concerned. I mean, he knows your work, but . . ."

If initially alarmed, Ashley was now calling "Mayday! Mayday!" She had arrived in Germany two months prior, ostensibly because of her leadership abilities, specifically around building a healthy team culture that delivered results, and now one of her bosses was telling her that her boss's boss was concerned about a coaching conversation she'd had with someone on her team.

"Listen," Ashley said, "I don't know what you mean by 'concerned,' but what I *do* know is that *you* know me. You've worked with me for long enough to know my approach with people, and I've done nothing to 'concern' anyone. I even got the endorsement from Elias before meeting with her. Frankly, this is textbook in terms of coaching."

"OK, OK, I know," he backpedaled. "'Concerned' may not have been the right word. I just need you to back off from Helen. Just trust me on this."

Perplexed, Ashley hung up the phone. She wasn't sure what she had stumbled into, but she tried to brush it off and get some work done. A few hours later, though, her on-site, direct-line manager asked her to come see him.

"Hey, Ash, did you have a conversation with Helen recently?"

Hold everything. How could a simple coaching conversation have turned into this?

"Yes, I had a coaching conversation with her. Her approach is tough to work with and was tearing down my team, which I've only just established and am trying to build up. I had more than a few complaints about her and observed her damaging behavior myself, so I spoke to her about it. I got the necessary backing from Elias first and thought she and I had a very decent, professional conversation."

He sat back, looked at Ashley, and said, "Yeah, I'm gonna need you to bring it down a bit. Helen has a certain style, and I need you to just back off that a bit."

"You know I've already gotten a call about this, right? With the same message. I don't understand. This is my brand-new team, and I'm trying to establish a climate of collaboration and trust, and you don't want me to coach someone whose behavior is not aligned with that? I'm totally confused."

"Yeah, with 'this one,' just bring it down a bit. OK? Good. I've got to jump on a call. Thanks for coming up. Everything else good? *Good.*"

And Ashley was excused from his office.

She immediately found her way to Elias's office, the colleague who had endorsed her approach.

"I just want to ensure you and I are OK on my approach with Hel—."

"No," he boomed, "we're *not* OK. You didn't even give her a chance. I mean, you just got here. Maybe it's *you* who people can't work with."

Ashley could hardly form words, much less get them out of her mouth, so taken aback and surprised was she by this verbal assault. He'd done a complete about-face.

Finger-pointing, he wasn't finished, "You haven't even been here three months, and you're already coming after Helen? She's like a sister to me, an aunt to my children, and you come in here in your first few months and have some problem with her? *You're* the problem."

Ashley tried to get a word in, but his rising voice and angry eyes cut her off as his whole physical presence bore down on her, never pausing for breath. Elias was on the attack and would not let up.

Ashley had never felt so dehumanized. She backed away from him and let herself out, relieved to be away from him.

By the time she made it back to her office and shut her door, Ashley was physically shaking. She thought, "How has a coaching conversation, something I'm known for and one I've done millions of times, turned into this?"

It didn't take Elias long to show Ashley he wasn't finished with her. In meetings, he went out of his way to contradict what she'd said, just for sport. He no longer said hello.

"Guten Morgen!" Elias shouted as he approached the table at which Ashley was seated. "Hello, Gio; Hello, Kirk; Hello, Fred . . ." He stopped for a beat to rest his cold stare at Ashley, before moving on. "Hello, Erik; Hello, Ben . . ."

When she was presenting to the leadership team, he settled into the back of the room, slouched in his chair, and wouldn't make eye contact. He proceeded to be disruptive, whispering and laughing with whomever he was sitting near, paying attention to his phone instead of Ashley's presentation.

At a global business meeting, Elias and Ashley were asked to present together, the two of them making the same presentation several times in one day, with groups rotating through. After the first group, Elias looked at her and said, "Hey, how about if you stop just repeating what I'm saying"—and walked away.

Ashley was beyond perplexed, disheartened, and disillusioned. She had just come off contributing to some of the best work the company had ever delivered, as affirmed by the executive team, and now she was being punished for doing something that had always been a significant strength of hers. Meanwhile, Hurricane Helen, fresh off a trip to global headquarters, was taking people out with renewed vigor and without any regard to her teammates, nor to the talk she and Ashley had. Several people who reported to Helen asked to be reassigned but were too scared to share the real reason they wanted to make a move. While they knew Ashley was a strong leader, they had seen and experienced Helen's tyrannical behavior go unchecked.

Where once Ashley felt confident and valued, she now felt like she was losing her footing. Something she had rarely thought about was now top of mind—she wondered if she would have been treated like this if she were a man. Her coaching approach, she thought, would have been appreciated for its exact intent, helping her colleague better herself to ensure her career runway was open and clear and the team dynamic was a safe and collaborative one. No one would have questioned Ashley's motives, and she would never have been spoken to in the way the three men spoke to her.

Ashley began to realize that the "good ole boy" network that she had always navigated, even embraced, because she never felt it excluded her, was now taking on a different sheen. Her male colleague was a member of a club to which she was not invited, didn't belong, and was beginning to understand she would never belong. How could she—it wasn't built with her in mind. Ashley was starting to see it as an actual club in which everyone operated in the same petty, bullying manner, and not only got *away* with it, but got *ahead* with it. She was surrounded by damaging and diminishing behavior.

After a while, Ashley decided to take the path of least resistance and forced herself to turn a blind eye to Elias's antics. *Adjust. Overcome the obstacle.* Just like her father had taught her. Instead of a leadership team where the members had each other's backs, it had become a command culture of "I say, you do." So Ashley *did*.

Regardless of what her colleague Elias thought of her or how he mistreated her, Ashley did her job well. She convinced herself that she didn't notice his disrespect anymore, even as he actually hung up on her during a rare phone call between them. Except she did notice. Every single day. And it was exhausting.

With some fight still left in her, Ashley marched up to Elias and simply said, "You wanna continue to act like a childish bully, go ahead, but don't ever hang up on me again. That's completely unprofessional and inappropriate." She walked away, but not before she saw the smirk forming on his lips with the knowledge that he was getting to her.

Yeah. Elias was getting to her. On a team-building trip, he and Ashley were assigned to the same team for a business-scavenger hunt. The answer to one of the clues was "maternity coverage," to which Elias commented while eyeing Ashley, "Yeah, maternity clothes. You should wear them!" Smirk intact.

A Much-Needed Ally

Finally, after a meeting with Elias and several other teammates, one of her friends stayed behind to discuss a particular direction and asked, "Ash, what's going on?"

Ashley paused, shutting her eyes. The situation with Elias had become untenable, and Ashley's colleague had picked up on the fact that he overlooked her in meetings, skipped over her contributions as if she hadn't spoken, and generally made her invisible. Since she had been ordered to back off, Ashley felt she had nowhere to turn, no support. Plus, she didn't complain. She worked. And yet she felt completely alone in this weird space she was taking up. Ashley was one of the key leaders of the European office. She was managing multibillion-dollar holdings. But she was on the outside looking in. She was not able to manage a member of her team in the hope of helping her become a better teammate on an even stronger team in which all members felt safe and respected. Ashley had been dismissed by one of her peers at every turn.

She confided in her friend.

"Oh, Ash," her friend said. "I'm so sorry to hear this."

"I know. It's awful. *He* is awful. It doesn't matter what I do; he is just a complete jerk."

"I've seen him do this to other people," her friend said. "He sets people up for a fall and then pounces. So maybe take some solace in the fact that it's not just you. I have your back."

"Thanks," Ashley replied.

And Ashley meant it wholeheartedly. It was the first time in over a year that someone—an ally—validated what Ashley was feeling. "I have your back" meant everything to her at that moment. It didn't fix the problem, but she felt seen and sane.

Meanwhile, Helen continued to run roughshod over Ashley's team, but Ashley's hands were tied. Ashley considered going to HR, but because the managing director, to whom both Ashley and HR reported, told Ashley to "back off," she didn't feel comfortable doing so.

Finally, a year later, Elias blessedly moved to another role but remained in the German office. His replacement was a friend of Ashley's, whom she had worked with throughout her career. During their first meeting, he asked, "Ash, what happened between you and Helen?"

"I honestly don't know." Ashley then proceeded to tell him her version of what happened. She still felt so completely in the dark and had come to learn that Elias was spewing nonsense about her every chance he got.

Ashley's colleague took it in, nodding as she spoke. When she finished, he said, "I was at dinner with a number of high-level people back at global headquarters, and this issue was brought up," he continued, "He made it known at that dinner that he was coming after you."

"Why? I don't understand this."

"That's all I know. Just let me manage Helen. Let me help you with this. Just stay clear of Elias. Let me do some PR for you with him and see if I can help. He doesn't know you like I do. He doesn't know what a generous leader you are, how good you are with your teams. I'm so sorry this happened. Just put some distance between you and Elias, and let me help with Helen."

The beautiful thing about allies is that they can show up when you least expect—and most need—them. "Let me help you" was an action statement made by a peer that not only meant the world to Ashley, but was carried out. He did help. He ran cover for Ashley with Elias and managed Helen in such a way that her outbursts at the team abated.

Although Ashley would never fully understand what she had stumbled into when she chose to coach Helen, a few things were made clear.

Helen was protected in a way that Ashley wasn't. She learned this the hard way. Ashley didn't have the support from those she thought she did. It was a binary choice: Helen or Ashley. Not only that, but it was also clear that the managing director and the rest of the executives had Elias's back, while no one had Ashley's. They were fine with Elias coming after her. Ashley felt she was on her own.

When senior leaders elevate an individual over the team, they seed several unhealthy markers. Although the vision may be clear, the mechanics to reach that vision are broken. In this example, problems were "solved" from the top down or were completely ignored. Ashley's entire team was made to feel undervalued, and misbehavior was rewarded. The result was a culture of disharmony, mistrust, and fear. In addition, by not allowing a team member to receive coaching from a proven leader who was willing to coach her, the organization undermined a healthy workplace culture in the making while stunting a future leader's development and growth. In other words, blind loyalty to an individual resulted in no one winning and an unhealthy culture taking root.

Additionally, although Elias had endorsed Ashley in providing Helen with feedback—" . . . here's a great quote from a book I'm reading. It will really work on her"—when she did so, she inadvertently electrified the system in such a way that drew attention to Elias's inability to coach his direct report. Ashley doing her job highlighted the fact that Elias hadn't been doing his. He was fully aware of how Helen operated. He had seen it firsthand for years—"that's just Helen." But he was unwilling to provide her—"she's like a sister to me"—with the feedback she needed and deserved. His own insecurity was then leveled at Ashley while being encouraged and permitted from above.

It's important to understand and respect the cumulative effect bullying has on targets. Just as all the positive work experiences we have add up to us being well suited for promotions, so too do the negative effects of bullying start to chip away at our abilities and confidence.

When colleagues ambush us, they set off a chain of events that can affect how we operate from that moment on. While Elias was intentionally keeping Ashley off balance and enjoying it, her chemical makeup was changing, her body's ability to process stress was malfunctioning, and her belief in herself began to plummet. Even if/when someone in the know validated that she was being mistreated, the damage to her as a human being and business leader was significant.

There were several moments during this experience in which allies jumped in and supported Ashley simply by listening, having her back, protecting her, and educating her. Those allies made it a point to connect with Ashley—even if there was nothing they could do about the problem—in a way that established trust. But there were more times when people who witnessed what was happening didn't jump in. In fact, in this example, Ashley was told to back off by the two people to whom she reported.

When leaders set that kind of example, it takes even more courage for others to become allies—and to help thwart the cowards. But what of the targets? By not going to HR, Ashley denied herself that avenue of potential support. It's clear why she chose not to—the big boss had told her to back off. There were two people who came forward and told Ashley they had her back; yet they never addressed what they were seeing to human resources or to the managing director. They witnessed both Helen's and Elias's disrespectful behavior and didn't send up a flare for help. Although it made Ashley feel better to have some people in her corner, keeping Elias's bullying behavior to themselves only served to enhance the unhealthy workplace culture.

DRILLS

- When was the last time you said something when you saw something happening that shouldn't be happening?
- What are the risks in doing so?
- What are the risks in *not* doing so?

10

Being Invited Is Not the Same as Being Included

You were never Little Red Riding Hood;
you were always the wolf.

—ABBY WAMBACH

The previous few chapters highlighted the relationship between leadership and workplace culture with a healthy result and an unhealthy result. At face value, it can be difficult to spot when unhealthy markers are taking hold. Even when organizations attempt to do the right thing, if a healthy foundation has not been set, the results can feel transactional and damaging. As you'll see in this example, sometimes what is damaging to one person can be inspiring to another.

Why am I sharing this particular story of workplace culture with you? And what does it have to do with bullying?

By now, you understand the connection between bullying and unhealthy workplace environments—cultures where inappropriate behavior is allowed to exist and perpetuate. You also are more familiar with the damaging and diminishing role that sexism and scarcity play. And so one of the most important things we can do to eliminate workplace bullying is to stop healthy workplaces from turning into unhealthy ones. All of us should be attuned to the health of the culture around us, and each of us has a responsibility to take action when we sense our organization's environment turning from healthy to unhealthy. This requires intention, heavy lifting, and courage.

For me, this shift came quickly, and I was uncertain what to do about it.

As a 27-year veteran, I sensed that the entire organization was experiencing a change, but I didn't understand it, much less see it clearly. I had run into workplace bullying, but it was like the perfectly executed pick and roll in a basketball game. You can see it coming, but you can't get through the screen fast enough without getting tangled up in it, which is exactly what bullies want.

The thing about workplace bullying is that it shatters what you know to be true. You start questioning your entire belief system. Showing up and doing your job well turns into this unfamiliar, uncomfortable, unforeseeable event each day in which you no longer know whom to trust or how you will be tested.

I had no time to think about what was happening. I just worked. After all, the NBA All-Star Game was upon us. My team and I would transform the NYC marketplace into a basketball "playground." Much as we had done in London for the 2012 Summer Olympics, we would employ a similar strategy in bringing innovative products, services, and experiences to life.

I was looking forward to the event for many reasons: I knew the preparation that we had worked on for months would be flawlessly executed and would set a new standard for Nike. I loved New York and all its smells and action. And I was definitely excited about the game itself. Better yet, I had figured out a way to bring my 10-year-old son, Spencer, with me. One of my brothers, Brian, was planning on being in New York for work at the same time and agreed to take care of Spence while I worked.

Like many working parents, I lived a dual life of hard-charging executive and "Mama," missing out on a lot of real-time conversations, walks to school, and tuck-ins at night. To bring my son and my work together in the Big Apple meant the world to me.

The team worked tirelessly and brought our vision to life as planned. The executive team was thrilled, and our brand was well positioned. Because I had been busy from dawn to dusk each day, I hadn't seen Spence yet, but on the day of the actual All-Star Game—and with my work wrapped up—I was looking forward to meeting up with my brother and Spence for an early dinner before heading to Madison Square Garden and the main event.

As we were completing our work, an email arrived from the president of the brand:

You've been invited to play hoops on the Jordan court. Tip off at 2 PM.

Whoa. Didn't see that coming. This wasn't the type of invitation that just anyone got. In fact, as I glanced through those on the invitee list, I saw the names of multiple senior vice presidents. So I had a conundrum.

Choice one: Turn off work mode and get ready for a fun time with my son and my brother. Since I was one of only two females on the invitee list, a polite refusal to play hoops would have been natural, perhaps even expected and appreciated.

Choice two: Meet "the guys" at the Jordan court and play some ball. I called my brother and painted the picture for him.

"You've gotta go play!" both he and Spencer said in unison.

Game Time

When I arrived at the court, still dressed in my work clothes, I made my way to a basketball court that was almost too pretty to step on. It was glistening white, with aqua blue filling the key, surrounding the iconic Jumpman logo, as well as bordering the court. It looked like untouched powder snow under a clear-blue sky. I had the same reaction I had when my dad took me on the "It's a Small World" ride at Disneyland for the first time as a child: the Jordan court took my breath away, and I knew it would be something I would always remember.

As I looked around at the men shooting hoops, I felt right at home. It was a basketball court, the cradle in which I was raised as a baby. I started shooting around with the guys. A young man approached our group of 12.

"Hey, guys, we have everything you'll need to play set up for you in individual lockers. Follow me."

Eleven men followed him, leaving me alone on the court, sweating in my pink cashmere sweater.

"Do you have somewhere for me to change?" I asked the young man when he returned.

"Oh, yes. We just had to take care of the guys first."

I stared at him, annoyed, and then said, "Well, yes, I can certainly see why that would make sense since there are 11 of them and 1 of me."

At that moment, I had a choice to make—stay or go. I could stay and wait my turn like the good little girl that I had always been or go—go and have fun with my son and my brother. A continuous loop played in my head—stay . . . go . . . stay . . . go . . . and just as I was about to leave, one of the men, a sponsor of mine, came out, dressed down and ready to play. He bounded over to me and noticed that I was still in my street clothes.

"What's the matter? Aren't you gonna play?"

"Yeah, but they had to take care of you guys first."

He hung his head, shook it, and said, "We really have to make this hard on you, don't we?"

"Seems like it."

Just then, all the men came out, high-fiving, laughing, trash-talking.

"I can take you back to change now," said a young woman who seemed to have appeared out of nowhere.

As she led me to the locker room, I heard the young man yell, "OK, guys, let's get you warmed up!"

Once in the locker room, I found a jersey and shorts, socks, and shoes, which had been laid out for me. No sports bra. I kept repeating to myself, "Just get dressed, Megan; just get dressed, Megan; just get dressed . . ."

Suited up, I joined the men on the court. Since they had warmed up, they were already playing five on five. Never shy around a basketball court, I immediately tapped in, tore down the court, and dished for a bucket. Transitioning back on defense, I stole a sloppy lob pass, dribbled to the other end, and hit a nice little jumper.

At one point, as I was taking the ball past mid-court, I heard the president say to another guy on the bench, "Well, she's clearly played."

That's right. I played. And now I *play*.

In my Natori underwire.

As the end of the game neared, I decided I would get to the locker room first to change. I had been struggling for so long at work due to bullying that the slight at the courts seemed like a "last straw" moment for me. The toxic work environment I'd been enduring, combined with the stress of All-Star prep on zero sleep, left me with nothing in my emotional tank. Then, when I should have been treated with the same respect and inclusion as the men who showed up to play basketball, I'd been made to feel like a burden, an inconvenience, an afterthought—at, of all places, a basketball court.

One of the highest points in my career, marked by bringing my son to see what Mama did for a living, had turned into one of the lowest points for me. I had busted my butt, and my team worked just as hard, to ensure our All-Star work was industry-defining. It *was*—not because anyone told me; no one did, but I knew it was, and I knew my value because of the work my team and I put into it.

The invitation to play basketball had been the cherry on top. I saw it as a gift that I was grateful to receive. It turned out, my gratitude so distracted me that I didn't notice yet another hook caught in my cheek to bait me into believing that I belonged. I did not.

I quickly made my way to the locker room—not in that bounding way athletes do after playing a fun game of basketball. Yes, I was sweating, and I was proud of how I had shown up. At 50, I could still get up and down the court, handle the ball, and hit my shot. But beyond that, there was no Springsteen "Glory Days" playing in my ears. No, I raced back to that locker room to get away. Away from this uniform that wasn't made for me. Away from these men who didn't respect me. Away from this place that suddenly felt foreign to me. Away from a system that wasn't built for me. I didn't need to be seen as special. I simply needed to be seen, period.

In a healthy workplace environment, moments like this often do feel special. They are a way for a team to bond, to celebrate, and to feel even more acutely a part of a larger whole. When every person on the team is respected and truly included, and every person feels a part of the team, fun outings serve to strengthen the team and strengthen each person's ties to it.

In an unhealthy workplace environment, these kinds of events and moments serve to simply amplify the larger disparities at play. Often there are a *series* of such moments and actions—but there may be one that perfectly crystalizes for you the state of your organization's culture. When I played in that basketball game on the Jordan court, there was more than passing, dribbling, and shooting on display. Sexism and scarcity were hard at work. There were two women invited to play basketball. Two. One showed up.

For targets of bullying, who are uncertain of themselves and have begun to question whether they fit into the company's mission any longer, a moment that even hints at communicating "you are not fully welcome here" can be devastating. It can have an impact that, to a neutral observer, may seem outsized in relation to the actual event. That's because it's the straw that breaks the camel's back—and the neutral observer hasn't witnessed all the straw already piled on that camel!

In this way, the effects of a sexist working environment can be similar to the effects of institutional racism. Until you are conscious of the structural reality, you spend a lot of time and energy wondering what's happening and why.

But the story doesn't end there.

Once back in my street clothes, cloaked in disappointment, with a side order of anger, I quickly made my way toward the exit, when three female employees approached me. One of them was the woman who had shown me to the locker room. The other two had been working behind the scenes.

"That was so cool that you played," said one.

"Yeah," said another, "thanks for doing that."

"You playing showed us that we could do that," said the third.

Their comments were like water to a lost soul in the desert.

"You're welcome," I said.

Workplace bullying is so damaging, and it results in targets subconsciously questioning our professional existence at every turn. It's hard to predict when our own feelings of disrespect and exclusion might actually serve to inspire those we don't even know are watching. When those women shared what watching me play in that basketball game meant to them, they acknowledged my existence and they validated me. In that moment, they signed up to speak up and to show up for others, and I knew that was a win. I was confident that they and you will:

1. **SUIT UP.** Put the kit on. Even when it's not easy in a system not built to support you.
2. **YELL FOR THE BALL.** Use your voice, especially when it's not easy in a system not built to support you.
3. **TAKE YOUR SHOT.** Bet on yourself in a system not built to support you.

The one positive that you can take away from such a moment is clarity. Clarity that your workplace environment is not going to suddenly, magically improve. Clarity that you aren't crazy. Clarity that your workplace culture really has shifted and really does tolerate behavior that a healthy workplace environment would not. Clarity about who your allies truly are. And clarity that you may need to forward the invitation to play or create your own pickup game.

That clarity will help you see what you need to do.

DRILLS

- When did you suit up, call for the ball, and take your shot? How did that feel? Was it easy? Difficult? Afterward, how did you feel? Alternatively, have there been times you wish you would have done so?
- How have you as an ally/leader dealt with bullying incidents you've either seen or heard about? How did you step in and step up, even when the culture of the organization made it seem like you were swimming against the tide? Did you persevere? What might you do differently next time?

11

What You're Experiencing Is Trauma

Even the largest, strongest, and fleetest person
may be driven to despair by bullying,
taunting, and constant insults.

—TED WELLS

This chapter describes the physical, emotional, and psychological toll that workplace bullying takes on targets. It may be triggering, and therefore it may be important for you to surround yourself with support. There is still such a societal stigma toward those suffering the very real psychological and physical effects of workplace bullying. It's this stigma that keeps targets covered in a shame storm of secrecy, lest we appear mentally unstable.

So let me be clear. This chapter is about me and the depths to which I fell as the result of having been the target of workplace bullying over several years. I'm sharing this in case you too find yourself in this situation. You are not alone.

———

There has been research into the negative consequences of workplace bullying. The statistics are grim.

According to a Workplace Bullying Institute study, targets of workplace bullying report a wide range of *physical* damage:

- 77 percent of targets report sleep disorders.
- 48 percent suffer migraine and tension headaches.
- 60 percent report cardiovascular symptoms, from hypertension through cardiac arrest.
- 33 percent suffer chronic fatigue–like symptoms.
- 37 percent report gastrointestinal distress.
- 17 percent suffer skin disorders.

And so on. Just as every person is unique, every target of workplace bullying processes the behaviors differently, and each target's body reacts to the stress of bullying in its own way. Taken in the aggregate, though, it's clear that targets frequently suffer *physically* from their bullies' attacks.

Similarly, studies show that targets suffer widespread psychological consequences. In a 2012 study, the Workplace Bullying Institute found that targets report a wide range of severe symptoms including:

- 52 percent suffered panic attacks.
- 49 percent reported clinical depression.
- 30 percent suffered PTSD.
- Fully 80 percent reported increased anxiety.

As well, targets reported intrusive flashbacks (50 percent), increased anger (66 percent), and even suicidal ideation (29 percent). A sense of betrayal was experienced by 74 percent of targets; 63 percent reported distrust of the organization.

For me personally, the physical and emotional consequences of the bullying behaviors I felt were real. I experienced a physical decline over the course of several years—but I kept working as hard as I knew how, and I tried to pretend things were normal. Two events finally served as a wake-up call.

On a work trip to Dallas, running on a cocktail of stress, sleep deprivation, and paranoia, I finally crashed. It was after midnight, and I was fumbling with my key card at the door of my hotel room, trying to slide it into the receptacle as I balanced my shoulder bag, a map of the hotel, an apple, and my focus.

A sudden movement down the hall caught my eye. Though I knew it was a hotel employee from the beige uniform, I was also convinced—as certain of this as I was of my own name—that the hotel employee was going to break into my room and try to kill me. I was so convinced, I hurried inside my room and immediately pushed against the closed, locked door the heaviest object I could find—the desk.

I felt numb and wired at the same time and spent the next six hours awake in my room, until it was time to lead a meeting the next morning.

Terrified, Anxious, and Paranoid

Soon after, I walked into my general practitioner's office for my annual physical.

She took my blood pressure and weight—and noted both were up—then cut to the chase.

"What is going on, Megan?

My weight was up partially because I had stopped exercising and couldn't seem to get enough food in my mouth at once. I had always considered myself "an athlete," often being asked if I was a soccer player or gymnast back in the day, because of my build, and now I wasn't sure I could even find the gym.

I shared with her what was going on at work.

"What other symptoms are you having?" she asked.

At that point, I came clean. I told her about the migraines. I told her about my lack of sleep. The nightmares I'd begun having that caused me to wake up screaming. The anxiety. The paranoia. The lack of energy. How I felt insulated, isolated, invisible.

I had turned into someone I didn't even recognize. The isolation I was feeling at work seeped into my personal life. Although I tried hard to put on a happy face and to participate in our family activities, I was cloaked in darkness, which resulted in me not feeling good enough about my work, my value, my ability to contribute, myself.

I was constantly sick. I didn't sleep. I no longer ran. I no longer worked out. I no longer sought out anything that might help me feel good about myself. Instead, I turned inward, walking invisibly through the motions of life, bingeing on *Grey's Anatomy* and *Downton Abbey* to comfort me. I needed to dance it out with Meredith and Cristina or become a member of the Crawley family to get through my days.

Finally, because I knew I had to, I told my doctor about the nightmare that had returned. The one I used to have every night after my mom died when I was 18. The one in which I was running through the house, following her voice, and never quite getting to her. I was emotionally depleted, deprived, and overwhelmed by the daily pressure I faced from workplace bullying. The return of that long-ago nightmare was an indication that something was terribly wrong.

The doctor, after listening to all I had to say—to what I now understood to be the whole awful truth of my nervous system in a complete free fall—left me with simple, yet powerful, words.

"You need to make a change."

Healing from Trauma

When I left my doctor's office that day, sadness overwhelmed me. Sadness and something else. Resolve. I accepted her words as the gift they were and committed to make a change, an immediate one. I needed to reverse the physical and emotional toll that years of bullying behavior was taking on me. It was destroying me and, therefore, my family, which I held most dear.

Although I didn't know what was happening to me from a physiological standpoint, I knew I was in trouble. Years later, I would discover that, along with my high blood pressure, sleep disorder, migraines, compromised immune system, chest pain, rapid breathing, and feelings of being uncoordinated, my brain was being flooded by the stress hormone cortisol.

I'm sharing this highly personal story because I want you to know that if you're in a similar position or know someone else who is, you're not alone. Maybe for the first time you're finding the connection between your health and your being bullied.

I would learn that a stressed brain gives a false reading of what's real and what isn't. A stressed brain struggles to perform until it can no longer perform.

Perhaps your sympathetic nervous system and parasympathetic nervous system are working overtime to get you out of fight or flight and into a safe place of rest, digest, and heal. Mine were.

Perhaps you are pushing down your feelings, making yourself feel worse and actually increasing your blood pressure and your risk of heart disease. I did.

Or maybe your feelings of receding and disappearing are your body's way of telling you that because of the level of stress you are experiencing, your body simply cannot complete its normal stress cycle.

Maybe you've stopped doing the very things your body requires in order to heal; for me, that included running, exercising, moving my body, socializing, and laughing.

If this sounds like you, my hope is that you can draw strength from the fact that you are not alone. Perhaps knowing this will give you the courage to take that first step toward gathering your support system. Who is that for you? For me, that step began with my family, and it wasn't easy. Give yourself a lot of space and a lot of grace. Start simple—reading books, meditating, walking—and then you may want to consider enlisting the help of a wellness team of experts. Where do you want to start? Perhaps a psychologist, or a functional neurologist, or an energy healer can help put you back together. One of the most defining moments of my healing was when a medical expert used one word to describe what she was treating me for: "trauma."

I wasn't making it up. And neither are you.

Know this: Healing from trauma begins with seeing it. So don't run away from the pain. Whatever the members of your support team look like, pull them close, and together you can start to chip away at it.

DRILLS

- Consider where you are in the arc of your own story. What help do you need?
- Start by reaching out to those you hold dear and vice versa. Let them know what is happening to you. No more suffering in silence.

PART III

STUDY

The Xs and Os of Workplace Bullying

Now that you've been introduced to the five types of bullies from 10,000 feet and you've read some examples of healthy and unhealthy workplace cultures in the making, let's come down to earth in this next part of the book for a close-up look at each: the In-Your-Face, Rat-Face, Two-Face, About-Face, and Gaslighter. Using real-life examples, let's look at how the bully might react to the four possible responses from the target: ignore, resist, comply, and enlist.

Like athletes studying game film, the idea is for you to analyze both the offense and the options you have in your toolbox to respond to that offense. In short, how do you defend against a bully, whether it's in the moment, afterward, or in preparation for your next encounter? It takes courage, quick thinking, and preparation.

So let's prepare.

Let's try and understand our bully's tactics, teammates, maybe even their motives. It will help us anticipate how we might counter in the future instead of getting trapped in a full-court press, fall down, and throw the ball away.

The shock of being the target of workplace bullying stunts our response options; we often default to compliance because our brain is sending "fear" signals to our body and history has taught us that not resisting is the safest play. But think about this. When a workplace team sees the strongest leader in the room—someone the team respects—constantly comply to a bully, it sends a message to those on the team: If that person can't stand up to this bully, what shot do the rest of us have?

Compliance begets compliance. If the people on your team don't see their role model challenge the bully, compliance becomes the only response. In a sense, compliance can be the most dangerous choice. But as you consider your possible responses, you need a new default that suggests other options are available.

So let's look at some examples of what those options might be. As I describe possible ways of reacting, remember that "could have" does not equate to "should have." This isn't about guilting people for wrong responses, but about offering options to those who might think compliance is the only choice.

As you read the examples throughout the next several chapters, be mindful that being a target of workplace bullying is not something that we allowed to happen to us. Not something that we deserved. Not something that we "asked for" because we acted, spoke, dressed, or did something else to somehow give permission for someone else to bully us. Don't let any language in this book or in your head make you think otherwise. You've already been bullied enough by others. Don't bully yourself.

Finally, a couple of disclaimers: For all the scenarios you're going to read, "Have you talked to HR?" will frequently, if not always, be the first question you're asked as a target of workplace bullying. Reporting the bullying behavior to HR is important for several reasons: (1) You may get the help you need; (2) by reporting to HR, you establish a record of the issue and of reporting the issue, which you will most likely need; and (3) there are boxes that targets need to check, whether we get the help we need to stay or walk away. Like baking a cake, there are certain ingredients that must be added before we can enjoy it. Simply put, going to HR forces the company to go on record about its response to your claims and allows targets to move on to whatever their next step is. Not reporting sends the message that we don't trust the system to protect us, and therefore we're going to withhold information from the function that is supposed to help us. If we don't allow ourselves that option, we've drawn a conclusion that may be inaccurate.

Remember Ashley from Chapter 9? She had been directed to back off coaching someone on her team. She then became the target of a workplace bully. When I asked her why she decided not to report the bullying behavior to HR, her response was, "I had just been ordered by the two most senior leaders in my organization to not do something that I was always so confident doing—coach. I then became a target of a bully. I didn't feel like I had anywhere to turn. HR reported to one of the two people who had told me to back off." Ashley may have been right. She saw the flaw that was contributing to an unhealthy workplace culture. One in which she didn't feel safe going to HR for help. This highlights the idea that HR is seen as part of the established unhealthy culture, because often, not always, the people in HR will position their allegiance to supporting the leaders who are misbehaving. When HR cannot, does not, and will not operate as an independent branch in support of those making claims, employees are left to find their own solutions. The flip side? By not going to HR, Ashley didn't check that particular box and therefore did not have a record of the incident, nor did she invite the body that is supposed to support her into the issue.

It's why this book is necessary. Many who have reported workplace bullying to HR have discovered that HR is fundamentally often part of the problem. If this resonates with you, the following response options may be helpful, which brings me to my second disclaimer.

The response options that follow turn out to be unsatisfying, at best. In other words, it feels like there's no way to win at this game the bully is bringing to the workplace. For many targets, there simply is not going to be a great option, and the most you can do is search for the least worst option. It's like Seinfeld's Olympic silver medal bit:

"Congratulations! You almost won. Of all the losers, you came in first of the group."

Being the target of workplace bullying is not remotely funny, but sometimes you need some Jerry Seinfeld humor to get you through it. Workplace bullying isn't an Olympics competition. The gold medal is that those in power take action that holds the bullies accountable for their misbehavior. As much as I'd like to promise you otherwise, telling targets to "shoot for the gold medal" is not sound advice. It doesn't mean we as targets shouldn't bring the issue to the attention of higher-ups, but don't count on leadership to elevate you to the medal stand.

We all dream of gold, but the real win is simply daring to run the race, giving it your all, and, if you decide to walk away, doing so with your head held high.

With that in mind, here are five scenarios involving bullies and how a target might react to each. Got it? Five types of bullies. Four response options.

12

The In-Your-Face Bully

"Put the #&*# slide back!"

The sole purpose of the public/overt bully is to denigrate
the target in a public setting. In-Your-Face bullies want witnesses.
They want everyone to know they're in power;
they're in charge. They're easy to spot in the wild.

Stella was presenting a quarterly business review to the 40-person global team. This wasn't a typical presentation. Stella and her team had worked on it for weeks. There were videos, editorial photography, storytelling at its best, all brought to life through a beautiful keynote presentation that had been heavily vetted, not only with Stella's boss, but also with other senior stakeholders. Stella had been in her role long enough to know that the "meeting before the meeting" would help to ensure that everyone was on the same page and that the presentation would go smoothly.

She began by painting the current state of business: "Inventory levels are high; cancellations are coming in at a rate beyond our estimates; the warehouse is going through a reset and—"

"Why," interrupted IYF, "do you have your SWOT analysis on page 8 rather than where we've always had it—on page 6?"

The room went silent.

"I'm sorry, what was that?" Stella asked.

"Your SWOT analysis. I like that further up in the deck, and you moved it back two pages."

"Oh," she replied, masking her disbelief, "we felt like the current inventory situation needed a bit more of a build-out, so we pushed it back a couple of pages."

Wait, her business was plummeting and IYF, who had already seen the presentation a day earlier, wanted to know why she had added a couple of slides?

"Put. It. Back," he replied. Dead stare.

"OK. We can certainly take a look at that." Stella's mouth had gone dry. The air in the overcrowded, air-conditioned conference room seemed to have gone stale. And she thought to herself, "What the—."

"Put the #&*# slide back! Now!"

"Gotcha. Consider it done."

The awkward moment was met with silence. No one stepped in. Stella was surrounded by smart, talented teammates, several of them, like her, vice presidents. Many, like IYF, had already seen and signed off on the presentation. But people didn't want to deflect the negative attention from her onto themselves. Rather than focusing on the issue at hand—business was going to be down due to sluggish sell-through—IYF was more interested in the order of Stella's slides. He was making an example out of her, and in doing so, he was able to dominate everyone in this situation.

His message was loud and clear: this was *his* team. Stella was just along for the ride and would be smart to—let's just cut to the chase—*do what she was told*. He decided early on that he must make Stella look bad so

Breaking down the game film:
Four tactics to respond to an In-Your-Face bully

TACTIC	STATEMENT	ADVANTAGES	DISADVANTAGES
Ignore	None.	Public friction avoided. The bully doesn't get the satisfaction of grandstanding that he's in charge. The target isn't humiliated in front of her peers.	The elephant is still in the room. The target might lose credibility with her colleagues because she wasn't willing to confront the bully.
Resist	"(Use the bully's name, because it reminds everyone that this is a human interaction), I hear you. The order of the slides is not going to be changed right now." Or: "(Name), we took your feedback, and the slides have been ordered in what we think is the most impactful way. Let's move on." Or: "(Name), if I were as good at keynote as I am at my job, I could probably abracadabra move those slides now. But I'm not. I am, however, very good at my job. So let's move on." Or: "(Name), what you're doing is bullying behavior, and it's making me uncomfortable."	The target asserts her responsibility as a manager and her courage as a human being. In so doing, she calls out the bully's behavior as inappropriate. This will likely score her "trust points" with the colleagues who aren't part of IYF's inner circle.	This might provoke the bully to double down on the target in a more covert setting.
Comply	"Yes, I'd be happy to change out that slide."	Embarrassing moment avoided.	The bully wins and, if his behavior goes unchecked, increases the chances that he will bully more.
Enlist	After the meeting, to potential allies: "Is it just me, or was IYF out of line? How did that interaction make you feel?"	There is potential for the target to build allies and increase chances for a sort of NATO response to a war of the bully's making.	The bully, if catching wind of this coalition building, might be inspired to make the target pay for what he could see as others teaming up on him.

117

that he could look good. He must pull her down to push himself up. This became Stella's new norm with him—her boss belittling her at every turn for his own pleasure and self-preservation.

This was so counterintuitive to Stella that she was slow in figuring out what was happening and what effect it might be having on her and on her team.

Stella didn't expect, and hadn't dealt with, someone intentionally wanting to harm her and make her look bad. Like a tornado victim, she didn't know what hit her. This In-Your-Face bully was not interested in supporting her so she could add value and help the team. Instead, he had found and targeted her.

Rewind. In this example, Stella started by "resisting" the bully with a couple of clarifying questions. We can assume that she was so taken aback by the bully's response in a business meeting, she may not have understood that an IYF bully was coming at her and using the order of her slides as his excuse. Stella may have thought he sincerely wanted an explanation for the order of her slides. He didn't. He just wanted to trip her up. This made it obvious that any further efforts to resist and hold her ground would result in him intensifying his bullying, which he quickly did with his demand, "Put the #&*# slide back! Now!"

That's the ball game. The IYF has thrown a tantrum and wants everyone to know that he's in charge of the order of someone else's slides. The IYF is the bully who wants to fight in the cafeteria in front of everyone to show us all what a big shot he is. Except the big shot is picking a fight over why you got five tater tots and he got four. That's how stupid the order of the slides is, but the IYF bully needs to let everyone know he's in control. Not surprisingly, there's often more to the story than meets the eye. You see, the irony is that Stella had inherited the role from the IYF. The decisions he and his team made put the business in its current state, and he clearly didn't want to hear about it.

If Stella had continued to resist, what would have happened? IYF had just dropped an F-bomb, so there was some aggression coming at her. Perhaps Stella was even feeling a bit threatened with that language. In this situation, with this IYF, this tone, and this language, we've clearly got a bully who is not going to back off. He *wants* the interaction to escalate. He *knows* no one in that room is going to step in and challenge him. This is sport for him. Further resistance, even with levity, will only fuel his fire. Compliance became the only choice—for now.

But Stella now knew she had a volatile IYF on her hands. She knew his play. He was acting unprofessionally, so responding unprofessionally would only add to his belittling her. For Stella, in that public setting, she chose to be professional.

If this is a pattern, follow up with a conversation with him and his superior and/or HR. Your goal is to frame up this incident in a context of professional respect.

As she prepares for this type of meeting in the future, Stella will take stock with some self-reflecting questions: "What is my position within the team?" "Do I have allies?" "Will they support me?" Stella must understand and acknowledge her own credibility and what she brings to the table. She must then leverage her credits and credibility. She may have more leverage than she thinks. That doesn't mean it's easy to punch through. But she needs to make the attempt; her team needs her to try.

One option. As she prepares for this type of meeting in the future, Stella will gather her three most trusted teammates, her allies. She will remind them of what happened at the last business review, and she will ask them to have her back if the same type of explosive attack comes at her again. "I am not going to comply and further feed this guy's bullying ego," she'll say. "I will be professional, and it may result in my asking for the room to be cleared. I will ask one of you to stay with me [she will let them know who], and the two of us will take IYF through the presentation, or we may end up rescheduling altogether. I need to know if you're comfortable with that."

Another option. As she prepares for this type of meeting in the future, Stella stops and realizes, "I don't have to accept his meeting request and subject myself to his bullying behavior." What would that look like for

Stella? She would let those in charge, including her HR business partner, know that she is no longer willing to put herself in the position to be attacked by an IYF bully. If one of them would like to be present during her business review, she would be happy to lead the group through it. Otherwise, she's done putting herself in the IYF's path.

See the table in this chapter for four tactics to respond to an In-Your-Face bully.

━━━━━━━

If you are dealing with an In-Your-Face bully, know that you have options. They aren't always obvious in the moment. In fact, with an IYF, you're immediately put back on your heels. When there's such obvious aggression and volatility coming at you, it's really hard to know what to do. But you've got some tools now. You've got some sound principles. Some response options. Recognizing what is happening to you is half the battle. You're no longer in the dark, and you no longer think you're being mistreated because of something *you* did.

In other words, you've got some plays of your own to make. So make them.

DRILLS

- What additional factors should Stella think about as she determines her next move?
- What advice would you give Stella?
- Have you ever experienced this type of bullying? If so, what did you do?
- Which response best resonates with you?
- What can or should an ally do in a situation like this? Is there anything an ally can do in the moment to defuse the bullying behavior?

13

The Rat-Face Bully

"We've got it."

What's different about the public/covert RF versus
the public/overt IYF is that the RF is sneaky.
RFs aren't concerned about time or place,
or about grandstanding; they just want to remind you
that they hold the power, and you don't.

Connor had just returned from sabbatical. He had needed it; not only was he burning the midnight oil, but he was also being bullied at work daily. It took him a lot to go to HR, but finally, prior to leaving for his much-needed break, he had reported the experience and was told there would be an employee relations investigation while he was gone.

Refreshed and renewed, Connor returned to work six weeks later only to discover that not only had the investigation *not* been concluded, but it hadn't even started. His first assignment was to attend an off-site meeting being hosted by his bully, who was ready to double down on her bullying tactics, having been told that Connor had reported her.

"We have a big meeting with the president coming up," RF said at a meeting. "He wants to get an understanding of the forestry business. *I'm* on point."

She said the latter with emphasis, while staring directly at Connor and implying that he wouldn't be. He showed no reaction because he knew that wasn't going to happen. His boss was crazy if she thought that he, the head of the Forestry Division, wouldn't be on point for a forestry business update to the president of the company.

Several of Connor's teammates approached him after the meeting. "What was that?"

"It's fine," he said, his voice belying his uncertainty.

Connor knew he had been put into his job because the executive leadership team didn't have faith in his boss's ability to do her job. She had been moved from job to job while Connor had a reputation for being able to work well with anyone, posting wins throughout his highly successful career.

The leaders also knew that Connor would be tested at every turn. Turns out, they were right, because now the woman whom Connor reported to was trying to ace him out of work that was his to drive. She wouldn't let him do his job as retaliation against him for reporting her to HR.

The next day, Connor followed up with RF and her strategic planner to discuss the meeting. He wanted to gain a better understanding for what "*I'm* on point" meant, assuming it suggested his team wasn't necessary—or competent enough—to lead.

"Hey, so you mentioned the meeting coming up," Connor said to her. "I didn't quite follow the part about you being on point."

"Yeah, we're gonna pull it together. You don't need to worry about it. We've got it."

Breaking down the game film:
Four tactics to respond to a Rat-Face bully

TACTIC	STATEMENT	ADVANTAGES	DISADVANTAGES
Ignore	None.	Friction avoided. The boss is affirmed.	The target and his team are made to feel inferior. The presentation is at risk of failing because the bully isn't the best choice to lead but wrongly thinks she is.
Resist	"(Name), because it's a forestry update, I rightfully assumed I would lead on the presentation." Or: "(Name), that's highly unusual. Why do you feel this is an exception to how we've always run the offense?" Or: "(Name), thanks, but we've got this. That's why you pay us the big bucks, right?"	This gives the bully a chance to see she "hasn't gotten away with it" and has a chance to rethink her "I'll lead" position. The target puts the spotlight on the bully to explain herself. With rational people, levity can diffuse volatile situations.	This only deepens the bully's desire to try to prove that she is competent and the target is incompetent. It will anger the bully. Bullies want the spotlight but only when they're in charge of it. Bullies aren't rational people. Odds are 30:1 that levity will not work with a bully.
Comply	"Sure, Boss, you lead. No worries."	Friction avoided. The boss is affirmed.	The target is forced to give away power and responsibility that rightfully belonged to him. The company is at risk of being represented poorly by someone who's not as competent as the people she ostensibly leads.
Enlist	After the meeting, to potential allies: "Is it just me, or are we like Navy SEALS who were just told the general is leading the raid?" He could mobilize the people on his team to put their own presentation together, vet it with key stakeholders, and be ready to present.	It's possible that others on the team who, unlike the target, aren't in the bully's crosshairs might remind RF that she's changing the play after the ball's been snapped. The political oomph might cause her to see that she doesn't have "numbers."	The bully, if her insecurities are unsettled by the team not falling into step with her, might make the target and other team members pay for what she sees as insubordination.

"I'm not following. A forestry update is the responsibility of me and my team. What do you mean, '*We've* got it'"?

"Oh, we've practically already got the presentation done."

From her desk, she pulled out a stack of papers thicker than the Manhattan telephone book. Connor was horrified at the complete disregard for his input as well as for the "less is more" approach he had always strived for in presenting to executives.

"Yeah, if we need you, we'll let you know. Maybe you should take another sabbatical. Thanks."

She dismissed Connor from her office. She and her strategic planner watched him leave.

Rewind. This wasn't managerial discretion. It was a shot across the bow. Welcome back! Connor's boss was stepping into Connor's lane, doing his job in a clear move of retaliation.

In this example, had Connor responded to RF in the public setting rather than chosen to approach her later, he would have publicly put his boss on notice, and he would have had witnesses to hear and see the exchange. The RF would have continued to do everything she could to box him out of something that was clearly his to run, but Connor would have represented himself and his team. Additionally, in his documentation of the event, Connor would list all those who witnessed the interaction.

Perhaps Connor felt that his choice to approach his boss with her strategic planner separately was the more professional option. It also allowed him some time to figure out what was going on. Although he had already reported the bullying to HR, he continued to be slow to recognize the workplace bullying happening to him. It's like Jamie Lee Curtis in *Halloween*. We know Michael Myers is in the house, and she wants to make popcorn, talk on the phone, and knit! That's the RF—easy to see on the big screen, tougher in person.

Connor knew he was in the presence of a bully. He had already reported her. But based on his high-road values, he chose not to call her out in public. What would have happened if he had done so? If he perhaps said: "Look, everyone here knows that update is the responsibility of me and my team. Unless there's something you're worried about in terms of us doing our job, we'll take it from here."

Remember, RF bullies are sneaky, covert. They're not as prone to public, overt outbursts as their IYF counterparts. This may have disarmed her enough for Connor to at least publicly represent himself and his team. That said, we know workplace bullies like to cross types, so Connor's RF may have some IYF tendencies that he may have already experienced, hence his decision to address her privately.

One option. Report the incident to HR immediately and pull in the employee relations people. Connor had already reported her as a bully, and now she was doubling down with a form of retaliation by managing him out of work that was his to do. He could double down as well.

Another option. Go directly to the president, who called for the update, and explain: "I know you want this meeting to be worthwhile, which is why I want you to know that I believe the wrong team is currently working on it and boxing my team out. The members of that team aren't qualified to lead this effort, and I'm enlisting your help in making sure the best team does so." Connor doesn't need permission to present. It's his business.

See the table in this chapter for four tactics to respond to a Rat-Face bully.

When Connor is able to reframe this situation, perhaps he would see that the right answer is to go to the president. In other words, don't fall into the trap of "I was put in this job to deal with this person; therefore I've got to do it on my own." Let those whose job it is to deal with mistreatment do their job. Don't let them continue to push the pile of XYZ back onto you. Return to sender. As a friend, who became an ally, told Connor in less euphemistic terms, "Remember the saying, 'Put the turd back in their pocket.'" Not elegant, but it certainly makes the point.

The friend went on to say, "If people do something that causes you angst, turn it around so it's their problem. They need to find a solution. It's not yours to do. It's not your problem. And I like the saying because it says exactly what it is!"

If you are dealing with a Rat-Face bully, know that you have options. No more second-guessing yourself. You have an RF on your hands. You know this type of bully is tough to operate around because the RF is so sneaky. Remember, the RF is covert and not necessarily prone to public outbursts. How can you use your understanding of Rat-Face bullies to your own advantage? They want to trip *you* up. What will trip *them* up? It's time for you to go on the offense.

You have your own moves to make to regain control. Make them.

DRILLS

- Do you know your company's policy about workplace bullying, and do you know its policy on retaliation once you've reported?
- Perhaps you've experienced something similar. What other advice do you have for Connor?
- What additional factors should Connor think about as he determines his next move?
- Have you ever experienced this type of bullying? If so, what did you do?
- Has an employee every brought a similar situation to you and asked for your advice or intervention? What did you do? What might you do differently today?

14

The Two-Face Bully

"Fire Peterson!"

The private/overt bully can be tough to spot in the wild
because this type of bully is first-team "all you" in public,
but will humiliate and diminish you in private.
Two-Face bullies want you to know they're in power;
they're in charge, and you're off balance.

T F and Jess met for their weekly update. A few days earlier, they
had copresented to one of their biggest clients, and TF had publicly praised Jess, thanking her for letting him "ride her coat-
tails." She was feeling great as he began their meeting.

"How was the team's meeting earlier today?" he asked.

"I received the update, and we're tracking well. I thought I'd spend the
bulk of this meeting updating you on that."

At this, TF glared at her, reminding Jess that she was wrong to think he actually wanted to know how the meeting had gone. He was running his own offense, the aim of which wasn't to help the team score, but to slam Jess into an incoming screen. She ignored his scheme and jumped in with her update, showing him the various tracking methods the team had put in place and the progress she and the team were making.

Jess went on, "The team is really—."

"Why don't you ask Peterson how today's meeting went?" he said, ignoring Jess's enthusiasm for her team's work.

Jess responded, "I don't know what you're talking about."

"I know you don't," TF replied, with a hint of amusement in his eyes.

"Is there something you'd like to share with me about *my* meeting, something you'd like to enlighten me with?" Jess asked.

The answer came in the form of a glare, a grimace, a scowl, and then the words: "No. Get that waste-of-space Peterson out!"

"What are you talking about? You hired him, and he's doing a great job."

"I want him gone. Fire Peterson!"

"That's not how things work here. What happened?"

"It's your team. You should know what goes on with it."

At that point, Jess gathered her things and said, "OK, how about I go. Just so you know, we are tracking well. The team is crushing it, and we're going to overdeliver and be under budget."

She made her way back to her building. Her body felt like it had needles pulsating from within. She passed Peterson's cube.

"Hey, Jeff," she said, "can you come to my office for a minute?"

Jeff was a talented, creative, likable guy who was hired by TF, the man who now wanted him fired for something that he apparently said in a meeting.

"What's up, Jess?"

"Hey, I am curious about today's meeting. I got the notes, and it looks like we're tracking well. Was there anything else that happened in the meeting that might have TF concerned?"

Jeff frowned. "Not that I can think of. I mean, I think I said something about the font we were using and wanting to make sure it was one he likes since that seems to be a hot spot for him. It was tongue-in-cheek, but not malicious. Nothing that I can remember though. Why?"

"No reason, Jeff. Let's just make sure we're staying focused on the work. It's so good, and we don't need anything distracting us."

"Should I be worried?" he asked, now looking worried.

"No. All good. Just curious. Thanks, and keep up the good work."

Jess felt like she was living in Springsteen's "Tunnel of Love" with the "crazy mirror showing us both in five D," except she wasn't laughing. She was struggling, and she realized TF wasn't just trying to trip her up; he was coming after her team as well.

Ever the optimist, Jess continued to believe she could work around him. She was convinced that she and her team would be successful regardless of TF's maneuvers. But it was difficult to anticipate his bullying moves and to disarm him. It was particularly tough considering she had people within her team who thought it was OK to alert him of a benign comment made by a teammate in hopes of building good favor with him. Jess realized that she was in deep and that her meetings were no longer safe, confidential places because of TF's foot soldiers.

TF's approach was chipping away at Jess's ability to see herself for who she had always been at work. Her normally confident, capable, curious self froze. She was so diminished by him that she started to feel relegated back to her childhood, always wanting to please those in charge. To that end, she asked TF to travel the market with her, certain if they could study trends together, talk to customers together, a bond would begin to form, and the team—the company—would win.

He declined her every invitation.

Breaking down the game film:
Four tactics to respond to a Two-Face bully

TACTIC	STATEMENT	ADVANTAGES	DISADVANTAGES
Ignore	None.	The boss grows weary of his own game.	The boss thinks you're playing dumb just to defy him, and likely doubles down.
Resist	"(Name), whatever Peterson may have said in a meeting is not pertinent to this discussion." Or more stridently: "(Name), Peterson is top drawer. You fire him, you fire me." Or: "(Name), you seem to have a particular interest in my meetings. Why is that?" Or: "(Name), sounds like you were a popular topic at today's meeting. Tell me more!"	The target makes the bully realize that he isn't God and can't expect that his wish is the target's command. The target matches power with power in a game of workplace "chicken." The target attempts to be in control. The target attempts to diffuse with levity.	This might set off the bully like a match to an M-80 firecracker. Retaliation would be not only a possibility, but a probability. This might get Peterson *and* the target fired. The bully may arm-wrestle the target for control. Bullies are humorless.
Comply	"Got it. I'll let Peterson know he's terminated as of today."	Friction avoided. The boss is affirmed.	Peterson, a solid employee, loses his job—and the company loses a good employee. The target loses even more power. The bully, the bad guy in this scenario, gains power by walking on the backs of the *good people*.
Enlist	After the meeting, to potential allies: "Peterson is doing such a good job, I'd like us to give him even more responsibility." Or: To those same allies, "It's not effective to meet one-on-one with TF anymore, so I'll be enlisting one of you to join me in the future."	Just like on the playground, bullies are at their worst when they're surrounded by supporters; they're weakened by detractors. If the coalition builds, the bully, not the others, may realize he needs to change or leave. The target controls who attends meetings with her, and by always bringing someone with her, she always has a witness to potential bullying behavior.	Sad but true, the bully, in his paranoia, might put a target on the back of everyone who's not anti-Peterson. It's not the target's meeting, so the bully may "excuse" the witness.

Rewind. Jess had a full-on, four-alarm bully on her hands, and yet she kept meeting one-on-one with him weekly. Little did she know then that she was setting herself up each time she met privately with him. She had no shot. Zero. Plus, she took the bait every time.

Bait: "Why don't you ask Peterson how today's meeting went?" he said, ignoring Jess's enthusiasm for her team's work.

Hooked: Jess responded, "I don't know what you're talking about."

Bait: "I know you don't," TF replied, with a hint of amusement in his eyes.
Don't take the bait.

Not hooked: "Peterson and today's meeting are my concern. If you're interested in having a professional exchange about the business, I'm happy to do that. If not, I've got better things to do."
Bravo! Jess just crushed Michael Myers in *Halloween.*

Would there have been a point for Jess to enlist help to ensure she wasn't meeting alone with the bully?

One option. Once targets realize they're dealing with a private/covert or a private/overt bully, enlisting support from an ally is not only a smart choice, but a necessary one. The targets realize that they are no longer effective in one-on-one situations and/or are not comfortable. By enlisting support, the targets attempt to control both.

Another option. When invited to a one-on-one meeting with a proven bully, decline the invitation. Don't give the bully a microphone and an audience of one to continue to manipulate.
See the table in this chapter for four tactics to respond to a Two-Face bully.

Prior to executing either of these options, let your HR business partner know what you're doing in a documented email. For example, "I've been working with [name your bully], and I'm concerned about how I'm being treated. [Provide examples.] Isn't that called harassment? It seems like he would benefit from some coaching, and I wanted to let you know that I will not be meeting with him one-on-one anymore. Instead, I will always have a third party with me, or I will simply decline the meeting invitation." With this approach, not only are the targets protecting themselves, but they're taking a stance. Instead of waiting for HR to *do* something— the cavalry ain't coming—the targets are taking their complaint to HR, using language that HR is legally obligated to address. In other words, the folks at HR put the company at risk if they don't get involved.

If you are dealing with a Two-Face bully, you know you have options. You know this because you've probably dealt with a TF somewhere else in your life. Perhaps a friend or acquaintance has shown up as a TF. So what did you do? You called the person out on it! You called the person out on it because you know you don't deserve to be mistreated. Why is the workplace any different? Something you wouldn't put up with outside of work, you'll accept at work? Why is that? Simplify this type of bullying behavior, and you'll begin to not only appreciate that you have options, but put those options to use.

DRILLS

- Have you ever been in a situation like this, one in which the team dynamic is compromised? What did you do?
- In this example, Jess involved HR using language that she thought would get HR's attention. What, if anything else, would you advise her to do/say?
- What about Peterson? Should he go to HR?
- What additional factors should Jess think about as she determines her next move?
- Have you ever experienced this type of bullying? If so, what did you do?
- Has a colleague ever asked you to help or intervene with a Two-Face bully? What did you do, and would you do anything different now?

15

The About-Face Bully

"My staff meeting takes priority over everything else."

Private/covert bullies are a special breed.
Tough to put your finger on because
their aggressiveness is nuanced, subtle,
hidden in the shadows. The About-Face bullies want
you to know they're in power. And they stay in charge
by keeping you guessing and off balance.

A t a global apparel company, managers were expected to lead, coach, and inspire. There were actual manifestos and core competencies that clearly spelled this out, including reminders like "Cultivate the best in others," and "Promote honest communication through inclusion," and "Trust your teammates to manage themselves and their time well," and "The workplace should be fun."

For Oscar, coming to work *used to be* fun. And then it became scary. He was being bullied by a cross-quadrant bully who mostly settled into About-Face mode. Oscar decided to confront him, after yet another one of his public IYF floggings. The beatdown was on the heels of the bully reminding Oscar that the bully's staff meetings had to take priority over everything else.

"Do you think I'm capable of doing this job successfully?" Oscar asked him.

The AF had one look; he wore it everywhere. It said any number of things: "I'm bored," "I'm annoyed," "I'm ecstatic," "I'm about ready to crush you." Greatest poker face ever.

"Yes. Oscar. I do think you're capable. I've been told you're the best GM in the company." It was said in such a tone that it suggested the exact opposite of Oscar being the best anything.

"OK, that's great to hear," said Oscar. "I need you to let me do it then."

"Do you not think I'm letting you do your job simply because I want things done in a certain way? How is that 'not letting you do your job'?"

"This isn't my first GM role," Oscar said. "It's my third—and I have my own way of working, managing my team, presenting. You seem to zero in on many decisions that are mine to make, and you've just told me that you think I'm perfectly capable. Instead of the results and strategic conversations, you seem ultra-focused on the format of presentations and the people I've chosen to send to meetings and on your staff meeting being placed above all else. You're micromanaging in a way that is getting in the way of us putting our best foot forward for one of the biggest innovation launches for the company. At times, we need to divide and conquer to ensure we get everything done. I need you to trust that I know what I'm doing and that I know how to efficiently deploy my team."

"There are things I want done a certain way," the bully replied, "and my staff meeting takes priority over everything else. And that includes any and all travel. You will be there."

"OK," Oscar said—and saw himself out.

Breaking down the game film:
Four tactics to respond to an About-Face bully

TACTIC	STATEMENT	ADVANTAGES	DISADVANTAGES
Ignore	None.	Only for the bully, who feels his kingdom is bolstered.	The bully's failure to recognize the target's abilities, and to use those abilities in the best way possible, weakens the company.
Resist	"(Name), if you honestly believe I'm a high-quality manager, then step aside and let me do what I've proved I've done pretty damn well—lead."	This gives the bully a chance to be a hero, in a sense. If deep down he realizes he's been an ass, here's a chance for him to humble himself and come clean. "You're right. My bad. I need to let you lead." One comment like that could absolve him of a lot of past sins.	Only secure people humble themselves. The insecure bully realizes, in the sensible resistance, that he's like the Wizard of Oz when the curtain is pulled away—but defaults to anger in a way the Wiz did not. Someone must pay for his insecurities. *Bottom line:* Revenge against the target is quite possible.
Comply	"Copy that. I'll cc you on my note to the staff saying staff meetings aren't to be missed, even in the event of travel."	Further friction avoided. The boss feels empowered.	Again, the company acquiesces to one unhinged individual— and a staff meeting becomes a legalistic "priority one."
Enlist	This is a slippery slope because good leaders simply *are*; they don't need to run behind-the-scene campaigns to convince others of it. But in subtle ways, the target can build support.	The target has a chance to make his case, to reason with his boss.	The only chance of success in the target so doing is if the bully is a person of reason. Most bullies aren't. What they see as reality and what others see as reality are often night and day. *Bottom line:* He isn't likely to change.

Rewind. This meeting backfired, but Oscar had to call it. Although AF sang Oscar's praises in public, AF's modus operandi was to control every-thing and that included how Oscar managed his team. Oscar thought by representing himself, he could get the bully to back off a bit and let him do what he was hired and equipped to do.

Not surprisingly, the bully's response was to tighten his grip on Oscar, retaliate, and double down on his bullying behavior. (See the notes in Chapter 14 on choosing *not* to meet with the bully one-on-one.)

One option. Oscar might enlist his allies toward broader and longer-term solutions such as having virtual staff meetings that all could attend while traveling. The point is, Oscar may not be able to confront the bully in the moment, but by enlisting allies, he might be able to make it through.

Another option. Oscar might be able to enlist HR in a collaborative, thought-partner way. By doing so, not only does he put his boss on notice, but he does so in a solution-oriented, team-first approach: "I'm trying to figure out how to manage a few different deliverables. Can you help me . . . ?"

See the table in this chapter for four tactics to respond to an About-Face bully.

━━━━━━━

If you are experiencing an About-Face bully, you have options. Even though the AF is tough to decipher because of his private/covert ways, you're now onto them. You're able to go through your checklist of recog-nizing, understanding, and identifying what you're dealing with. That's a huge step because you're no longer trying to figure out *if* you're being mistreated. You've confirmed it. More difficult is, of course, what to do about it. But don't you feel better just knowing you've got an AF on your hands? Isn't it a bit empowering to know? It is. So use that to your advan-tage. That "I'm onto you" swagger is just what you need to figure out your move against an About-Face bully. So make it.

DRILLS

- Have you ever been in a situation in which you feel like you're not able to do the job for which you were hired? What did you do?
- Why is the staff meeting so important to the AF in this example?
- What additional factors should Oscar think about as he determines his next move?
- What advice would you give Oscar?
- Have you ever experienced this type of bullying? If so, what did you do?
- Have you ever seen a colleague be targeted with this kind of bullying behavior? If you encountered that now, how might you intervene?

16

The Gaslighter

"He said he let you know."

Within the covert bullying family is a particularly disturbing
strain of bully, the Gaslighter, that lands somewhere
between the Rat-Face and the About-Face.
Gaslighters are the ultimate
at head games. Like their covert cousins,
they want you to know they're in power;
they're in charge by keeping you guessing and off balance.

One day, Charlie was supposed to meet her boss in his office to receive her performance evaluation. He set the meeting for 7 a.m., knowing that she tended to get in closer to 8 a.m., because she had mentioned to him that she liked dropping her kids off at school on the way into work. Mistake.

She raced to his office, arriving a few minutes before 7:00, sweaty and red-faced.

"Is he here?" Charlie asked his assistant. "I have a seven with him."

Breaking down the game film:
Four tactics to respond to a Gaslighter

TACTIC	STATEMENT	ADVANTAGES	DISADVANTAGES
Ignore	Refuse to engage. Go to the cafeteria for breakfast. Or: Sit in the Gaslighter's office for 15 minutes; then send an email rescheduling because he never showed.	The target refuses to engage in the spontaneous cross-campus bootcamp class of the bully's making. In doing so, she pretends that the bullying is not happening with an "Oh, you made a mistake and forgot the meeting. No worries; here's when I'm available later in the week." The target knows he was bullying her, but does not acknowledge it in any way.	The target's failure to say "How high?" when the bully commands her to "jump" may result in the bullying being intensified.
Resist	"Hey (Name), I guess you wanted to ensure I got my workout this morning!" Or: "(Name), I thought it was hard enough to keep track of my kid's schedule; now I've gotta keep track of yours, too!" Or: "(Name), we're going to have to reschedule the meeting since you didn't let me know." Or: Tell his assistant to let him know you're on your way; then take your sweet time getting there.	This lets the bully know the target is onto his games. It gives the bully a chance to acknowledge the paces he's put the target through without being direct about it. The target attempts to match power play with power play.	Gaslighters are master manipulators. *Bottom line:* Revenge against the target is most likely.
Comply	None. Setting a new course record for a cross-campus run.	Further friction avoided. The boss feels empowered.	Acquiescing is dangerous business because it only adds fuel to the Gaslighter's fire.
Enlist	The target documenting these experiences to highlight the additive nature of this type of bullying is important.	The target takes a documentarian approach and is able to stay in the real world rather than in the upside-down one the Gaslighter is building.	When the target makes her case to HR, HR does not support her. "So what; he changed a meeting location and forgot to tell you."

"Oh, he decided to hold the meeting in your office instead. He said he let you know."

Charlie nodded, thinking to herself, "Of course, he decided to do that, and no, he didn't let me know."

This was a challenge because "In your office instead" meant a half mile away from where Charlie had just landed. A former athlete, she sprinted to her office, arriving out of breath and, again, red-faced.

The Gaslighter was sitting alone in her office with the lights off.

When she mentioned the mix-up in location, he replied, "Yeah, I thought it would be nice to meet in your office."

Her performance evaluation was glowing. He had written that she was doing a great job and proceeded to tell her whom she could and couldn't trust that week. Shifting into power-play mode, the Gaslighter finished the meeting by slipping in the fact that one of her male colleagues was making twice the salary she was.

Rewind. Everything is a test with a bully and especially with a Gaslighter. The bully's reason for being is to push targets toward insanity. The layers of control are obvious now but are difficult to see in real time. An important first step with gaslighting is catching on to the fact that you are a victim of it. This can take a long time and many encounters. But once you see it, you can then consider more creative responses.

"Gaslighter? Hey, it's me, Charlie. I'm at your office for our seven o'clock meeting." "No. It was scheduled for your place, so I'll just wait here for you." "No. I'll be here unless you want to reschedule." Charlie's not playing that "Gaslighter, Denier" game.

Charlie didn't understand that when the Gaslighter showed interest in the lives of her children, it was just a pretense; in this case he was able to turn "I like to drop my kids off at school in the morning" into a tactic to control her schedule. Everything she shared would be used against her.

Note to targets: Bullies are not our friends. They don't get the privilege of knowing about our personal lives. Full stop. Also, beware of the innocent-looking assistant who was of absolutely no help to Charlie. She could have reached out to Charlie to let her know about the meeting.

She chose not to. (Probably because she'd been bullied into submission.) Charlie sprinting across campus to barely be late for that 7 a.m. meeting was a classic "pleaser" move. And that's what often happens when targets are bullied. Our stress response is to up our please-o-meter to our own detriment. Charlie's review was glowing because the team's results were glowing. Trying to mess with her review would be too obvious for the covert Gaslighter.

One option. Enlist the support of HR. But enlisting the support of HR when a Gaslighter has targeted you is tricky—and, unfortunately, unlikely to lead to a positive resolution. The same slipperiness that makes the target of gaslighting question what's happening also presents a challenge to an HR professional trained to try to see both sides of a conflict. In most situations, HR will default to blaming a miscommunication or misunderstanding rather than calling out gaslighting. Without explicit documentation, without witnesses to the repeated action, and without an HR business partner who is well versed in the head games that Gaslighters play, going to HR about gaslighting will probably be unsatisfying.

Another option. If you see yourself in one or more of the scenarios in this or the previous chapters, you may also have noticed that the options available to you are less than compelling. But there's only one other option, and in the end it's the only one you will fully control: walk away.

That's not quitting. That's refusing to acquiesce to an organization that no longer deserves the privilege that is you.

See the table in this chapter for four tactics to respond to a Gaslighter.

If, at this point, you feel a bit overwhelmed by these examples, don't worry. It *is* overwhelming. But like a basketball coach showing his team game film from a 40-point loss, you can't hope to survive until you understand what exactly is happening on the court. Or in your case, in the office.

I'm hesitant to use the word "opponent" to describe your bully, but by your bully's own choice, that's what they are choosing to be. You're not defining your bully; bullies define themselves. Workplaces work best when people are all on the same team, but when some people don't want to play team ball, it's not your fault that they're in opposition to the very people they need to have succeed.

As I land this thought, it reminds me that when I'm presenting to a company and we come to the Q&A portion, I'll almost always hear: "This might sound like a weird question, but what about those of us who've never experienced bullies? What can we or should we be doing, if anything?"

It's a great question. And I readily admit my five "box scores" from the previous chapters are aimed specifically at the target's possible responses. So here are three things for witnesses to bullying:

First, be there for someone who perhaps *is* being bullied. Listen. Encourage. Advise. Defend. Document. Help the person understand that, like that famous line from the psychologist played by Robin Williams in *Good Will Hunting,* "It's not your fault."

Second, as I tell the audience, "Use CPR." That will prompt a lot of say-what? looks.

"Yeah," I'll say, "you need to take a CPR class to prepare you. Just because you're not being bullied now doesn't mean you won't be in the future. And so you need to be ready to know what to do in an emergency. How you can survive an 'accident.' Bullies benefit from panic. So get yourself prepared."

Third, enlist HR on behalf of the target. As an objective third party, you are potentially in the best position to calmly and reasonably share what you're witnessing.

Meanwhile, leadership within the company needs to publicly take a position. Take the leap of faith. Call it for what it is. Witnesses know it's not right when they see it happen. Acknowledging makes "the undiscussable" become the discussable—an issue that needs to be formally addressed.

Otherwise, the bullies, like termites, will ultimately eat away at the foundation of the entire company.

DRILLS

- What additional factors should Charlie think about as she determines her boss's next move?
- What advice would you give Charlie?
- Have you ever experienced this type of bullying? If so, what did you do?
- Which response most resonates with you?
- Have you ever witnessed a colleague suffering from gaslighting by a manager or other colleague? How might you have intervened?

IDENTIFY
Bullying in the Wild

Coach was running us at basketball camp one summer day. We had just started our drills when I noticed this kid jump out of line and head to the drinking fountain. It was like in the movies when the music of dread plays—like, "What is this kid doing; does he want to *die*?" Big Dave's huge shadow loomed over him as the kid started to put his hand on the drinking fountain button.

"Son," said Coach, "what do you think you're doin'?"

"Uh, I was getting a drink of water, Coach."

"So you're feeling OK, are you?"

"Yes, Coach, just thought I'd get a sip of water."

"Son, we play together and then we take our break together. As a team. Now *get back* in line!"

I wouldn't have known it at the time, but my personal *brand* was "Coach's Daughter." I walked tall with the importance of that. "Coach's Daughter" meant I would act a certain way, play a certain way, and study a certain way. "Coach's Daughter" governed my work ethic— coachable, hardworking, tough as nails, the kind who, if knocked down, would get right up again.

Most notably for the context of this book, "Coach's Daughter" didn't complain.

Stories of Bullying

Up to this point, you've become familiar with how to recognize and understand workplace bullying. You've been introduced to the five types of bullying and to the importance of having sound principles in our toolbox as we ignore, resist, comply, and/or enlist. You've gained an understanding of the role a company's leadership principles play in creating a healthy workplace, and, conversely, what happens when leadership fails and an unhealthy workplace culture takes root. I've provided you with some "game film" to further understand the Xs and Os of workplace bullying.

But here's the deal: there's nothing neat and tidy about workplace bullying. No Geneva Convention rules of engagement. Bullies don't follow the sharp delineation of a court with baselines and sidelines. You know this. Bullies are consistently out of bounds. Bullies jump over, around, and through any and all "types" to mess with us.

So Part IV, "Identify: Bullying in the Wild," focuses expressly on how bullying shows up in the workplace by presenting examples as shared with me by targets representing various levels and various companies around the world—people who have been bullied in the workplace. Their stories will allow you to practice your skill at recognizing, understanding, and combating workplace bullying in all its untidy, grimy messiness.

Those who participated in this book are a spirited group. They're a bighearted, got-your-back, talented-beyond-belief cauldron of badasses that really show up for each other.

They are new friends and former colleagues who see each other, support each other, and share their experiences with each other. They've inspired me.

They are gay, straight, married, divorced, mothers, and fathers of two-legged and four-legged children, daughters, sons, sisters, brothers, aunties, uncles, cousins, and friends.

They played sports, danced on stages, grew up in the United States and beyond, lived in houses and trailer parks, were raised by single parents, several parents, no parents, and grandparents.

They come in all different shapes, sizes, and skintones, and they identify as binary and non-binary.

They are independent thinkers, competent, likable, ethical, honest connectors who lead with kindness, smarts, empathy, and advanced social skills.

In other words, they are the perfect targets for workplace bullying.

In the hope of helping those going through similar experiences, they've shown great courage in sharing their stories.*

*As requested, names and places in the following stories have been changed.

17

Playing Small: Bullying Robs Us of Who We Are

What did you do to prompt this behavior?

When Casey joined the renowned advertising agency, she was elated.

"I loved starting out at the agency," she shared. "We were all on equal footing in a collaborative environment. No one had power over anyone else, and we were all just learning from and supporting each other."

A couple of years later, when Casey moved into an account director role, she considered it her dream job. The competitive environment, a staple throughout the organization, spoke to her own competitive spirit. And she embraced with gusto the concept of "triad," a group of three functional experts who represented accounts, creative, and production.

A high level of accountability came with the account director role. Casey was singularly responsible for shepherding the creative process from early insight all the way back to the clients in the hope of exceeding their expectations.

She was well suited for the role. Her cool confidence allowed her to be an effective "triad general," running her team the same way she ran the offense playing ball at a Division I university. Alas, "triad" would ultimately speak to her in a more sinister way—in the form of workplace bullying.

Personality psychology researcher and professor Delroy Paulhus, along with fellow researcher Kevin Williams, cocreated the term "dark triad" to describe people who exhibit three traits: Machiavellianism, narcissism, and psychopathy. Along with a host of associated behaviors, ranging from aggressiveness to manipulation to perceived superiority, the dark triad, initially camouflaged by high achievement and charm, was about to descend on Casey's work life in the form of a male colleague.

Healthy competition, or "healthy tension" as it was referred to at the agency, often brought out the best in people. Think of great sports rivalries: Steph versus LeBron, Stanford versus UConn, or one from my era—Chrissy versus Martina. Like any great rivalry, players pushed each other to be better in the spirit of, "You won this one, but don't get complacent, because I'm going to work twice as hard to beat you the next time we meet."

The head of Casey's account team, whose clients were from the sports and fitness industry, was well suited for the role. After all, he had been an All-American athlete whose old-school approach was more Bobby Knight than John Wooden. He pushed the staple of "healthy tension" beyond recognition, stripping it down into just plain old tension in which internal competition between teammates was the norm.

In this climate, jockeying for the boss's favor and angling for that next big promotion became the singular goal. This was no one-team, one-dream approach. Instead, it was about individual success, served up with a daily dose of fear and intimidation, gaining momentum at the behest of the leaders' operatives who egged on an offense of public humiliation toward those who wouldn't participate.

Enter Casey. What started out as an equal, peer-to-peer, friendly relationship between Casey and a colleague quickly shifted into one filled with stinging jabs veiled as teasing and characterized by aggressive behavior and a daily serving of sexual innuendo. She took it in stride—and with a 6'4" frame, she set the pace.

"I can do locker room, and I'm always going to compete," she told me. "So I just pushed off all the inappropriate stuff coming at me and kept doing my job, which I loved. I'm not going to lose on the court or in the locker room."

Her colleague's inappropriate behavior escalated—including his own claims about having "weapons." When things got to a point where Casey was feeling unsafe, she approached her boss. "You know, this is becoming a little out of hand," she remembers reporting. "I mean all this talk about guns, knives? He's got a bow and arrow, and he just tore down one of our best creative designer's divider walls because he was so mad about something."

Her boss's response? "Casey, it's fine. He's edgy. But he's kind of like a rock star, you know? Sometimes the rock star is going to destroy the hotel room. You ignore it because he's so talented. That's what we've got here."

At the fall account meeting, Casey was tasked with presenting content to the agency's national team. Always prepared and comfortable on the big stage, she nailed it. At the post-meeting "teardown," her boss not only highlighted her work but used her presentation as the high-water mark for others, fertilizing the competitive environment he had seeded.

Her male colleague didn't like that. He pulled her aside. "You may have won this round," he hissed, "but it will be the last time our boss praises you."

Casey was stunned. She'd already heard he'd pulled an X-Acto knife on their manager, the guy who had previously likened him to a rock star. Now he seemed to be threatening her.

Because of her upbringing, she knew that the best defense can be a great offense. She simply continued to shine. But—conscious of it or not—she never again tried to outshine him. At least not publicly.

Casey didn't need anybody to point out what was happening: he wanted her to pay the price for accolades that, amid his insecurities, he clearly thought he deserved. Casey stood for something he only fantasized about—being a Division I college athlete. He made up stories about having played major college football, but those who played for the school he attended said they'd never heard of him. Another time, he presented himself as having played football in Europe. As a former college athlete, Casey was the real deal—which seemed to make her even more of a target. If his web of lies, constant threats, and subtle innuendos weren't enough, the "box-cutter incident" and a more recent choking incident were never far from her mind.

"He kind of scared me 'cause I heard about the box cutter, but I was in my dream job and succeeding," she said. Still, she felt off balance. Meanwhile, she continued to put up with the daily dose of demeaning comments.

"I always felt like if I didn't keep up and jab back, I was going to be out. Even when we had this big meeting and we were all given T-shirts with nicknames on the back. Black tees, with each guy's nickname on the back in white font. Mine said 'BLT.' When I asked the guys what it meant, they snickered and giggled and finally told me, 'boobs, legs, and teeth.' I got the impression they had several things BLT stood for, and that was the one they had the guts to say to my face."

In other words, in addition to the most threatening bully, Casey was surrounded by colleagues who not only didn't protect her, but actively assisted in her mistreatment. Casey could thrive in give-and-take, even in a male-dominated workplace. But when the give-and-take crossed over into something toxic, with no ally in sight, she was at a loss for what to do.

"I just put up with it and got back to work," she said.

Some years later, this well-known bully made the coveted title of vice president. Casey took the high road, sending him a congratulatory note. Her kindness once again triggered his dark triad traits, now taking on an even more aggressive, humiliating, and sexual tone. He asked her to lunch "off-site," reminding her to "bring your triple D's and sexy heels 'cuz I want those up by my face."

Casey knew reporting this to her boss would lead nowhere. She thought briefly about reporting the incident to HR. But she assumed nothing would come of it—after all, the man had just been given a big promotion—and she didn't want to do anything to jeopardize her own career. So she stayed silent and tried to simply avoid being around him in the office.

Not long afterward, she was selected to lead a big presentation to Duke University. She approached the task as she always had. Prepared and excited to see Coach Mike Krzyzewski, a personal hero, she was hitting her stride when she saw her former colleague, the bully, in the back of the room. In an instant, she felt her heart sink. She wrapped up her presentation, but to avoid him, she took her time leaving the room. As she was slowly gathering her things, she felt anxiety start to build. Sweating and shaky, she made her way to her car, where once inside, she broke into tears; the man's presence in the meeting stalked her even as she drove away.

Once home, she shared her day with her husband. She was effusive while talking about Coach K, then caught herself mid-sentence as she started to tell him about trying to leave the meeting without being seen.

"What are you talking about?" he asked. "Why would you need to do that? Did he make you uncomfortable? You've worked with him forever. What's going on?"

She was speechless; she'd been caught in her own deception. Like the victim of domestic abuse who feels as if it's her fault, to talk about it was to remind herself that she'd somehow asked for it. She'd let this happen. And she didn't want her pain to become her husband's pain. That would turn her guilt from bad to worse.

Now, however, the floodgates were open. She shared the whole story with her husband, who also worked at the agency.

"If you're going to start keeping things from me, we're going to have a tough time," he said, concern written all over his face. "You know that, right?"

"Please don't tell anyone," she said, as if believing she were to blame. "I'm going for that big role soon, and I don't want this getting in my way."

Her husband did the only thing he knew to do, the only thing his particular DNA allowed him to do: he went straight to HR. An employee relations investigation was conducted, though it turned out to be more salt in the wound than "doing the right thing."

Guess what she was asked in the investigation?

"What did you do to prompt this behavior?"

She remembers the moment clearly. "Umm. I can't even believe you're asking me that," she replied. "Let me see. I didn't sexualize him in any way. I didn't ask to see his penis, nor remark on its size. I did nothing to make him think interacting with me like that was in any way OK. Nothing that would have led him to believe I wanted those kinds of advances."

Casey wasn't backing down. Wide stance; box out; secure the ball.

When the investigation was complete, nothing was done to Casey's bully, nor was the overarching culture that allowed such behavior explored by the company in any way.

"It was clear I had no support from above. Yet he was protected by executive leadership," she said. To Casey, it felt like a business-as-usual beatdown. "Even though I was told that he was feeling the sting of his actions, I'm the one that went through a character assassination. Maybe he didn't get as big of a bonus that year. Basically, the organization was saying, 'It's OK to operate that way. It might cost you some money, but that's all.'"

Casey regretted coming forward and, at the same time, wished she'd said something sooner. The result? She began to "play small."

"I no longer had the drive or the competitive spirit I once did," she told me. "I just wanted to be off the radar."

"I always wear heels,"—and for a 6'4" former basketball star, that's a *statement*. But after the last incident with her bully, Casey was so belittled and humiliated, she became a shadow of her former self.

"Why did I shrink?"

Losing One's Sense of Self

When considering the effects of bullying, we sometimes miss one of the most devastating results: identity theft. As targets, we are robbed of who we are. It causes us to become someone we are not—even someone we don't want to be. People in power—or with powerful in-house allies—are able to continue being who they are, while those who are bullied are rattled to the point of total discombobulation, picking up the pieces of their former selves for years to come.

Reading Casey's story, you may feel saddened and angry, but not at all surprised. When a group of—in this case—men, many former athletes or athlete wannabes, try to re-create what they had "back in the day," not only does it fall flat; it leaves tremendous carnage in its wake in the form of heartbreak and betrayal.

The beauty of sports competition had been chewed up and spit out into something that resembled a fight club environment. This, combined with the fact that Casey was a shining star, actually earning accolades, was a recipe that her bully couldn't handle. It resulted in his jealous, arrogant, vengeful responses to her. Not only that, but he was also able to leverage the dark triad as his superpower for many years to come, even being rewarded with bigger roles and titles while she plateaued.

And then there were the actions of those above and around her. Let's look at these one by one, and then let's imagine what these leaders and allies might have done differently.

Her boss dismissed her fears, defending the bully. What if he had, instead, prioritized Casey's rational fears, and either confronted her bully or initiated an HR intervention? It's likely her bully's career trajectory would have changed, not Casey's. It's also likely that kind of intervention would, in the long run, have strengthened the organization, eliminated risk, diminished the harm caused to Casey and others by the bully, and retained talent, including Casey.

Her coworkers made it clear: they didn't see her as an equal, or someone worthy of respect (or even common decency). What might have happened if a single male colleague in that setting had spoken up, called out his male coworkers, and put an end to the sexist, offensive games? Certainly Casey would have felt seen and supported. And, possibly, publicly calling out offensive actions as offensive may have decreased the likelihood these actions reoccurred. Often, just a single ally speaking up can make an enormous cultural impact.

Casey's HR department seemed more interested in *her* actions, and then let her bully off the hook. But what if the HR team had instead investigated this matter with an open mind, and talked to colleagues and leaders across the department, rather than settling for a he said, she said stalemate? Quite likely, if HR had conducted anonymous interviews with colleagues who worked with Casey's bully, HR would have heard the same alarming stories of the bully's propensity toward threats and violence the rest of Casey's coworkers had heard. And if HR then took appropriate action, it would have protected the company from risk, helped alleviate bullying, and helped the targets of inappropriate behavior find a reason to remain loyal to the company.

But none of this happened. It's really no surprise that this talented, powerful woman reacted by not only playing small, but walking away.

DRILLS

To recognize workplace bullying, it's important to start observing what is going on at work. What is going on with you, to you, and around you? How would Casey answer the following questions?

- Is there an overall climate of fear and intimidation?
- Are the values of the organization you joined being bent to accommodate misbehavior or overlooked completely?
- Does everything run through a singular filter—the bully?
- How are others feeling? Most important—how are *you* feeling?
- Have others validated your observations of bullying behavior?

Switch perspectives back to you again and answer these questions:

- Which type or types of bullying can you identify?
- When does healthy tension and/or healthy competition become unhealthy? What should you be on the lookout for?
- What other avenues for help could you tap into if you were in a similar situation?
- As leaders and allies, what steps could have been taken to help Casey?

18

Suit Up for Battle: Bullying Wears Many Faces

It was death by a thousand paper cuts.

Targets of workplace bullying often talk about how the emotional toll actually propels them back in time, reverting them to their childhoods and, along with it, childlike responses to stress.

"I felt like I was always trying to prove myself," Shawna told me about her longtime career as an educator at a prestigious university. "Almost like I was a kid. Then the paranoia sets in, and you start applying meaning to things that don't even exist."

Like me, Shawna describes her career—and her life—in two distinct parts, BB and AB: before bullying and after bullying. Before, she was a gregarious, multisport athlete, the older in a family of two girls.

"I was a hustler," she said. "I didn't come from much, so I was always looking for ways to earn. I was clear about two things early on—education was key, and I would have to pay for mine on my own. I did."

But over the course of her time at this job—AB—she became an introverted shell of her former self, often only finding solace in the extremes—running, consuming nothing but coffee and popcorn, and spending money.

What happened? She experienced a long series of incidents that, collectively, diminished and demoralized her. As she put it, "It wasn't any *one* thing. Workplace bullying is the culmination of a lot of 'one things.'"

For starters, because Shawna was often the only woman in the meeting room, she found that she altered how she operated.

"I felt like I was playing a role every day. I'd turn it on when I arrived at work. In fact, I started 'suiting up' for work in the best clothes, best shoes, best handbags. It was like my armor until I could turn it off at the end of day. It was exhausting."

Different rules seemed to apply to the men and women around her. Female colleagues who were single, who had husbands who were stay-at-home dads, or who had older children were putting more and more hours in; she herself was stretching things as far as she could, getting up at 5 a.m. to make lunch for her small children before getting into work by 6:30 a.m.

On the other hand, during one weekly meeting held from 6 to 8 p.m., her male counterpart consistently left at 7:30 p.m. to their boss's applause. "Look at Scrimms, best dad ever, getting home to his family." Shawna stayed until the meeting came to a close, often as late as 9 p.m.

Even successes felt demoralizing. Excited about a recent promotion, she felt optimistic when she received an email inviting her to her new boss's office for a 6 p.m. one-on-one. But she was congratulated and threatened all in the same few minutes.

"I'm going to personally hold you accountable for the health of this department," her new boss told her. "I will fire you if anything goes wrong."

Race and Appearance

Race dramatically deepened her sense of isolation. During another meeting, she was told that one of her coworkers, another Black female, "has a problem with a Black woman doing well." When she approached the other woman, who was a friend and mentor, the woman told her, "I never said anything like that."

The idea of men pitting women against women—and race against race—to create division further added to the illusion of scarcity many women already felt.

"There weren't many of me," she said. "So now I'm supposed to arm-wrestle another Black woman for the one spot at the leadership table? No thank you."

The hits kept coming.

"OK, thank you, Whoopi," she was told after sharing a point of view in one meeting. "This is not *The View.*"

"Can we see your other side today please—your *white* side?" a male colleague sarcastically asked her during another meeting.

Commiserating with another nontenured colleague during a reduction in force, she was told, "Of course you're staying. This company needs people of color." No credit was offered for her talent, experience, and hard work.

Later came yet another reorganization, one that negatively transformed the workplace from one of healthy interdepartment competition, merit-based promotion, and competency-rewarded talent to a new structure that, by its very design, alienated people and diminished the opportunity for community.

During a meeting with a potential multimillion-dollar donor, she was batting cleanup in the line of presentations. When she got up and introduced herself, her department head whistled.

"Wow! Look at Shawna and how pretty she looks in that red dress. She's like a Christmas tree all lit up!"

Shawna felt undermined and sexualized; her confidence plummeted. He had not commented on anyone else's appearance.

"I started to think, 'Well maybe I don't belong here,'" she told me.

Her clothes had become like body armor, at least in her own mind. Designer handbags. Beautiful shoes so she might tower over others. And the clothes—stylish designer clothes from all over the world. Underneath it all, she was a limp rag of insecurity. Her job no longer brought her joy, nor did it align with her personal values.

Yet she stayed.

"I was making good money," she shared. "I was working with young people on exciting material, adding value."

But the toxicity of the workplace was everywhere—even coming in the form of less-direct, passive-aggressive bullying from women.

"Female bullying feels more sneaky. They're gonna go to your boss and complain but be nice to your face. They're gonna make sure there's not a seat at the table for you, literally. Assign your work to others. Undermine your credibility. Men? They're more in your face about it," she said.

"The university was at its best when there were clear external threats. It gave us something to go after. But when enrollment was up and we received national attention, held the number one spot, the competition really turned inward. Department against department. Level against level. Teacher against teacher."

During a particularly important meeting, she and her team were experiencing some technical difficulty when her boss exclaimed, "We should just cancel. You guys clearly don't have your sh*t together."

A Thousand Paper Cuts

This was about the time Shawna's running miles increased and her caloric intake decreased. The gap between her highs and lows expanded. She lost track of her wine intake each night. She began to fight insomnia and to turn to antidepressants. Her body was letting her know something had to change.

"The weekends were almost the toughest because I'd get emails on Saturday and Sunday that I needed to respond to but would have such angst that I hadn't said the right thing," she recalled.

All the while, the place that she had come to know as home was speaking out of both sides of its mouth, simultaneously. "We care about our people," and "Why the hell weren't you at the 7 p.m. meeting?"

Despite the multiple years of increasing demoralization, Shawna still was able to find enthusiasm for opportunities there. "I thought I hit the motherload when I was invited to take on added responsibility, and got to work for someone who used to be a peer. I was so excited."

But her excitement was short-lived. Her new boss was a bully of the covert, two-faced variety. He sang her praises in public while privately he beat her down with "Just do what I say" dismissals. There was zero collaboration. Zero guidance. Zero strategy. Her new boss, who'd been a friend, was more concerned with how he looked to the university president than effectively leading the team.

Although it stung when she was released during a "downsizing," she had known her days were numbered.

Things had gotten so bad that when she was let go, she was relieved. "I look back on it now and realize what a low place I was in," she said. "It was death by a thousand paper cuts."

After leaving, Shawna realized she would get to be who she wanted to be, not who the university wanted her to be. She was immediately courted and hired by another college, one that was a better match for her, not only in terms of alignment of values but also in terms of her area of expertise. It turns out, Shawna as Shawna was exactly what the college wanted, a win for both.

Bullying Takes Many Forms

Shawna's story highlights the fact that workplace bullying doesn't necessarily have to be dramatic, in-your-face, wildly inappropriate behavior. In fact, it rarely is. More often, it is, as Shawna described, "subtle and nuanced and hard to explain." But that kind of insidious bullying has a huge impact; and especially over time, the additive effect is just as devastating as the overt public brand of bullying, if not more so. The outcome is the same: decreased productivity, increased health issues, and, ultimately, loss of talent.

When it comes to bullying, the means are less important than the end. Yes, some bullies like the public acclaim; they get a charge out of having an audience watching them pick a fight on the playground and showing how tough they are. Others are satisfied with just looking in the mirror and knowing they are tough; they need only convince the person across the desk from them that they are the boss, and the target is not.

In Shawna's case, the bully coerced her into being but a shadow of the talented employee she used to be. She was forced to be someone she was not. Remember when she said, "I felt like I was playing a role every day. I'd turn it on when I arrived at work"?

Healthy workplaces allow people to be who they are in safe, inclusive, and diverse environments. One of the biggest head-scratchers about organizations that look the other way regarding bullying is that—how else can I say this?—they're being stupid. Real people want to be real people at work versus suiting up for battle.

Repeatedly, Shawna's colleagues failed to intervene or to appreciate the consequences of inappropriate behaviors, and were complicit in the hurt these behaviors caused over time. Ask yourself what might have happened if one white colleague had turned to another and explained that asking a Black colleague to act more white is inappropriate, racist, and outrageous? Surely the person making the statement would think twice before doing something like that again. And in the moment, perhaps Shawna might have felt seen, heard, and supported.

If you are an ally, you have an obligation to act, to speak up, to intervene.

And if you're a manager, care enough about your workplace to hire and nurture smart leaders. At no time did Shawna believe that a manager would be willing to intervene on her behalf. As a leader, you must make clear that you will not tolerate inappropriate behavior, first by talking about it and then, when confronted with the actions of a subordinate, by taking swift action. If you oversee other managers, then make your expectations clear to all of them that they are to do the same.

DRILLS

To recognize workplace bullying, it's important to start observing what is going on at work. What is going on with you, to you, and around you? How would Shawna answer the following questions?

- Is there an overall climate of fear and intimidation?
- Are the values of the organization you joined being bent to accommodate misbehavior or overlooked completely?
- Does everything run through a singular filter—the bully?
- How are others feeling? Most important—how are *you* feeling?
- Have others validated your observations of bullying behavior?

Switch perspectives back to you again and answer these questions:

- Which type or types of bullying can you identify?
- What are some of the ways being the target of workplace bullying has affected you?
- Why is it so important for targets to document what they are experiencing?
- What role does race play in workplace bullying?
- Of the reasons Shawna chose to stay, are there ones with which you most identify if/when you stayed in an unhealthy workplace culture?
- Have you experienced a workplace that allowed you to be who you are? What was that like? How did that feel?

19

The Facade: Bullying Comes from the Top

It was like that point in the movie where the music
is suddenly replaced by the sound of the needle
being scraped across the album. It happened that fast.

As the regional director of a well-known cosmetic brand, opening five doors in less than a year, Hud took pride in the workplace culture he established. It was one in which the team came above all else. Roles and objectives were clearly defined, measurables were studied and shared, mistakes were used as opportunities to learn, and victories were celebrated along the way.

A culture of trust and connection had been established, and the results he and his team posted over the next three years were industry-defining.

"I did my best to create an inclusive culture in what can be a very exclusive industry," he said. "I always believed that my job was to lead by example and push those on my team to end up beyond me. The team thrived, we were successful, and we had a lot of fun along the way."

When a new, inexperienced regional sales manager came in, she took a different approach. The result was cracks in the culture that Hud and his team had worked so hard to create.

"We were rockin' and rollin'—selling beauty and having fun—and then it was like that point in the movie where the music is suddenly replaced by the sound of the needle being scraped across the album. It happened that fast."

What had been a team-first approach almost immediately morphed into a culture of internal competition. An already fast-paced work schedule moved into warp speed. Celebrating the team was replaced with berating the team. The culture became one of penalizing, patronizing, and pettiness.

His new manager made a move that is typical of managers who lack confidence in their own skills and competence: she aligned herself with the head of human resources. It's a proven tactic that bullies take to ensure their own security when they start running roughshod over the team.

"When I saw that move," Hud said, referring to his manager's intentional closeness with HR, "I knew we were in trouble."

Because he had always loved working with clients, he decided to step down and move back into the position from which he had been promoted—a personal artist.

"When my boss said to me, 'I wish I had met you years ago, so I could have trained you properly,' the writing was on the wall," he said.

Without Hud's protection, the entire team started to feel the manager's wrath. The culture had devolved into one of fear and intimidation with overtones of control, top-down autocratic rule, and people with no regard for anyone but themselves.

When emails became belittling in tone and arrived in people's inboxes at all hours beyond the normal workday, one employee started recording his one-on-one meetings with her. In one such meeting, she is heard "losing it" at him to the point that he later shared it with those in charge, including her ally in HR.

It was determined that he was a disgruntled employee and was fired. Meanwhile, she stayed on and was sent to sensitivity training. Stymied, Hud looked on as these horror stories repeated themselves. He offered what support he could.

"I had no move to make other than to be an ally to those who were being mistreated. I sought out those who were targeted and simply told them, 'I am here for you. I am 100 percent on your side. I am a witness to what is happening to you.' I started documenting everything that I saw, but I had no receptacle for what I was seeing happen to my teammates, to me. HR had proved itself not to be a safe option."

After one 22-year-old artist took a leave of absence because of the emotional strain of working in such a toxic environment, the bully boss was finally let go.

On her way out, though, she sent a note to Hud, telling him, among other things, that she knew he had thrown her under the bus on more than one occasion and that she protected him while he "stuck a knife in her back." His "character flaws," she warned him, would catch up to him.

"I had no more fight in me on this one. She was all about the blame game, took no accountability for her own actions, and spewed hatred while on the job and while exiting. It was awful for everyone."

So much so, that Hud decided to leave the company he had worked so hard to build up.

If you are reading this book as an ally to a target of workplace bullying, or perhaps simply a witness to such behavior, Hud's story may resonate with you. While you may not have been the focus of a bully's actions, those around you have been affected; often the whole team suffers consequences.

While Hud eventually lost his energy to keep fighting, it's important to note two things Hud did well.

First, he offered support directly to the bully's targets. He spoke with them, confirmed that he too saw the inappropriateness of the behavior, offered his complete support, and maintained a relationship and open channel of communication.

Second, Hud began documenting everything he saw. While he wasn't comfortable actively going to HR—because he and the team had seen their colleague terminated for taking this route—he did continue to document the actions of the bully boss. Had there been an independent investigation, or an investigation ordered by someone with authority over the HR department, Hud's detailed documentation would have been valuable in supporting his colleagues' stories.

What else might you do as an ally to the target of bullying behavior?

- **ENLIST YOUR OWN ALLIES, MENTORS, AND SPONSORS.** If going to HR is not a path that seems available to you, and if the bully is the boss, consider what other people in the organization you could safely approach, either formally or informally, to let them know what's going on. Perhaps this is simply a manager or director in another department. Perhaps it's someone you trust, who has the credibility (and connections) to take the matter to a high-level leader without fear of consequences. Simply advancing the ball, then letting someone else carry it a bit farther still, is worthwhile.

- **NAME IT.** Help the targets of bullying behavior understand exactly what is happening, and help them consider what to do. As you've learned in the pages of this book, so often targets of bullying have a difficult time articulating and processing bullying while it's still actively occurring. By naming it ("Our boss is a bully, and what she is doing to you is called 'workplace bullying'"), you help targets not only feel seen, but take the first step toward comprehending their reality and their available choices.

- **REMAIN A CONSTANT ALLY.** Letting targets know you're on their side is important, but to really be an ally you should continue to communicate as often as you can with your colleagues. Let them know, frequently, that you are there to support them, that they can come to you any time, that they are not imagining the bullying—and also that it probably will not end until either they or the bully moves on. Take any subtle steps you can, when you happen to encounter the bully and target together, to redirect the bully and the conversation. Being an ally is more than a single moment and more important to the target than you'll ever know.

A Battlefield of Victims

When organizations don't value the work that goes into building a high-performing team—one that fosters trust, commitment, and celebration—either they don't have a clear understanding of the work required to create such a culture, or they don't care. In Hud's case, both were at play, and the result was loss of productivity, loss of talent, and loss of reputation.

Instead of learning from the previous managers' mistakes and successes, newcomers often take a spray-the-infield approach, tearing down to start fresh. To rebuild from a culture that has been leveled is not insurmountable, but an honest assessment must be executed, evaluated, and understood by all parties. Otherwise, companies put themselves at risk to be in a vicious cycle of revive, repair, reverse.

The new boss who came in had no interest in leveraging the healthy culture and great work the team had established. Instead, her own fear got in her way as she showed no regard for the team or its accomplishments.

On an individual level, it's hard enough for targets to find justice even when HR seems to "get it." But in this case, when the bully convinced HR that she wasn't the "bad guy" in this situation, any hope for resolution vanished. In many cases, "sensitivity training" is a code phrase for someone getting community service instead of the more severe penalty that was really deserved.

The only silver lining in the dark cloud here was that the bully ultimately exited, though she left behind a battlefield of victims, Hud among them.

DRILLS

To recognize workplace bullying, it's important to start observing what is going on at work. What is going on with you, to you, and around you? How would Hud answer the following questions?

- Is there an overall climate of fear and intimidation?
- Are the values of the organization you joined being bent to accommodate misbehavior or overlooked completely?
- Does everything run through a singular filter—the bully?
- How are others feeling? Most important—how are *you* feeling?
- Have others validated your observations of bullying behavior?

Switch perspectives back to you again and answer these questions:

- Which type or types of bullying can you identify?
- How might workplace bullying show up differently in startups versus well-established companies?
- Why would a new manager choose *not* to leverage those things that are working well on a team?
- What role could HR have played in this example?
- What other steps can allies take to better the workplace environment?

20

Can I Get a Witness? Bullying Affects Everyone

Bullying steals your hope.

argets aren't the only ones whose careers can be leveled by bullies: so, too, can those of innocent bystanders. Colleagues of the target. People like Shelley, a manager, who was an accomplished leader for an international beverage brand for more than a decade.

At 40, she was meeting with big hitters, decision makers from major events and broadcast networks around the world.

"It was problem solving at its best," Shelley said, "because I had a boss who let me run."

She was living the dream. She had worked on product for six major brand campaigns, and because she spent 13 years in the same role, she instilled great confidence in the external organizations with which she worked.

"I thrived on the adrenaline rush," she said.

In 2011, she moved to a senior director–level role and immediately loved it.

Shelley recalled: "I was surrounded by enlightened men and women who recognized that I brought something special to the table. They let me do my job."

Until they didn't.

A woman she reported to emerged as a workplace bully. Her target was one of Shelley's peers on the team.

"He was so good at what he did, but our boss absolutely came at him," she said. "Before meetings, he would send our boss material to preread, and she wouldn't bother with it. Instead, she would berate him in front of the team, asking for information that he had already sent to her."

The target, who was described as "one of the smartest, nicest people on her team," professionally provided the woman with the required information; yet he continued to take the brunt of her attacks.

Shelley felt the only way to survive was to keep her boss as far away from her business as possible.

"I really didn't want her in my business," Shelley said, "but I needed to be on her good side to be successful. She would completely humiliate someone in front of 50 people, 100 people. It didn't matter to her. For her, she tried to justify her bullying as a 'teachable moment.'"

Because of the onslaught, people became paralyzed and stopped sharing ideas. It's like the nail that is sticking up. It gets hammered down, and no one wanted that. No one wanted to stick out and become a target. As fear increased, creativity decreased. People not only stopped talking; they stopped asking for what they needed.

In one meeting, the boss yelled at one of Shelley's male teammates, saying, "You clearly don't know what you're talking about." But he did.

During another meeting, she was on the attack again, berating a female colleague. When the colleague tried to speak up, the boss yelled, "Don't you interrupt me. I'm not finished yet." Colleagues—men and women—would come to Shelley in tears, and she would do her best to calm them down, but everyone's confidence was shattered. Everyone's spirit was broken.

After one particularly difficult meeting, Shelley approached her teammate, the man who took the bulk of their boss's bullying.

"I know that was really rough for you," she said.

He nodded in resignation. "I'm not sure how much more I can take."

Because Shelley worked on a part of the business with which her boss was well versed, she was put into the unenviable position of being considered the boss's favorite—a no-win situation. .

"When we'd travel, I became her go-to person—always by my side, shared the same taxi, sat by me at the meetings, grabbed coffee with me," Shelley said. "I was the person she tethered herself to."

It was on such a trip that her boss confided in Shelley that she had been bullied as a kid.

Mystery solved, but Shelley's problems were just heating up. In a surprising power play, the boss—Shelley had done her best to stay on her good side—overrode a performance rating for someone who reported to Shelley, a woman who had had an exceptional year.

Shelley recounted, "When she lowered a performance review of someone on my team, someone who reported to me—that was a low point for me because it was a move that just said, 'I'm in charge. You're not.'"

When Shelley returned from a well-deserved break, she discovered that her boss had promised the person on Shelley's team who had covered for her that he would receive a bonus for doing so.

"This was such a bizarre move by her," Shelley said. "First, she selected a person to cover for me. That in itself was odd since it's my job to do that. Second, the person she chose would not have been my choice. He came across as a very entitled guy. More style than substance, and I was actively coaching him on that." Her boss decided that, rather than the clear developmental plan he was getting from Shelley, he deserved a bonus. All without consulting Shelley, who didn't feel that going to HR would accomplish anything but potential retaliation against her.

Still, her boss's "about-face" bullying moves started to stack up: information was withheld, and work was sabotaged. Shelley felt a distinct new chill and concluded that her opportunity to go to HR had passed.

In response, Shelley stopped sleeping, lost weight, and began to throw up before work each day.

Thinking back, she said: "I lived in constant fear. Fear of my boss. Fear of her boss. And fear of HR. I hadn't been targeted, but I knew I could be and most likely would be."

Her fear was coupled with the paralyzing shame of not having stepped in to help those who had been so mistreated. Her premonition came true: Shelley was now a target.

"I was trapped. I wasn't good enough. I could no longer drive myself. I was completely broken—physically, mentally, emotionally." Long after she left the company, Shelley continued to suffer both emotional and physical symptoms of the trauma caused by her bullying boss, until finally she reached an epiphany with the help of a therapist.

"Bullying steals your hope," Shelley said. "I learned that I needed someone to hold my hope for me until I was ready to take it back, and I did take it back. I get to decide what seeds to plant in my life. I get to curate my own life."

Survivor's Guilt

Shelley's story is an important one in illuminating how workplace bullying doesn't just affect targets, but also affects the witnesses to the bullying. Their feelings of complicity are overwhelming and ultimately health-harming. Bullies choose "favorites" for a variety of reasons. Though as Shelley pointed out: "I wasn't her favorite. I was someone she didn't dislike. There's a difference."

Shelley worked on a part of the business that the bully was familiar with, was comfortable with, and wanted to be involved in. So neither Shelley nor her business was a threat to the bully. It makes sense that the bully would gravitate toward her.

Witnesses choose not to step in for various reasons—as Shelley said, she wanted her boss to stay out of her business, but also needed her support to run her business. Ideally, in this situation, going to HR would be a viable course of action; but in organizations like Shelley's, where the HR department is regarded as unable to effectively intervene, often a target feels she is on her own, left to solve her own problems. Like Shelley, her male colleagues felt the same way. Unfortunately, not one target of this substantial bully communicated what was happening to HR. Perhaps no single complaint would have gotten traction, but a series of consistent stories might have grabbed HR's attention.

Instead, staying on her boss's good side was the only way she could do her job and remain relatively unscathed—or so she thought. What finally happened? Why was she not able to sleep or eat?

"The fear that it would come my way," she said. "This turned acute stress—stress my body was wired to manage—into chronic stress."

The shame of watching others being bullied and of not having stepped in was too much for her to bear; in a sense, it was survivor's guilt. And when her body finally gave in, the stress of all of it added up to an erosion and shutdown not only of her nervous system, but of her confidence, decision-making, and value.

"I had so much cortisol pumping through my system," she remembered, "my adrenals were burned out. I could no longer 'hack' mother nature."

You may have found yourself in the position of witnessing bullying, but not experiencing it as a direct target. Many of us in that situation would be tempted to do nothing. Getting involved—whether through supporting a target, or making a report to HR, or even confronting the bully—may seem like a losing proposition nearly certain to focus the bully's wrath on a new target: you.

But the lesson you should take from Shelley's story is that doing nothing may eventually catch up with you. Usually a workplace bully is also a serial bully. And unless someone intervenes, it may be just a matter of time before the attention falls on you.

For Shelley, the anxiety of anticipating that the bullying boss would eventually turn on her, combined with guilt that her colleagues bore the brunt of the bad behavior while she remained untouched, proved to be just as traumatic as being the actual target likely would have been.

If you are in Shelley's "pretarget" position, consider this: you have greater credibility now with anyone in authority (including HR) than you will once you've become the target, and thus greater ability to spur an appropriate intervention. Rather than pretend you can lay low until the bullying blows over, you're far better off taking action.

DRILLS

To recognize workplace bullying, it's important to start observing what is going on at work. What is going on with you, to you, and around you? How would Shelley answer the following questions?

- Is there an overall climate of fear and intimidation?
- Are the values of the organization you joined being bent to accommodate misbehavior or overlooked completely?
- Does everything run through a singular filter—the bully?
- How are others feeling? Most important—how are *you* feeling?
- Have others validated your observations of bullying behavior?

Switch perspectives back to you again and answer these questions:

- Which type or types of bullying can you identify?
- Have you ever witnessed workplace bullying? If so, what did or didn't you do? Why?
- Why did this bully choose to bully some and not others?

- Why do you think she turned her bullying attention toward Shelley?
- What effect does micromanaging have on an individual? A team?
- Have you ever felt paralyzing shame at work? If so, what caused it, and what may have helped you to move beyond it?
- Have you ever thought of quitting as a win? If so, when? If not, why not?

21

Amateur Hour: Bullying Distorts Doing the Right Thing

I had never been in an environment that was so quick
to label and then pigeonhole people—you're the foreigner;
you're the tomboy; you're the gay.

The post-meeting slap across her ass startled Isoke into silence.

"Good job in there," he said, flashing a slimy smile as she turned around to face him.

Months before, when Isoke had joined an investment bank, she was a young, Black woman fresh out of Florida A&M, where she'd been a sprinter and scholar. She'd grown up on an island, and her voice had the lilt of the ocean waves in which she'd swum as a young girl.

This was her dream job.

"The lights were bright," she said. "I was working in a highly charged environment with highly charged personalities."

She quickly learned the lay of the land, working on significant deals, getting to know her teammates, and understanding how the multibillion-dollar institution worked. She also came to realize that her gender would always make her the "odd person out." She wouldn't be invited to boys' poker night, lengthy lunches, or weekend golf games. She accepted that inequity, deciding she'd compensate with the smarts and work ethic she'd learned from her parents.

But she could never accept how her coworker, Steve, treated her. A favorite among male colleagues, Steve was an unabashed flirt, creating a highly sexualized work environment. He earned the nickname "ten-to-three-Steve," to match the hours he put in at work. His sexual escapades were well known throughout the team because he peppered his meetings, conversations, and one-on-ones with his latest exploits, often involving one or more of the women on the team. Although he had tested the waters with Isoke on more than one occasion, she showed no interest and thought that would be the end of it.

"I had never been in an environment that was so quick to label and then pigeonhole people—you're the foreigner; you're the tomboy; you're the gay. It was a way for those in charge to quickly determine who would play ball with them and who wouldn't."

As an analyst, Isoke was required to submit her work to the underwriting department, where Steve worked. Ensuring the accuracy of all the paperwork she filed was not something Isoke took lightly, but Steve had a different idea and would let reports stack up, bringing the workflow to a halt. Ironically, Steve influenced how much risk the bank was willing to absorb.

"I really felt like I had landed in amateur hour," she said. "I was new, and because of that, I was smart enough to know that Steve's eyes and experience were required as I got up to speed. I also quickly figured out, though, that I would have to do my best to compensate for Steve's incompetence."

As the pattern continued, Steve connived ways to hide his mistakes. In short, he blamed Isoke. He verbally prodded and poked: "You gotta get these to me faster." "You screwed up this one." "What are you doing?" "You need to stay late and get this stuff done."

"We're falling behind," he said at a team meeting, while looking directly at Isoke. "But, hey, don't blame the new girl! Right, It's-O-kay?" mocking Isoke's name with an ill attempt at an island accent.

Isoke responded the only way she knew how: by working harder, even though she knew she was pulling her weight and he wasn't pulling his. To protect herself, she minimized interaction with him, which seemed to further fuel his rage. When a multimillion-dollar deal was delayed because of an error, the disconnect between Isoke and Steve came to a head. The mistake hadn't been Isoke's. But Steve used the screwup—caused by him transposing two numbers—to diminish her and elevate him.

He fired off an email to the team that didn't name Isoke but might as well have. Its subject was "Messy Close!" At the next team meeting, Steve took the gloves off and berated Isoke in front of her colleagues, placing all the blame squarely on her shoulders.

Isoke's response was to shut down, to not speak, and to become small.

"Steve treated me terribly in the meeting with everyone looking on," she said. "When the meeting ended, I walked toward the restroom to splash some water on my face. As I was opening the door to go in, I felt a sting across my butt. I turned around to see Steve standing there with a creepy smile on his face. He had just slapped me across the ass."

"Good job in there," he said.

She went to a teammate for guidance. He suggested she let her boss know what had happened. She agreed, but first went to Steve's office.

"What just happened out there," she said to him, "can never happen again."

"I thought we were cool," Steve replied.

"We are most definitely *not* cool," Isoke said—and left.

Although she shared the incident with her boss, she prefaced the story with, "I don't want you to do anything about this." She didn't want to earn another label.

"I felt like my boss was relieved when I told him not to do anything," she said.

A year later, when Isoke joined another team with another manager, she was finally ready to talk in more detail about what had happened to her. She was still visibly shaken by what had transpired but felt like she was in a safe place to do so. Telling her story to someone completely unrelated to the experience helped her process what had happened. She thought that was the end of it. It wasn't.

Her new manager took her information to a human resources business partner, and after an investigation into the incident, Steve was terminated.

Isoke felt vindicated but never fully recovered.

Steve was so popular among his male colleagues that when he was fired, the blowback on Isoke was significant. Although she went on to secure bigger roles, she never fully regained her balance from that first experience and the smear campaign that followed her. The developing narrative was that she was trouble. Anything she asked about or challenged wasn't just her way of trying to better the operation or defend herself; instead, it was her way of playing the victim card, of having an inflated sense of her worth, of being the troublemaker many thought she was. It got so bad she submitted a formal complaint to employee relations. That sealed her fate.

"My teammates distanced themselves from me," she said. "The investigation took months, and it was handled so poorly. I realized that when you stand up to a bully, you absorb the label that comes with it. Coupled with the fact that where I was living, I saw no diversity, had no community, I knew the only choice for me was to leave."

After five years—her time on the job peppered with bullying, inequity, and sexual harassment—Isoke left the company.

"I realized it wasn't healthy for me to stay," she said. "It took things getting very bad for me to look at my identity and to realize how much of my life and my happiness was centered on how things were going for me at work. I walked away, and I've never regretted it."

Failure to Act

Looking back at Isoke's story, the "what-ifs" are difficult to avoid.

What if, instead of taking Isoke's "I don't want you to do anything" literally, her boss would have instead known exactly what to do? What if he had taken Isoke's story to HR then and there? What if, instead of showing relief that Isoke didn't want him to do anything, he instead had been trained to provide a better answer? The right answer?

"I know you don't want me to take action, but what happened to you was terrible and inappropriate, and we don't accept that here," he could have said. "I not only want to report this to HR; I'm obligated to do so."

The message to her colleagues and to all bullies-in-training: Isoke was right. Steve was wrong. This better not happen again. But when the organization and HR don't hold the bully or the bully's enablers accountable, talent walks.

If you are reading this book as a manager, learning about workplace bullying and what to do when it impacts your team, you probably already know that it can be hard to take action—especially when someone has asked you, even told you, not to. I understand this situation from my own personal experience of not reporting something when I should have. I get it. But with years and experience, it's easier to see the consequences of inaction more clearly, and the risk-reward ratio is obvious.

You might even be tempted to react the way Isoke's first manager reacted: by ducking. Isoke, fearing blowback, let him off the hook—and he was quite happy to do nothing.

When employees approach you, no matter what they say, they do in fact expect you to act. You are likely the first (and possibly the only) person they will entrust with an incident they've clearly found troubling. Employees in this situation may not know yet exactly how they feel; they may not see clearly what happened or why or what they ought to have done, much less know exactly what the company ought to do next. It's not the employees' burden to ask you to do something specific. That's your job: to think clearly about how to intervene, or about where to take the matter in order to elevate it and to see that it is dealt with appropriately.

If you, as a target of bullying, approach a manager, be clear that you expect this leader to take action on your behalf. Do not diminish the inappropriate behavior, and do not signal to the manager that doing nothing is the option you'd prefer. Remember, the inappropriate behavior is probably not going to end all by itself. You have to play an active role in ending it. Being firm and clear with your manager is important.

Isoke was an extraordinarily talented hire who had landed in her dream job. She is someone that her company should have wanted to keep around for the next 25 years and who wanted to be around. But her employer lost this talent because there was:

- A culture that enabled bullying and made Steve believe it would be acceptable, even encouraged, to behave as he did without consequence
- A lack of understanding at the manager level of what response was appropriate upon learning of the incident
- A badly flawed HR response that led to the target being ostracized further
- A complete lack of support, guidance, or organizational response that would have led Isoke to believe she was valued and had a future within the bank

DRILLS

To recognize workplace bullying, it's important to start observing what is going on at work. What is going on with you, to you, and around you? How would Isoke answer the following questions?

- Is there an overall climate of fear and intimidation?
- Are the values of the organization you joined being bent to accommodate misbehavior or overlooked completely?
- Does everything run through a singular filter—the bully?
- How are others feeling? Most important—how are *you* feeling?
- Have others validated your observations of bullying behavior?

Switch perspectives back to you again and answer these questions:

- Which type or types of bullying can you identify?
- How might assigning labels or even nicknames play a role in a healthy or unhealthy workplace culture?
- If favoritism is an ingredient in an unhealthy workplace culture, have you ever experienced the positive effects of being favored? How do you reconcile that?
- What avenues can more junior employees take to find the support they may need?
- Have you ever been in a workplace culture in which you, like Isoke, shut down, did not speak, and became small? Why did that happen, and how did you feel?

22

Say My Name: Bullying Marginalizes Through Microaggressions

Getting my name wrong equates to questioning my agency.

W hat's in a name? Everything.

Your name is literally you—the first marker of your identity.

It's personal. It's important.

So when people in power can't bother to get your name right, they are saying, "You're not worth remembering. You're not worth my time. You're an outsider." Not getting your name right is a subtle yet powerful form of bullying. It's another potent ingredient in the recipe for diminishing and demeaning behavior.

For reasons that only my mom and dad know, my name is pronounced "Mee-gun," not to be confused with the more popular pronunciation, "May-gun." I use a gauge to determine if I'll correct someone who mispronounces my name. If we are going to be working together and/or seeing each other on a consistent basis, I will do my best to find a tactful way to correct you. If not, I tend to let it slide. I am called "May-gun" 100 percent of the time upon first meeting someone. Even when I introduce myself saying my name, "Mee-gun," the response is "May-gun?" as if I actually don't know how to say my name. I make the correction, which is usually followed by a noncommittal "Huh, interesting."

My experience in the workplace—more than 30 years—suggests that at least some readers will think this is much ado about nothing. I get it. When it comes to workplace bullying, aren't there more egregious sins upon which I could be focusing? Certainly. But the cumulative effect of the so-called little things can be as dangerous as the grand-slam slap on the ass. I've seen plenty of people whose careers died by a thousand small incidents that began with something as seemingly innocent as an intentional refusal to call people by their preferred name.

My friend Pamela is frequently met with confusion when she introduces herself with the name she was given.

"Why do you want to be called 'Pamela'?" she's often asked by colleagues and supervisors.

Or "What happens if I call you 'Pam'?"

And her favorite, "What does your family call you?" To which she deadpans: "Are we family? My family calls me whatever they want!"

"I know it's not unusual for others who share my name to shorten it to 'Pam'; however, I prefer not to do so," she said. "I didn't see anything controversial about it because I've known others with even longer names who don't go by a shortened version—Michael or David, Katherine or Christina. It takes me aback when people question why I prefer to be called 'Pamela.' After all, it is my actual name!"

In the workplace, when your name is mispronounced, it's not just a sign of plain old laziness. It's an indication that you are being disrespected. It's a sign of flat-out arrogance, the idea that the other person assumes he or she knows better than the owner of the name what the best version might be. Done repeatedly, it's a sign that you may very well have a bully in your midst who wants you to know she, he, or they have the power and control, even when it comes to your name. The unspoken message to the person being disrespected is "We both know what you prefer to be called, but the fact that I refuse to call you that is a wink-wink 'agreement' that neither of us thinks you're worthy to be called that. I gain the power because I repeat the slight; you lose the power because you're afraid to call me on it."

It's yet another not-so-nuanced effort to diminish a person's position in the workplace. We saw this play out in the 2020 vice presidential race—the intentional mispronunciation of Kamala Harris's first name along with talking over, interrupting, and otherwise disrespecting her. Then there's the 1994 Jim Rome incident, in which during an on-camera interview, the sports talk-show host insisted on calling Los Angeles Rams quarterback Jim Everett "Chris," as in "Chris Evert," the female tennis player. This was like a double Yahtzee of low blows because Rome was disrespecting not only Everett—whom he'd often referred to as "Chris"—but women in general and Chris Evert specifically.

The inference was that Jim Everett was soft, feminine. Everett famously warned Rome not to do it again, and Rome defied him, calling him "Chris." The interview ended with Everett flipping over the table that separated them, lunging for Rome, and lumbering off the set. But what was an expected—perhaps accepted—response from a professional athlete isn't an option for an employee.

"I've tried many different techniques to reinforce my choice while trying not to make it a big deal," Pamela told me. "Anytime I introduce myself to someone, I shake their hand, and say, 'Hello, I'm Pamela.' If they respond, 'Hi Pam,' which they most often do, I don't let go of their hand. I let them know, 'I go by Pamela,' while still holding onto their hand and looking them in the eye. More recently, I've tried to get in front of it and simply introduce myself as Pamela, while adding, 'and I go by Pamela,' very matter-of-factly with no drama."

It's a great technique, but, she says, "Then I contend with those around who feel the need to comment—'Oh nooooo, don't call her Pam!' or 'Oh, is she ever a Pamela!'"

The two of us discussed why our names become about the other person. For Pamela, a Black woman, it's just another way for people to emphasize her "otherness."

"Getting my name wrong equates to questioning my agency. It's a microaggression that just adds up to feeling marginalized. I mean, why would anyone question my name? It's the name my parents gave me. It's the name I affirmed as an adult."

That's the thing about microaggressions. We experience them throughout our lives, some more than others. And they are additive in nature. Pamela was not only coping with the bullying within her current work environment, contending with people mispronouncing her name; she was bringing every previous microaggressive bullying behavior with her into that environment. For targets such as Pamela, it eventually leads to exhaustion.

Back to the Jims—Rome and Everett. It was expected of Jim Everett, this big, tough, professional male athlete to react to Jim Rome's taunts in the way he did. Many would have thought less of him if he hadn't gone after Rome. At the very least, few thought badly of Everett for losing it. Yet we expect employees, and especially women, to laugh it off. To ignore what's happening. And if they so much as correct the Jim Romes in their lives, it's the targeted woman who is then criticized.

"The whole experience serves to make me feel that somehow I'm the problem and I have to go out of my way to ensure people are not offended that I go by my name," Pamela said. "That is so backwards! If anyone should be offended, wouldn't it be me? But as a woman in corporate America, and a woman of color in particular, this is yet another instance where speaking up could mean being labeled as too direct or aggressive or confrontational."

"And as you know, if you speak up too much, you're out."

You Aren't Important

Pamela's story is a reminder that bullies will stoop to anything to diminish someone they deem unworthy. But would they stand for someone doing the same thing to them? Would a manager named Robert be OK when he was introduced to someone, if that someone said, "I think I'll just call you Bob."

This is not nitpicking; this is yet another microaggression that when repeated, adds up to a message to the subordinate that says, "You aren't important to me." Businesses thrive when employees respect each other; they die when insecure managers marginalize others.

Similarly, many of us make clear what our preferred pronouns are, and acknowledge and respect the choices our colleagues make. Yet we're often faced with colleagues who either insist on applying the pronoun they prefer, or are blind to the importance of the appropriate, preferred pronoun to the listener. Ignoring your colleague's preference sends a clear message: you aren't important, your choices aren't important, and I don't see you as a person.

Our identity, including what we call ourselves, is hugely significant. Pamela's concerns are legitimate concerns that a healthy workplace culture would heed.

If you find yourself in a workplace that doesn't respect your identity— whether your name, your preferred pronoun, the way you dress or wear your hair, or any other aspect of what makes you *you* and the way you prefer to be in the world—there are a few steps you can take.

First, embrace and insist on your identity. The easiest way, the path of least resistance, is to try to ignore the microaggression. But pretending it's not happening is the surest way to ensure it will continue to happen. When people ignore, challenge, or disrespect your identity, professionally but firmly correct them.

Second, if they make the mistake again, correct them again.

Repeated disregard for you, once you've directly corrected and confronted the behavior, is intentional. It's not a joke, though the person doing it may claim they are just kidding or it's "not a big deal." Rather, it is intentional, and it is bullying. You are correct to perceive it as such and to take the appropriate steps you've learned in this book.

DRILLS

To recognize workplace bullying, it's important to start observing what is going on at work. What is going on with you, to you, and around you? How would Pamela answer the following questions?

- Is there an overall climate of fear and intimidation?
- Are the values of the organization you joined being bent to accommodate misbehavior or overlooked completely?
- Does everything run through a singular filter—the bully?
- How are others feeling? Most important—how are *you* feeling?
- Have others validated your observations of bullying behavior?

Switch perspectives back to you again and answer these questions:

- Which type or types of bullying can you identify?
- What are some of the ways those in power can show employees that they are worth remembering? They're appreciated? They're valued?
- When have you had to correct people about the pronunciation of your name or something else at work? What was your approach?
- Why is the mispronunciation of one's name an indicator that an unhealthy workplace culture may be taking root?
- Are there ways that you've either seen or experienced "otherness" emphasized in the workplace?

23

The Setup: Bullying Strikes on Day One

The bully set my reputation before I even had a chance to.

Max was a never-quit guy.

Part of that determination came from a maternal grandfather who worked the graveyard shift at a Texaco plant and cut grass all day in the southeastern Texas heat—to support his wife and his eight children. Six-year-old Max helped him cut that grass.

And part of that determination came from a father from Bogotá, Colombia, who got his master's degree in chemical engineering while studying English as a second language. "I've never known a more intellectually curious and smart person," said Max.

So committed to the concept of team was Max, that after a stellar high school soccer career, having declined several Division I offers, he was surprised to *not* be selected for the University of Colorado's club team.

"Never-quit" Max immediately volunteered to serve as the equipment manager. And that's what he did. Set up cones, inflated soccer balls. Whatever needed to be done, Max did it. On the third day, when he showed up to do the same, the coach told him to suit up. He had made the team.

As a first-generation immigrant from Colombia, he had been raised on winning and applied this attitude everywhere he went—from the soccer pitch to the classroom to the hospital he joined as an operations analyst.

Max jumped into his job, and less than three months in, he was told not only would he be attending an upcoming global meeting, but he'd be responsible for presenting data to the entire risk management team, led by his boss.

Once he landed at the meeting, he declined the extracurricular golf outing, knowing he needed to review the numbers. He was told, "We're golfing. *You're* golfing."

"I knew I wasn't ready for what was being asked of me," he said. "But I golfed, and then when I was told we were going to the bar afterwards, I snuck back to my room instead. I stayed up all night. Literally. I somehow managed to get the reports done, printed, three-hole punched, and put into binders for the team. But I didn't have time to review them."

There was a mistake in the report.

"I still remember it to this day. I spotted it right away. There was a glitch in one of the Excel spreadsheet tables, which meant the total sum was off."

His boss "flew off the handle" and told the team of 20 to pull the report out of the binder, wad it up, and throw it on the floor.

They did just that. In unison. While Max sat there and watched. Humiliated.

"This was the first time I was meeting these guys. My first experience. It ended with my boss saying to me in front of all of them, 'You can go home. You're out. Leave.'"

The next day, with the meeting still in full swing, Max flew home, by himself.

"It was a terrible moment for me, and it set the tone for my experience with that team."

Once his boss returned, he told Max he had three months to "turn this sh*t around or you're done." From that day forward, he showed up each day, scared he was going to be fired. He was shown that mistakes weren't tolerated. Embarrassing him, humiliating him, bullying him continued to be the norm.

"That whole experience translated into me being weak, being someone who those in charge could beat down. Once the tone was set, I had no shot."

The bullying that Max experienced is a form of "mobbing," whereby a boss's underlings pile on the target to win favor with the person they report to.

The bully lit the match, and the rest of the team fanned the flame. Max was wadded up like that paper, cast aside, and thrown in the garbage.

"It was really tough," he said. "No one on that team was inherently unkind, but no one stepped in on my behalf, so the bullying behavior went unchecked."

When he finally spoke to his father about what was happening, the message was always one of support.

Max said: "My family was so proud of me, but they had sacrificed so much. I felt the need to compartmentalize and downplay what was happening. I didn't want to let them down, so I persevered."

His desire to deliver, to "win," kept him going back each day, where he was belittled, demeaned, and embarrassed.

"The bully set my reputation before I even had a chance to," he said. "I already respected hierarchical structure, but now I overrespected it. Overdeferred to it as the bullying gained momentum. I lost all sense of who I was."

The New Employee Trap

Of all our stories, none illustrates the snap-judgment sin as painfully as this one. Max was pigeonholed as a failure from the get-go. Never mind that he really didn't have a chance; he was set up to fail. That's not on him; that's on the managers who did absolutely nothing to prepare him for a big assignment right out of the block.

When bosses like Max's ask the impossible, then erupt, it's less a reflection of the employee's incompetence than the boss's lack of confidence, bitterness, and lack of courage. Angry, discontented people hide their disappointment with themselves by berating others. Bitterness, it's been said, is like taking poison and expecting the other person to die.

In workplaces, people who demean not only don't "get well" by doing so; they get worse. They throw good people off their game. It took years for Max to recover from feeling as if he were a failure. And it cost the company because of that.

Companies would be wise to hire people who set up newcomers for success. Given his background, Max was a diamond in the rough, the kind of no-quit kid who could have helped the company soar. But when they turn a blind eye to managers who demean, companies and their leaders are basically saying, "We wanna be like the bully, not the no-quit kid."

New employees like Max are particularly vulnerable to being bullied because they have no support system in place, no allies to start with. It's a testament to his perseverance that he found a way to survive—and a mark against the company that allowed a bully to make it so difficult for him to succeed.

As a result of workplace bullying, Max's fear of failure kicked into overdrive and fueled his anxiety as he tried to determine the right answer, the right move, the right play. Anxiety replaced confidence and clarity, which had always been staples in his life.

If you find yourself in Max's position, the most important thing you can do is to recognize what is happening. If you have a single ally in your new workplace, conduct a reality check with that person, and seek the person's guidance regarding the right steps to take—whether that's consulting HR, a senior manager, or some other entity; perhaps an ally with greater knowledge about the organization will be able to help point you in the right direction.

When those in charge set a tone of toxicity and hostility, all the others fall into the role they play in that scene. Those witnessing the bullying, even unwittingly enhancing it, are relieved they aren't the target. The behavior gains momentum, the target can't find their footing, and the imprint has been made.

Max had overcome barriers his entire life. He was lucky to have the support of his family, who continued to encourage him even as he received nothing but negative messages from his employer. Max would overcome workplace bullying as well, moving on to bigger and better roles, but not before the bullying took a significant toll on him.

"To this day, when I'm around some of those guys, it's like we still take our place in the scene. We still hit our marks. I'm still the new guy."

DRILLS

To recognize workplace bullying, it's important to start observing what is going on at work. What is going on with you, to you, and around you? How would Max answer the following questions?

- Is there an overall climate of fear and intimidation?
- Are the values of the organization you joined being bent to accommodate misbehavior or overlooked completely?
- Does everything run through a singular filter—the bully?
- How are others feeling? Most important—how are *you* feeling?
- Have others validated your observations of bullying behavior?

Switch perspectives back to you again and answer these questions:

- Which type or types of bullying can you identify?
- How does where you come from influence how you operate in the workplace?

- Has an attitude of "never quit" and/or of always putting the team first ever been considered a negative for you?
- Have you ever made a mistake that set the tone for all that followed? What was that like, and how did you overcome it?
- Have you ever observed, participated in, or been the target of mobbing? What was that like for you?
- In this example, how could the team have helped Max?

24

Subtle and Oblique: Bullying Seeks Control

The most painful type of bullying actually eats away
at your spirit slowly and methodically.

n July 2013, Belinda received one of the best performance reviews of her career. Both of her bosses agreed that her ability to lead teams and execute good work made major contributions to the company. "The sky is the limit for you," one wrote.

One year later, she left the company, saddened and disappointed.

"What transpired in that year was not bullying in the obvious sense," she told me. "Instead, each day I endured efforts by my boss to control and minimize my contributions in the organization."

For Belinda, it began when a new boss asked her to "cc" him on every email she sent out, which struck her as a glaring lack of trust. He also wanted access to her calendar so he could see where she was. She declined both requests.

Under her previous two bosses, she was given the freedom to run things as she deemed necessary. The new boss saw things differently. He wanted control of all the work and insisted that she was to no longer have meetings with senior members of any team without him. On the surface, it seemed like a harmless, if odd, request, but he used it to push her out of leadership meetings and covertly took over work that traditionally had been hers to run. This created confusion on the team.

When she spoke with him about it, he said, "Get used to it."

In the months to come, she received some negative feedback from the team. "They felt I was too outspoken and negative at team planning meetings," she said. "Truthfully, I was—and deserved the feedback. I think I was trying to make up for feeling controlled by my manager."

But instead of working with her on that, her boss asked her to send him a recap of every meeting she attended without him and to send a weekly recap of her work to him and the leadership team.

"In addition, he was overly critical and would offer me up as the reason behind anything and everything bad that happened on the team— whether I worked on the project or not," she said. "He would also verify that I was in meetings by walking by to see if I was in the meeting rooms."

Over the next few months, her boss continued to tighten his grip around her in this exhausting game of cat and mouse.

"I decided to take action and spoke with both his boss and his boss's boss, both of whom I believed were advocates of mine. Although they said all the right things in the meeting, nothing changed."

After several months of this, her boss put her on a performance plan.

"I was shocked and went to a high-level person who was my ally to share what had happened. Upon hearing the story and reading the performance plan, she got involved. She told the head of HR that I could sue the company for what had transpired and that it needed to be fixed, and fast."

Two weeks later, my boss retracted the performance plan and instead delivered a midyear review that seemed fair and balanced. But it was too late.

"I decided to leave. I realized that a single individual was allowed to undermine the nine years of solid contributions I had made to the organization. At no point in these four months did leadership try to understand what was happening to me or demonstrate concern for my well-being. I was not supported and realized that this type of thing only happens to people that the company does not really see or care about. To me, this was the sign that my future there was limited."

Prior to giving her notice, her boss had organized a "360 review" for her.

"I welcomed it. The coach's assessment was, 'There are three things that are very clear. You are well liked and respected by your teammates. You do not have good role clarity. And you have a major problem with your boss.'"

The coach's advice was for her to find a new role. Soon after, Belinda resigned and moved to another state.

"I have more obvious examples of bullying at that company," she said. "Yes, I have been singled out and yelled at behind closed doors. But I think that the most painful type of bullying actually eats away at your spirit slowly and methodically. It is intended to reduce your confidence and intimidate you into complying with someone else's view of you. I had to leave to realize how much damage had been done. It took me at least five years to begin to feel like a whole person again."

The experience, she said, left a bittersweet impression on her: "There are many things about my experience there that were absolutely exhilarating, and I cherish all of it, even the pain. It was a life-changing experience that only a select few get to be a part of, and I am grateful for how it binds us all together. That said, leaving was also the best thing I have ever done."

Insidious Bullying

Belinda's story reflects what I've said elsewhere in the book: bullying often is subtle. When it stays in the shadows, it's more difficult for outsiders to detect. And if called on the carpet, it's more difficult for the target to accept that this is, indeed, bullying. We live in a sort of shock radio world where the "out-there" stuff gets the attention.

But remember, bullying comes in all shapes, sizes, and colors. It's often insidious, flying beneath the radar of everyone, perhaps even of you. What determines whether it's the real deal isn't its overtness, its obviousness, or even its perceived intent. When others repeatedly demean you in order to lift themselves up, you're being bullied.

What might you do if faced with Belinda's situation?

To begin, you could seek guidance from your HR department.

Next, check with your manager's direct reports. Are they subjected to the same controlling, micromanaging rules and requests? Or are these behaviors directed only at you? Your boss's boss and your HR department are likely more interested in (and better able to intervene in) a case of a subpar manager taking down an entire team.

Seek out opportunities for other, neutral observers to encounter your manager's controlling ways. For Belinda, that included a 360 review opportunity—which led a neutral source to advise her that her best option was to leave the manager. Similarly, a neutral observer may help verify your perspective and help you understand available options.

In the end, just as for Belinda, your best option may be to walk away. Targets of bullying often can do all the right things and yet still wind up feeling as if they, not the bully, paid the price. But not every workplace will be like the one you are experiencing now. Not every manager will be a bully. And when you have the courage to walk away, as Belinda did, you put yourself in a position to find such a place.

DRILLS

To recognize workplace bullying, it's important to start observing what is going on at work. What is going on with you, to you, and around you? How would Belinda answer the following questions?

- Is there an overall climate of fear and intimidation?
- Are the values of the organization you joined being bent to accommodate misbehavior or overlooked completely?
- Does everything run through a singular filter—the bully?
- How are others feeling? Most important—how are *you* feeling?
- Have others validated your observations of bullying behavior?

Switch perspectives back to you again and answer these questions:

- Which type or types of bullying can you identify?
- Have you ever experienced your energy being diminished? What were the signs, and what did you do about it?
- Why is it so important to document your experience as the target of workplace bullying?
- Why did those who could have and should have advocated for Belinda choose not to do so? What was the cost in not doing so?
- Do you view Belinda walking away as a win or a loss? For herself and for the company? Why?

25

Dopamine: Bullying Kills Careers

We all felt so humiliated,
our work dismantled and delegitimized.

Working for an organization on a revenue moonshot can be both amazing and terrorizing. For Sawyer, it was, at its best, the most inspiring and innovative place to be, and at its worst, an environment where the misbehavior of promotion-crazed leaders ran rampant. The result was a climate of bravado, jockeying, and internal competition that, left unchecked, turned the environment toxic.

"Public humiliation was a sport at my company," Sawyer, a steely-eyed, 21-year employee for a materials manufacturer, shared with me. "Actually, an everyday activity."

Sawyer, in her late fifties, has an affect that is equal parts grit, grace, and goofball.

"I worked for incredible leaders, had talented mentors, and tough bosses who pushed me to be better," she told me. "They put me into situations and roles before I was ready because they supported me. I knew they had my back so I wasn't afraid to jump."

She went on: "I had 18 amazing years and three really lousy ones. I drank the Kool-Aid of every inspirational internal brand video ever shown. The joy of athletes performing written all over their faces. It was like a shot of dopamine every time we saw our materials being used or worn by athletes. It was like we were right there with them."

When Sawyer became a vice president, she stepped in with the same exuberance she had for every other role she had previously held. Only this time, she was immediately hit with what she saw as an unrealistic revenue target, along with a decrease in full-time employees and a sarcastic, "Oh, you're one of those 'serve the consumer, lifer' people. Good luck."

Something Sawyer had always been proud of, being a committed, long-term employee, became a weapon used to humiliate her. Somehow she was now considered damaged goods because she had not been hand-picked and brought in by the current ruling power structure.

Sawyer's materials team was responsible for all hard-goods product, including balls, bags, gloves, and socks. Her team's work was, as she shared with me, "on every fan reel."

Every time we see a one-handed stretch to catch a football on game day, no matter the level, that glove, ball, sock, and so on, came from Sawyer's team. That soccer ball we see being batted around by the best "footballers" in the world came from that same team, along with the shin guards on bodies and bags on the sidelines.

It was one such soccer ball that would prompt perhaps Sawyer's biggest heartbreak.

The team had been working on a soccer ball innovation two years in the making, and Sawyer was thrilled that her team's work would be part of the big brand story for the season. A first for Sawyer and her team. The presenter asked Sawyer for a sample of the ball, along with some technical highlights, so the product could be properly introduced at the all-employee meeting, a coveted opportunity for any product team.

In front of hundreds of people in the audience and thousands more streaming the meeting, the executive strode onto the stage, ball in hand, editorial-style sport images flanking the stage. As she hit her mark, she stopped, turned to the crowd, tossed the ball in the air, and caught it a couple of times.

"Do we really need to be making these?" she asked with a sardonic tone. Time stood still. Sawyer's mouth went dry. She stared in disbelief.

With eight words configured into one loaded question, Sawyer's entire team, along with two years of painstaking work, was blindsided by what felt like betrayal—from "one of their own."

"I heard from every member of my team," she said. "Even those who hadn't worked on the ball. We all felt so humiliated, our work dismantled and delegitimized." Suggesting the team's work was not valued also suggested the team was not valued.

Not only that, but the executive now had her operatives in place with seemingly one goal in mind—to make Sawyer feel so alone and so uncomfortable that she would self-select out or accept a demotion to simply get out of the bully's crosshairs. The executive wielded her power in such a way that those watching from the sidelines were too scared to come to Sawyer's aid, lest they become the bully's new target. Taking it a step further, to stay in favor with the bully, many joined in on the bullying behavior, which only further alienated Sawyer.

"It got very nasty," Sawyer said. "Blood had been drawn, and the sharks were circling."

Public humiliation or not, she forged ahead, deciding that she would work even harder to hold her own on the all-male team with which she worked. When her twentieth work anniversary came and went without any sort of acknowledgment, it stung. When her annual review came and went with no regard for her team's accomplishments, it stung. When her name showed up on an Excel spreadsheet inadvertently shared with her, highlighting plans for her demotion, it not only stung, it felt like another public shaming.

But she continued to forge ahead.

Sawyer's determination and love for the brand propelled her forward to a one-on-one with her boss, who told her she needed to be more visible across the organization and more social after-hours during team travel.

"The 'You should be socializing more after-hours feedback' was a turning point for me," Sawyer said. "That's code for 'we executives don't choose to see you and will not let you into our club, so don't bother.' The writing was on the wall. My team's work had been literally tossed to the side at an all-employee meeting."

Sawyer was willing to take a lot, and she did. However, when the product review meetings her team held became particularly toxic, she realized that her diminishing personal stock at the company was negatively affecting her team.

"Come after me, I'm gonna dig in and work harder. Come after my team, I'm gonna dig in and protect them," Sawyer said. "What I realized was that I no longer was being of service to them."

In one particularly rough meeting, Sawyer's product director was presenting the latest innovation in socks, a product line that had proved to be incredibly successful, when a global vice president launched into a verbal beatdown unlike anything Sawyer had ever witnessed or experienced.

"Here's one of my guys doing a great job, leading us through the spring product line," she recounted. "He's cheerful; he's hardworking; he knows his stuff. He's got the boards, the samples, the math—all in a beautifully kitted-out room. We're coming off double-digit growth, margins through the roof; you name it. And then a 20-minute tirade ensues."

To this day, Sawyer is convinced it was an "inside job," meaning it didn't matter who or what was presented that day; her direct manager and the global VP had decided that it would be an opportunity to further humiliate her by coming after her teammate.

In a conference room full of nervous energy, all sense of professionalism and civility was ignored; a colleague launched a flurry of F-bombs at Sawyer and her team.

The In-Your-Face bully loves to publicly denigrate all, to flex his "I'm in control" muscles and distribute a beatdown, while others look on. That's what was happening. Most watched in horror, some in awe. Coconspirators on the perimeter of the conference room sat silently, smirking through the barrage.

Knowing it's time to walk away and doing so are two different things.

"I knew I could probably stay if I petitioned other leaders from other functions for help or if I was willing to continue to endure the public beat-downs, the resource, staffing, and work sabotage by my own supervisor," Sawyer said. "I had no air cover, and therefore my team was vulnerable. It was time to get my ducks in a row. After that meeting, I knew we had lost our way in terms of how people were allowed to treat one another."

The Feeding Frenzy

One of the more disturbing, and heartbreaking, effects of workplace bullying is the intentional sabotage of the work accomplished by the targets and their teams. Even if the product or project is launched, the bully has managed to publicly suggest that what the targets have done isn't valued, needed, or on strategy. So the targets take a double hit—being humiliated and being told, often without words, that they're alone. They have no support. Their allies, mentors, and sponsors are either long gone or nowhere to be found, and those who should show up as advocates are too busy or too scared to step in.

Sawyer knew something about allyship, having leveraged her position to drive salary equity for women within the company. It was an unpopular position to take, and her challenge was made more difficult by managers who erected budget-cutting roadblocks in her path. She would later wonder if her activism had led to her ultimate demise. For now, Sawyer forged ahead with her signature grit and grace, but somewhere along the way, the indelible values she held so dear were publicly scoffed at and denigrated.

If you find yourself the target of a bully who publicly humiliates you and your team, there are a few things you can do.

First, it is important for your own emotional health to talk openly with the colleagues impacted by the bullying behavior. If these are team-mates, commiserating is important; if these are your direct reports, it's vital to help them process the bullying outburst, and to comfort them and help them, not only to understand their options, but also that you will do your best to protect them.

Second, confront the bully. Be clear about the consequences of the bully's behavior in terms of lost time, team motivation, unclear strategy, and so on. Explain that what just occurred was a management *failure*—and not yours. Before the conversation, create a specific action plan, and present that plan to the bully as the steps that you will now take to resolve and repair these consequences.

Third, call out the bully's behavior as bullying. Name it, across the organization. HR needs to know, your team needs to hear the word "bully," and managers up the line need to hear it described accurately, along with the consequences and your cleanup plan. Create the narrative that a bully has attempted to inject toxicity into the organization, but you will provide the cure.

Fourth, call out the bully's allies. In Sawyer's case, it was the smirking executives sitting on the edges of the room. Speak with them individually. Explain to them the consequences of the bully's actions; tell them that you have apprised HR of the situation, that upper management has likewise been notified, and that you were disappointed in their apparent support for the bully's toxic behavior.

If you can do all of that, you may—repeat, may—be able to counter-act the bullying behavior.

The other option, and often the better path available to you, is to seek out a role where you no longer report to that bully. So as hard as it may be, and as unfair as it may feel, consider walking away.

DRILLS

To recognize workplace bullying, it's important to start observing what is going on at work. What is going on with you, to you, and around you? How would Sawyer answer the following questions?

- Is there an overall climate of fear and intimidation?
- Are the values of the organization you joined being bent to accommodate misbehavior or overlooked completely?
- Does everything run through a singular filter—the bully?
- How are others feeling? Most important—how are *you* feeling?
- Have others validated your observations of bullying behavior?

Switch perspectives back to you again and answer these questions:

- Which type or types of bullying can you identify?
- Have you ever been placed into a position at work before you felt ready? What were the circumstances, and what did it tell you about the workplace culture?
- Is it important for leaders to integrate "lifers" like Sawyer with those who are external hires so both feel equally valued? Have you ever experienced this happening well? Poorly?
- Have you ever been on a team where the team members had a difficult time building trust with each other? What was getting in the way? How did it feel? Was the issue resolved, and what role did you play?
- What are some of the ways leaders' insecurities can show up in the workplace, and what is the effect on the team?
- Do you view Sawyer walking away as a win or a loss? For herself and for the company? Why?

PART V

NAVIGATE

The Bully Culture

The conversation I had with my children, Jackie and Spencer, was not an easy one for me.

"Hey guys, I need to talk to you about something," I said. We were standing around the kitchen island, where all important family conversations happened. Their faces reflected looks somewhere between "Are we in trouble?" and "What's wrong with Mama?"

"It looks like I won't be working in Baske—"

"What?" said Spencer.

"Why not?" asked Jackie.

"You know about bullies, right? We've talked about how we don't tolerate bullies at school, right? Well, we don't tolerate bullies at work either."

"Why do you have to go? Why doesn't the bully have to go?"

"Because sometimes life deals us a bum hand that we don't totally understand, and this is one of those times. But as long as we remain true to who we are, it's all good 'cuz that's all we can do."

"What are you going to do?" asked Jackie.

"I'm going to spend a lot more time with you two."

Two smiles, three counting my own.

26

As You Think About Walking Away

Don't go away mad; just go away.

—NEIL EVERETT MORFITT

The chance that your bully is going to change is slim. For some of us, HR intervention is a plausible and effective solution, or at least the preferred initial strategy; for others, an effective HR response is less likely. The chance that leadership will do the right thing is frequently zero. So where do you put your hope?

You put your hope in yourself, not in the circumstances of your workplace. It feels like there's a fourth *F* to the fight, flight, or freeze scenario. The fourth *F* is "face it." Find your way. Figure it out. Forge your own path. OK, that's more than four, but you get the idea.

As you contemplate your best move—and whether you ultimately decide to stay with your current employer or walk away and find a new opportunity—there are a number of things to consider and to do. A longer, more detailed list appears in the Appendix, but at a minimum you'll want to consider the following:

- Untangle your personal life from your work life. Make sure you are using your personal email address only for personal communications and your work email only for work-related communications. The same goes for devices—do your best to separate your work phone, computer, and other devices from those you use for personal matters. On social media, take care to consider your identity and what you post about.
- Consider contacting an attorney both to discuss the possibility of a workplace claim and to get advice on your rights to pay and benefits upon leaving your job.
- If you haven't already, start looking for your next opportunity. I get it: it can seem overwhelming to job-search when bullying has worn you down. But even small, manageable activities like updating your résumé and LinkedIn profile, and exploring job search sites and tools like Indeed, can be a useful head start when you decide to walk away.
- Decide what your story will be. If you do decide to walk away, your friends, family, and professional acquaintances will all wonder why. This is especially true if you do not have a new job waiting for you when you leave. So think through what you will tell them. For me, a simple "I want to spend more time with my children" was enough to satisfy those who asked.
- Envision your last day, and consider how you will actually exit. My hope is, you'll choose to leave in as dignified, graceful, and proud manner as you possibly can. In any event, you'll leave with head held high.

For me personally, the internal process took many months, eventually resulting in a disappointing and vague outcome. Several months later, the company offered me a position well below my last role—an offer I immediately declined.

As if on cue, a new narrative took shape.

"Megan is difficult," the whisper campaign began.

"She has an inflated sense of her trajectory within the company."

"She isn't a team player."

"We asked her to take another role, and she refused."

And the one that stung me to my core, "She couldn't hack it in basketball."

Upon declining the lesser role, I was given the option to step into a project-based role to allow the corporate leadership team a few months to find me an appropriate landing spot. Ten months later, the leadership team had made no progress, which led me to the only reasonable conclusion I could make: the organization was fine with me leaving. So I gave them what they wanted.

I resigned.

Does any of this sound like your situation? If the answer is yes, you've got some decisions to make. Perhaps in addition to: Face it. Find your way. Figure it out. Forge your own path, we add the most important F: friends. You're not alone in this even though you now may be feeling like others are part of the squad and you are not. You may even conclude that not everyone is equal, certain people are untouchable, and it is no longer about the work. There is no new position or promotion that is salve enough.

But even knowing all of this, we still must try. We must demand an investigation when we find ourselves as the target of workplace bullying. We must push for what is right and fair. We must make it about us. Our experience. Our smarts. Our future. Our voice. After all, the truth will be brought to light, and justice will prevail. Right?

Not always. In the end, bullies are often protected in a way that targets aren't. Maybe it's their connections. Maybe it's their gender. And maybe it's a moment in time.

Take your pick of reasons. With all the earnestness of my younger self ice-skating at Cannon Hill Park, I couldn't understand why bullies spray-painted their insecurities masked as hatred for me. I had trusted in all the things my grandparents, parents, and siblings had taught me: work hard; play fair; fight through the screen; get 'er done.

And lost. Or so I thought.

I was slightly emotional as I wrote the farewell note that I would send out to those with whom I had worked for nearly three decades, starting all the way back in Wilsonville with my oldest and dearest friend, Marcie, who was at the top of my "To" list.

They say that "home is where the heart is." Never has that saying been so clear to me than now, as I think about where my heart has resided over the last 29 years. Nike is the place I have felt most at home for more than half my life.

The experiences that I've been afforded are second only to the relationships I have coveted. And that's where you come in.

Thank you for the role that you have played in making this the fullest, richest, best-ever time for me. The places we've seen, the work we've delivered, the fun we've had—it is all embedded in my heart, always.

Now a new chapter begins. One that is focused on my two not-so-little humans: Spencer Everett and Jacqueline Murphy. They have loved sharing me with Nike, but I will say, their glee upon learning that Mama will be around full time has left me wondering what I haven't been providing in their first 12 and 10 years, respectively.

If this reads a bit like a love letter, it's by design.

I love Nike. I love you.

Thanks for all of it. I will see you around.

Meegs

DRILLS

- Imagine your exit. What might it feel like to walk away from your job? Who would you want to talk to on your last day, and what would you say? Write it out.
- How have you combined your work and personal lives? Do you use devices provided by your employer? Do you use work email, phone, or social media for personal communications? Identify the specific ways the distinction between work and personal may have bled together so that you can consider how to separate the two.
- What do you imagine yourself doing the day after you quit? Five years after you quit?

27

Recognizing That Respect Has Turned to Disrespect

Who wants to see us today?

—MOM

t was a typical day for me. My new normal—going grocery shopping, finding some special treats for Blue, then picking up Spencer and Jackie, ages 12 and 10, from school. As the kids jumped into the car, settling their too-big backpacks next to them and sharing the highlights of their day, they asked, "What did you do today, Mama?"

"I had lunch at Nike today with a really nice woman."

"Do they want to hire you back?" they asked in unison.

"No, that's not what we talked about," I replied. "We talked a lot about what's going on there, and it made me think about all that I've learned through the experience that I went through, you know? How about you guys? Did you learn anything from all of that? I mean, you were right there with me, going through it all. What did you learn?"

There was a long pause, and then, from the backseat, Jackie said, "Stand up for yourself."

Her eyes locked with mine in the rearview mirror, and I was amazed, not for the first time, by her. To my right, Spencer chimed in, "And keep standing up for yourself." His blue eyes fixed on me.

R-E-S-P-E-C-T

That mindset—one of having self-respect and insisting on your own worth—is going to be important, whether you decide to stay in your current position or leave.

All our lives, we've been conditioned to believe that standing up for ourselves also means digging in our heels—that insisting on our own value equates to winning a fight. While that's sometimes true, it's not always true; in the case of targets of workplace bullying, it's almost never true.

Let me tell you two stories that may help you find the mindset to work out what to do next.

My upbringing was one of rules, roughhousing, and respect with two working parents and Mrs. Gilmore. We would never have thought to use the more sophisticated label of "nanny," but by definition, that's what she was. Easily in her sixties when she started caring for us as small children while Mom and Big Dave worked as full-time high school teachers, Mrs. Gilmore would do some light housecleaning and look after us for a few hours when we came home from school.

With my Mrs. Beasley doll sitting next to me, I would pound a glass of ice-cold apple juice and tell Mrs. Gilmore all about my day. While getting her work done, she was always laser-focused on me and all that was going on in my young mind.

One day, some girls came home with me after school, and to be funny, I called Mrs. Gilmore "Mrs. Babysitter." My friends laughed at that, and Mrs. Gilmore gave me a look that said, "We'll talk about this later," which came more quickly than I would have liked. I had never before seen Mrs. Gilmore mad or hurt. She was both. Still, her gentleness remained intact.

"Do you think that was a nice way to address me, Megan Ann?"

"I don't know," I answered, squirming in my seat.

"Do I have a name?"

"Yes."

"And what is it? What is my name?"

"Mrs. Gilmore."

"That's right," she said. "Would I ever refer to you as 'that child I watch?'"

"No."

"And why wouldn't I?"

"Because my name is Megan."

"That's right. Your name is Megan, and mine is Mrs. Gilmore, and we show each other respect by using each other's names, don't we?"

"Yes," I replied. "I'm sorry I did that. Chantelle thought it would be funny."

I had almost done well enough for us to be done with this conversation.

"Did Chantelle make you refer to me that way, or did you choose to do that all on your own?"

"I chose to, Mrs. Gilmore. I'm sorry."

I was now in tears as I realized that I had hurt my beloved Mrs. Gilmore. I had disrespected her, and I was just now beginning to get an idea of what that actually meant.

"There, there," she said in her gentle Mrs. Gilmore voice, pulling me into her baby blue cashmere sweater that smelled of the cinnamon and sugar toast she had made for me earlier that day. "I appreciate and accept your apology."

I learned at an early age that disrespect of any kind was not tolerated. I also learned what it felt like to be surrounded by people who were on my side, had my back, and would take the time to teach me life lessons.

Mrs. Gilmore's lessons were alive and well as I made my way through a long and successful career. Even when I ran across abrasive people at work, I was always able to find my way through, respectfully.

And then, like the other targets of workplace bullying who contributed stories for this book, no amount of respect, professionalism, or other tactics I deployed put a dent in the bully's desire to harm me. It was as if a new set of rules applied—rules that I didn't understand and that didn't seem rational. I believed wholeheartedly that the world operated on a simple baseline of respect toward everyone around me. And then I encountered workplace relationships where that was just not true.

Meeting Kobe Bryant

Now consider a second set of words of wisdom.

It was August 2014, and my first signature athlete meetings were approaching. Showrooms were built out, calendars were cleared, and catering was booked. I had met athletes before but never in this way. I would be at the table with the highest level of Nike executive leadership as Nike's vision was discussed with each athlete. Product direction was highlighted, and in turn, each athlete would share with us what was on his mind, where his brand was headed, and what he expected of Nike.

First up was Kobe Bryant.

At age 17, the soon-to-be-drafted basketball maelstrom, Kobe Bryant, signed an endorsement contract with Adidas. Eight years later, in 2003, he joined Nike with the hope of forging his own path. Kobe participated in the cocreation of one of the greatest collections of footwear, apparel, and equipment the Nike brand had ever designed.

Prior to the official meetings, Kobe decided he wanted to say good morning to Nike employees. He was positioned in the information hut at an entrance, smiling and waving at unsuspecting employees driving into work.

I had never met Kobe and expected him to be standoffish, protected by several layers of "his people." Your basic diva. In other words, I was not anticipating that I would like Kobe Bryant.

Except that I did. Immediately. Kobe was professional in our meetings and had a clear vision about his brand and his plans post-basketball, which were being discussed.

As Nike's general manager of North America Basketball, I was in the room with one of the greatest players of all time, a five-time NBA champion, two-time MVP, discussing the business of basketball. Kobe Bryant was a visionary who was direct and directive, but also listened and probed for understanding. He was, indeed, surrounded by his people, and they couldn't have been more professional and supportive.

Later as we had lunch, I was seated across from him. I was no longer talking to "Mamba," one of the all-time fiercest competitors in NBA history; Kobe was now just a dad, discussing how his girls were doing as they geared up for school. As he was smiling about raising daughters, I was thinking to myself: "This is the guy that, on the night he tore his Achilles, tweeted, 'If I get in a fight with a bear in the woods, pray for the bear.'"

"Tell me about your family," he said.

"We've just repatriated from Holland. My daughter is doing great, but my son, Spencer, is having some difficulties finding his way at his new school as a fifth grader."

"That's tough. I still remember when we moved back from Italy. Man, I didn't fit in. It was like my clothes weren't right, my hair wasn't right, my music wasn't right. I felt totally out of place other than on the basketball court."

"I bet that was tough. I'm so glad for the experience that both my children had over there. It's hard to watch him struggle though, you know?"

He nodded.

"This is something I tell my girls when they're going through something particularly tough," he said. "I ask them, 'Can you cut down a tree with one strike?' No. You can't. You take that ax, and you chip away at that tree, and pretty soon, that tree comes down. That's life. Anytime it serves up obstacles, you chip away at them. Just like that tree, you gotta take some whacks at it."

"Thanks for that," I said. "I'm gonna share that with Spencer."

I did. Tucking him into bed that night, I told him that I had gotten to meet Kobe that day.

Head perched on his Star Wars pillow, he smiled at me and said, "You got to meet Kobe Bryant today, Mama?"

"Yeah—and guess what we talked about?"

His eyes widened, "What?"

"We talked about you," I said. And then I told him what Kobe said.

Spencer snuggled in. "Mama," he said, "I'm gonna take some whacks at that tree tomorrow. Just like Kobe."

Value Yourself and Others

There is a lesson that connects these two stories: Treat people well. Treat people with respect. Connect with people to show you care about them. And when a bully has targeted you, and you've tried all that you can try, take some whacks at that tree.

You now know what that looks like:

Recognize that something is happening to you. In other words, you're not making it up—whack!

Understand how an unhealthy culture is at the root of workplace bullying taking hold—whack!

Identify bullying in the wild so you can pick some moves to make—whack!

Navigate your way to understanding and accepting that being the target of workplace bullying may very well lead to you exiting the company that is allowing the mistreatment to happen—whack!

The process, of course, spells out "ruin," which is what you taking action is prevented from happening to you. You are refusing to stay under the thumb of someone who has only their own, not your, best interest in mind.

Exits can be long, messy, and unsatisfying, but ultimately they are what frees us.

I don't want to guilt anyone who's been, or is being, bullied. But you can't wait for the cavalry to come save you; in most cases, it's not going to happen.

As Kobe said, "That's life." And yours is too important to let indecision or acquiescence keep you from being all you were meant to be.

We live in a world that values money, position, and prestige above all else. But our challenge is to understand that deeper things are in play. Fast-forward and ask yourself what, at your celebration of life, do you want people to remember you for: that you climbed high on the corporate ladder or that you were a person of integrity? You want them to remember that you had the courage to refuse to let others control you. That you cared about others. That you cared about helping make a better world by connecting to yourself and others in a deep and meaningful way.

Don't misunderstand me: having money, climbing high, and getting accolades for your success aren't bad things. They only become so when, to attain such things, we give up the most important thing in the process: ourselves.

Think about who you are and what you stand for, whether that's because of your upbringing or despite it. Be intentional about valuing yourself and others. When you look in the mirror, remind yourself that the person staring back at you sets the pace of your life. No one else.

DRILLS

- By now, you should have a clear understanding for the terrain on which you work. What have you discovered? How are you feeling about it?
- When have you taken "whacks at the tree"? What were the circumstances?
- Think about your own "Mrs. Gilmore." Do you have one? Perhaps you are one to someone else?
- How are you valuing yourself?

28

Considerations

Clear the mechanism.

—BILLY CHAPEL

f you are contemplating walking away from your current role, I suggest four additional considerations that may help you sustain the strength, willpower, and dignity you will need to see it through.

Activate Your Allies

First, do everything you possibly can to assemble and activate your allies and friends.

Shortly after leaving Nike, I was blessed to be invited to help establish a group called "The Wing Women." We decided that former Nike employees, who identified as female and needed a network, would band together and, taking a page from "wingman"—as in "I got your back"—would create a group. At our quarterly meetings, we devote our time to personal connection, as well as philanthropic, professional, and political discussions.

The Wing Women immediately meant something more to me than a networking group. It was and is a female posse, my huddle, as author Brooke Baldwin highlighted in her book of the same name, that I rely on for advice and, most of all, the support I needed as I moved on from my previous life. The Wing Women would become one of the most important ingredients in my recovery from the trauma of having been bullied.

Plan Your Final Act

Second, even if you eventually decide to stay in your role, an incredibly useful exercise is to consider exactly how you would want to exit the company.

Do you want to leave quietly, with a simple two weeks' notice and your final paycheck?

Is it important to you to try to get the attention of someone—anyone—in leadership to help the company see it is losing a talented, hardworking, successful employee for no good reason?

Are there people you would want to meet with before you go, to help them understand why you are leaving? And if so, what exactly do you want them to understand, and why?

For me, the most important person to talk to before I left was none other than Mr. Knight. I knew I had to see him one last time.

"Well, first of all," he said to me after I told him I was leaving, "you're way too young to be retiring. What's goin' on?"

We were in a small, private conference room adjacent to one of Mr. Knight's offices in the Mia Hamm building on Nike's sprawling campus.

I had presented to him in large and small settings, each time feeling both the privilege and nerve-racking enormity of having him in the audience—like saying prayers aloud in front of the Pope. But this was the first time during my 30-year career at Nike that I had an audience with just him.

"Thank you so much for making time for me today, Mr. Knight." My formality wasn't a sign of capitulation, a hypocritical about-face. No, it was a simple sign of reverence, gratitude, and respect. He hadn't bullied me; others had.

And this is where it gets tricky. Where exactly does the buck stop? Did companies bully me and the others interviewed for this book, or did people within those companies do so? How do we distinguish one from the other? After all, it was Mr. Knight's "never say die" approach that afforded me a career full of exceptional experiences, friendships, and memories.

Perhaps both things can be true.

We can't assume that a company is bad because of the presence of some bad apples, but when those people are put into leadership roles, an unhealthy workplace culture is not far behind. As the *New York Times* would report in its article "At Nike, Revolt Led by Women Leads to Exodus of Male Executives," that is ultimately what happened—it's just that the exposé and the exodus happened too slowly to benefit me.

Mr. Knight's question about my leaving gave me an unexpected opening, but not for a nanosecond did I think of venting to him. When he was guiding the ship, the waters weren't this kind of choppy. When he left day-to-day management and put others in charge, a lot of his ideals walked out the door with him. He wasn't the guy in the hot-air balloon flying over the campus, watching how those he handed the baton to were managing the company.

I had set up this meeting for a singular reason. A one-on-one with Mr. Knight was a big deal to me, and I would use it for its intended purpose only, which was to say thank you. There would be no airing of dirty laundry, no unhinging of negative emotions, and no unleashing of injustices. My mother hadn't raised me to complain; she had raised me to write thank-you cards. And today was just that—a face-to-face thank-you note. But she also raised me to speak up, to use my voice—for me and those around me. And that, of course, is what this book is about.

"It's time," I said to Mr. Knight about leaving. "I've got a seventh grader and a fourth grader. I'd like to spend more time with them."

"Well, that's the best reason you could give," he said.

"I really just wanted to thank you." My voice found its way through the corridors of emotion that the most heartfelt thank-you elicits. "Thank you for never quitting. You had so many opportunities to do so. Yet you never did, and because of that, I'm here, sitting with you, after almost 30 years working at this great company that you built. I so appreciate what you did."

He listened intently, this innovator, dreamer, and entrepreneur who operates from a place of humility and generosity. As our conversation covered the contours of lives spent at Nike, I sank further into the plush, dark leather chair and let him know I had just read his book, *Shoe Dog*. It dawned on me that his words and recollections were helping me say good-bye to the love-at-first-sight Nike I had joined in 1988.

I guess that's what I wish I would have shared with him. That his story was providing me with the permission to write my new story. It had filled me up with the fuel I needed not only to walk away, but also to understand that my win was in walking away.

When I got up to leave, I hugged him a final good-bye. I knew I had just had the most bittersweet 29 minutes of my 29-year Nike career. As trained, I took the high road and gave thanks, because thanks were due. As I made my way to the door, I was cloaked in gratitude. Gratitude under a haze of anxiety, exhaustion, and sadness, but gratitude nonetheless.

That was the right choice for me in that specific conversation. There were other meetings, with other people, that took a different tone.

You'll likely have the same experience. There will be a variety of people you may want or need to meet with before you walk out the door, and a variety of goals you may have for each conversation. Think about what you want to say in each setting, and what if anything you'd hope that listener would do based on your words. Being highly intentional about these last conversations can help you see even more clearly whether walking away is the right decision for you.

Be of Service to Others

Third, appoint yourself the *CEO of Yes*.

That's right. The CEO of Yes.

I made myself the CEO of Yes mainly because I was having a hard time functioning. I was having a hard time getting out of bed. I was weepy, tired, and depressed. I knew that putting myself in a position to help others was going to be a positive for me. It would hold me accountable. It would allow me to get outside my head, which was playing tricks on me. It would help me feel some value.

Saying yes to coaching Jackie's youth volleyball team was more about me than the fact the kids needed a coach. I needed them. I needed to be around the life force that is children at play. I started saying yes to all the things that I had always said no to or that people just simply stopped asking me for because I was too busy, or I was out of the country, or I didn't respond.

You need help moving? The CEO of Yes is ready to pack boxes.

You need help finding a school for your son who is struggling in public school? The CEO of Yes is available to learn everything there is to know about alternative options.

You need help with your carpool days because you're sick? The CEO of Yes not only will take your days but will be part of the meal train set up to deliver food to your door.

It feels so good being of service to others. It's freeing to put our own needs aside and to be available to those who are in need. I was getting invited to luncheons and actually attending. I was finally someone my friends could count on to be available and present, not checking my phone and in a rush because I was so busy with all my work stuff. It was amazing. When I started listening to Shonda Rhimes's *Year of Yes* while on my daily walks with Blue, I knew I was onto something. It felt good to say yes. It was awesome, the answer, the elixir!

Hold up. Maybe that's going too far. Saying yes helped so much. It gave me purpose. But finding my footing didn't happen overnight.

Initially, I thought I was trying to find my footing back to the me that was me before workplace bullying kidnapped the me that was me.

And, no, I didn't say yes to everything. What I did do that I hadn't done in a very long time was to start to listen to my body. I started to pay attention to what I needed. Many of the targets interviewed for this book talked about needing some space, some peace, some quiet. Most of us sought out some form of counseling to start talking about what had happened to us. Most of us were diagnosed with PTSD from chronic stress. Many, if not all of us, talked about our "wellness tribe," those we enlisted to support the process of putting us back together.

"I did it all. I needed it all," many said.

In addition to weekly counseling sessions, we sought help from naturopaths, massage therapists, functional neurologists, chiropractors, cranial sacral therapists, acupuncturists, yogis, Reiki, Rolfing, and energy healers. Movement, music, and no longer muscling through equated to the healing power of walking, listening, and resting.

Anticipate Struggle

Fourth, you can be sure that if and when you do walk away, you will continue to struggle with the fact that you experienced bullying behavior, and it will likely take a long time to process and find a sense of peace and resolution around what happened to you.

Outwardly, I put on a brave face, slipped into some cool shoes, and moved on. I jumped into being "Mama" and tried to love it.

I made breakfast, volunteered at the kids' school, and listened to my children tell me about their days when their days actually happened, instead of a week later when I returned from somewhere I'd forgotten. I tried out new recipes, settled us into a new house, walked our new puppy, Blue, and became part of our new community. I hosted small yummy mummy gatherings, took some yoga classes, and tried to find my way.

But here's the deal: inwardly, I was stuck. Perhaps you are too.

What do we do without the pace and adrenaline of our workplace?

For many of us, we begin the tentative steps of peeking out of the protective shell—equal parts paranoia, self-doubt, and fear—we had built around ourselves while being the targets of workplace bullying. It is a slow, painful process. There were days when I didn't want to get out of bed, and in fact, I went back to bed after my children were delivered to school and Chris was at work. I tried hard to limit those days, but I had too many of them to count.

After all, what I had done for a living was the signifier of my identity. "Megan from Nike" said everything I was willing to know about myself. "Megan from Nike" said everything I was willing to allow the world to know about me. I didn't know who I was without Nike, and I had no idea what my value to my family could be without it. Not only that, but Nike had defined my approach to everything for over half my life. How I lived, breathed, worked out, traveled, mothered, wife'd, ate, slept, interacted—all to the beat of Nike.

I was finally realizing that in my status as being "Megan from Nike," I had lost sight of being me.

So start now, even before you make the decision to walk away, to find help in understanding and processing this trauma.

DRILLS

- Who are your allies and friends, and how will you rally them? Are you reaching out to them for support? How will you do so after walking away?
- Who are the people you most want to meet with as you exit? What are the specific messages you want to communicate to each? After thinking about these conversations, do you feel more ready to walk away, or less?
- How are you listening to your body and what it needs from you? How have you begun processing what has happened to you? How will you find help, whether from friend or family or from healthcare professionals?
- Is there an opportunity to be of service? What might that look like for you?
- Do you need help? See the Further Resources section at the end of this book for suggestions.

29

The Re-Definition of Winning

The way to avoid weeds is to grow good grass.

—BOB WELCH

For years, I still had this nagging question I couldn't shake. You know the one: How could someone like me succumb to bullying? Someone with my supportive upbringing and strength of character. Where did things go wrong? What had I done wrong? What was the flaw in me? I was crafty. I was a leader. I was tough.

I know you've had it too. Even though we've already covered this topic, it's worth repeating. My friend Bridget said it best via a pointed text to me:

I hear you speak and kind of shaming yourself for saving yourself. You did not succumb to a bully; you chose to get yourself out of a horrible situation. You reached out for help and nobody responded. You fought like hell and you couldn't do it anymore. Stop apologizing for removing yourself from that toxic situation. Stop talking about yourself as a quitter. Nothing could be further from the truth. Stop second-guessing yourself. That was a brave and fearless decision you made.

Why is that so difficult for those of us who have been targeted to understand, accept, and believe? Why is it so difficult for targets to understand that, as another friend shared with me, "No one should have to learn how to tolerate abuse"?

A qualifier before I continue: I'm not sure that my decision was made out of courage as much as desperation. But I am sure of this: It was easier for me to walk away than it might be for some others. I was coming from a position of power and privilege. After nearly three decades in the business, I'd made a good income. My husband had a good-paying job; our family of four was financially comfortable. The people who deserve the "brave and fearless" label are those who walk away despite not having such support: the single mom or dad with children to support, for example.

Honor and dignity are equal-opportunity pursuits. Read actor/producer Viola Davis's book, *Finding Me*, or others about people who overcame hardships, and you're reminded that deep character transcends economic status. Davis became a success because, despite an abusive childhood rooted in poverty, she refused to be defined by her circumstances. She clung to her personal dignity through thick and thin.

And that's what walking away to win is all about: regardless of who you are, refusing to let others define you. Instead, trusting in your own integrity to guide you to work situations where you are valued for who you are, not demeaned for who you aren't.

But in life we're taught to either win or lose. To do your best over and over. To try your hardest over and over. To suck it up over and over. When we do all this and still come up short, it feels like losing.

Yet to stay in a situation in which you are being demeaned, diminished, and disrespected is to acquiesce to a system, a culture that is not set up to support you. So here's what we learn from all this: *The win is in walking away.*

Not that it's at all simple. Witness the binary decision that targets of workplace bullying face: Do I stay, or do I go?

Stay and continue to wait it out. Maybe the bully will be moved. Maybe I will be moved to something fulfilling. Maybe not. Maybe my health will continue to decline, and I will no longer be of value to anyone, especially my family. Maybe that will be the case because maybe I will no longer be alive.

The other choice is to go. Leave. Quit. Fail. Lose. We see only two choices in front of us. One that we categorize as winning and the other as losing, failing, quitting. In one, we continue to be a winner, and in the other, we become a loser, a failure, a quitter.

What will determine whether you win or lose is not your years at the company, your income level, or any other economic status. It's how you value yourself. Your dignity. Your courage.

So don't play small. Don't give in. Don't think you have no other choice but to be bullied. Instead, head held high, find a place where you belong. Find a place where you are valued. Find a place where your "me" isn't cast aside to fuel some insecure boss's fragile ego.

For far too long, not only did I not see walking away as a win; I saw it as a devastating loss. Waving the white flag of defeat. Letting the bully win. What I saw was what I was experiencing—high stress, low energy, less productivity, more sick days, inconsistent engagement, and zero satisfaction—with a chaser of fear, shame, and paranoia. Like one of the women I interviewed said, "I had lost hope."

That's the thing about workplace bullying. As targets, we are only able to see what is happening to us, and it starts to feel hopeless. There are all kinds of physiological reasons for this. Our stress response has lost its ability to operate and is on high alert. It's taken our brain captive, so we are having a difficult time thinking clearly. Thinking logically. Thinking through things the way we previously had and normally would.

One interviewee said it well: "There was a time, a long time, that I was crafty. I was quick. I was able to make decisions on a dime. More than one at a time. And then I ran into workplace bullying, not once, not twice, but three different times, and I discovered, only with the assistance of distance and time, that being mistreated over and over took such an additive toll on me that one day I went to work and it was all gone. All my craftiness, my quickness, my decision-making ability. It was all gone."

Perhaps the decision is no longer a binary one. Perhaps the in-between place is one in which targets enlist their allies from within the organization and externally and get the help they need. Perhaps today's targets will feel more equipped, empowered, and entrusted to seek help. Perhaps today's targets won't be told, when they reach out for legal advice, "It's not illegal to be an asshole." Perhaps today's targets will band together, rise up, and demand change. Perhaps psychological safety isn't a pamphlet dropped off by an organization whose name you can't remember. Perhaps diversity, equity, and inclusion actually mean fair and equal treatment. Perhaps you don't have to be a particular "way" to grow in a company. Perhaps organizations will start to take workplace bullying seriously and treat the problem versus simply moving the bully or the target. Perhaps bullying intervention becomes a thing along with employee assistance programs for bullies—they're the ones who need the assistance to stop bullying. Perhaps companies assign their own 911 hotline to a function that is not human resources, but is set up to listen to and help targets of workplace bullying, instead of protecting the company's status quo.

Perhaps companies will take workplace bullying seriously and recognize that the emotional impact of allowing, modeling, even encouraging the psychological assault of employees is significantly damaging. Perhaps they will understand and embrace the idea that you can be competitive and kind and that the truest measure of a company's success is not its bottom line but the health and well-being of its people.

Perhaps then targets will realize it isn't we who are flawed, and it isn't all of company XYZ that is flawed. It is individuals who acted horribly and lost sight of what doing the right thing really means.

DRILLS

- What is your definition of winning? Write about it. Talk about it. Think about it.

30

Advice to Players in the Bullying Drama

We've learned that quiet isn't always peace.

—AMANDA GORMAN

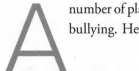number of players take the stage in this drama called workplace bullying. Here are some final thoughts I'd like to offer each.

To Those Doing the Bullying

I'm honored that you had the courage to get this far in the book. Seriously. Good job. Great first step.

There are many of you out there, and you're causing a lot of distress, anxiety, and harm to innocent people. In some cases, you're ruining people's lives.

But by now you understand, don't you? We are onto you. The world is changing. The workplace culture is changing, led by targets like me and others. And as this new movement grows, you're not only going to find it impossible to get away with what you've been doing; you're going to be drummed out of this industry and that industry. Your reputation is going to follow you like a hungry vulture—and eat you alive.

But there's hope for you if you have the courage to change. You shouldn't be defined by the worst thing you did; that said, it *is* part of your story. Acknowledge it, and make amends.

Get the help that you need. Full stop.

Meanwhile, return to an individual contributor role. In other words, you're not capable of managing others until you're able to stop taking out your own childhood trauma, tortured past, insecurities, lack of talent, or whatever else you're bringing into the office each day and inflicting on your innocent coworkers. The people with whom you work are *not* the problem. The problem is looking at you in the mirror each morning and each night.

Deal with that person. If you don't, you're destined to live a life of bullying people to compensate for your own unhappiness. And is that any way to live?

To Witnesses of Bullying

Try not to be so hard on yourself. In interviewing people for this book, those who were witnesses were just as traumatized as the targets, if not more so.

It makes sense. Witnesses feel helpless. They are in the eye of the damned-if-you-do, damned-if-you-don't storm. They are experts on survivor's guilt.

Often, they have tried to intervene only to be met with no response, or a vague or insufficient response, or a punitive response. Of those I interviewed, not one witness said that the intervention helped the target or the situation. It made the witnesses feel better that they stepped in, but there was no lasting effect on the workplace bullying. Sad? Yes. Surprising? No.

What seems to have more of an effect is when witnesses address what is happening with the target and let the target know they are seen and heard, even going so far as to say, "I'm documenting what I'm seeing from my perspective because this is indeed happening to you." Several targets I interviewed shared how much better they felt when someone noticed what was happening and commented on it. "I hate it when he belittles you like that. His ego can't help it. Know that it's not you." Or "I wish I would have said something, because I saw you change—physically. I'm sorry I didn't. I know she was causing you harm."

None of the targets I interviewed held any sort of grudge against witnesses, nor did I hold a grudge against mine. In fact, we expressed our gratitude that someone was in our corner, even if that someone was not able to positively affect our situation—or "came late to the game." It's so hard as targets to be sure we perceive the situation accurately; we begin to doubt ourselves. Simply sharing with the target that you, as a witness, read the situation the same way can be incredibly affirming.

As with targets, witnesses must evaluate the workplace culture in which they find themselves. Observing not only what is happening to the target, but also what is happening in the workplace, is important. Is there a pervasive culture of fear and intimidation? Are good people being forced out?

Here are some extra-credit assignments for witnesses: think of it as the "what *not* to say" list:

- "Well, she/he/they have never bullied me." *Respect the idea that your experience is not someone else's experience.*
- "Maybe if you . . ." *Targets are already feeling unwarranted guilt; this just adds to it, making them feel as if the problem, and the solution, is their responsibility. Neither is. Targets want to be listened to and respected, not finger-wagged.*

- "Have you thought about . . . ?" *Ditto.*
- "Wow! That person is really nice to *me*." *Again, bullies are fully capable of being fair to one person and unfair to another. This only foists more "my-fault" guilt on the target.*
- "In fact, we had your bully over to dinner." *Bullies often hide their "sins" with charm galore.*
- "This, too, shall pass." *This does nothing to validate the target's hurt and need to be listened to.*
- "Only the strong are bullied." *Bullying is bullying, regardless of the strengths or weaknesses of the targets.*
- "At least she/he/they are paying attention to you!" *The issue isn't attention; the issue is the* kind *of attention. A healthy workplace fosters healthy attention, not "I've got you in my crosshairs" attention.*
- "Suck it up." *Not helpful. Targets need allies, not Little League coaches who hide behind tough talk.*
- "Don't let the bully win." *Review your definition of "win."*

Instead, witnesses, just be there for targets. Show your support through your own actions of seeing, hearing, and documenting.

To Leaders of Businesses or Organizations

The old way of pulling the pin, dropping the grenade, and fleeing the scene to watch from the sidelines is no longer an effective leadership practice. Back in the day, you used this approach to thin out the herd, knowing that the strongest would pick up the pieces. Employees are not interested in you inflicting chaos and calling it a performance review. You won't need to show today's talent the door. They will find it themselves.

Sustaining profits matters. Sustaining a healthy workplace culture matters more. How are you engaging, inspiring, and ensuring a healthy, safe, and thriving working environment? You not only need to establish rules and referees around workplace bullying. You must model those rules.

But first, evaluate your current workplace culture. Measure the healthy and unhealthy markers that are stacking up within your company, and if you find that an imbalance exists, put a game plan together to combat it.

Be honest in your evaluation; if necessary, bring in an outside team to ensure as much. Workplace bullying doesn't just happen. It feeds on a culture of missteps, microaggressions, and mixed messages. Listen to your workforce. Do people sound joyful? Or are they telling you, "Administration is distant if not invisible; communication is sterile, emotionless; abusive leadership is rewarded; it's all about status and protecting one's job," as one interviewee shared with me.

When they tell you there's a bad seed in a function, evaluate that seed and find the seed the help they need. It may mean the bad seed is stripped of managing others and is shepherded back to an individual contributor role where they can do less damage. It may mean the bad seed is let go. Make player trades. Admit when you get it wrong. Lead with courage.

Ensure that your employee handbook has a clearly stated zero tolerance for bullying. Many companies employ a chief cultural officer, separate and independent from their chief human resources officer. Usually, human resources is tasked with just that—resourcing the organization with humans—that means hiring people, firing people, administering benefits, and protecting the company. Companies that want to walk the walk around culture need to have a more explicit organizational design to uphold the company culture and, with that, combat real-life bullying at a practical level.

Workplace bullying is pervasive, and the toll that it takes on a company's culture is directly tied to the toll it takes on a company's bottom line. Leaders, you cannot overcommunicate the values of the company, your assessment tools for the organization's culture, and the alignment between who you are externally and how you treat your employees internally.

Putting "muscle" against workplace bullying is simply talking the talk. Putting "teeth" against it through clear rules and referees with accountability and repercussions is walking the walk. This means an annual checkup of your workplace culture resulting in an accurate and honest diagnosis, a treatment plan, and frequent follow-ups throughout the year. Similar to the patient that goes in for checkups, so too must workplaces be scanned for behavioral abnormalities.

Seek help. See the Further Resources section at the end of the book to find options.

Write this down; put it somewhere that you'll see it every day; memorize it: *The culture of any organization is shaped by the worst behavior the leader is willing to tolerate.*

What is the worst behavior you are tolerating? Perhaps it is your own. It is defining your workplace culture.

To the Allies

You know who you are—not necessarily witnesses to bullying, but people willing to help a target. Yours is not a passive role. It's an active one. Often, it's an uncomfortable one. You're the see-something, say-something, do-something crew, and you play a critical role in the whole drama of workplace bullying either continuing to happen or being smoked out within your company.

That's right: *you.*

You have a voice at the decision-making table about workplace culture and within that how people are being treated. How they are being rewarded. How they know they are valued.

So pull your head out of your golf bag, EBITDA, or cocktail long enough to observe what is happening around you and who may need your help. Take note, and put your company on notice when you don't see diversity around your executive table, when you see others not getting to finish their sentence, when you observe someone playing small. Be curious.

Find out what is going on with other people beyond yourself or your circle within your organization and take a stand.

Reference material for allies can be found in the Further Resources section at the end of this book.

To the Spouses/Partners/Friends of Targets

We know you. We thank you. We love you.

Your ability to listen, to show patience, and to provide reason during such an unreasonable time provides us with exactly what we need. And you alone know that we are incapable of taking on much more than we are already dealing with at work.

We're not fully functioning in our relationship with you anymore, and your ability to understand that, to hold us close, to give us space, and *to just be* is exactly what we need.

It's tough, right? You've told us to be done with this nonsense. You've told us we're not in a safe place, a nurturing place, a place in which we're valued. You've let us know that, together, we can do anything we want to do. But when we get home from work and you see the shield come over our eyes, when "Fine" becomes the extent of a conversation, followed by the dreaded, "I just need an hour," you know what we've been through; and you know that all you can do is support us, love us, and give us space.

But what about you? How do you find the help you need? We know you don't agree with what's happening to us, so you must find an outlet for your own frustration at the situation in which we find ourselves.

Discuss what is happening with those you trust. Maintain the things in your life that are bringing you happiness and energy. And know that you doing those things is helping both of us.

Even while you feel so helpless, watching the person you love most in the world be beaten down. It is so hard on you, the one who loves us most. Thanks for sticking with us and helping us so that we can, once again, find joy in the things that give us joy.

Most specifically—you.

Finally, to the Targets

I hope you feel seen, heard, and understood.

Recognize that you are by no means alone.

And let's stop suffering in silence.

I said it before, and it bears repeating:

- **SUIT UP.** Get your uniform on and represent.
- **YELL FOR THE BALL.** Use your voice. No more doing the same thing and expecting different results.
- **TAKE YOUR SHOT.** You know what you're doing. You've hit that shot thousands of times before. Square up, get your look, release, follow through. As the great hockey player Wayne Gretzky said, "You miss 100 percent of the shots you don't take."
- **AND, ALWAYS, ALWAYS, ALWAYS FOLLOW YOUR SHOT.** Box out, bang the boards, throw some elbows.

You've got it in you. And if the game's rules and refs don't align to your ability to play your game? Then hold your head high and walk away. You've maintained your dignity, your integrity, and your identity—words and ideals that don't represent the place you work. A workplace with a bullying culture doesn't deserve your integrity and identity.

One of the most devastated targets I interviewed was a woman who admitted that it got so bad that she seriously considered driving her car into a concrete embankment. But listen to the rest of the story she offered:

Years later, I had recovered from my bullying experience. I found a way to rebuild my mental and physical health. It took years, but I now had the confidence, strength, resilience, and courage that someone else had taken from me. I had proven that my stability, mental health, and joy can stand unwavering in the face of bullying, diminishing, and marginalization, which I still witness, or encounter, in the workplace and other groups I engage with. I stand in my power every day and advocate for others to stand in theirs.

But in a similar way to how one recovers from serious injury or trauma, scars remain. Memories remain. They just don't cause pain anymore every time you feel them. But you know they are there. Although healed, these scars have reshaped the way I think, I listen, I judge. I also now have complete empathy, along with the sadness, for those for whom attempts at suicide are successful. I am no longer that person that wonders "Why?" or "How could they?" "It couldn't have been that bad."

I know it can be, and it is possible to see no other way out.

And I also know that I don't want what I experienced to happen to anyone else; I don't want anyone else to lose themselves, and enable others to take their power, agency, and joy. To make them feel unseen, unvalued, invisible. We can't stop bullies, just like we can't stop all villains. But we can thwart their efforts and diminish their effect if we empower others to recognize when it is happening, and be strong enough to stand up for them, with them, and ourselves."

Another target I interviewed said after leaving, it was easy to second-guess herself. So she created a huge list of "things to think about when I think I've made a mistake in leaving" or when "I'm wondering, did I just leave the greatest job at the greatest company in the world without a good reason?"

Remember that feeling when:

You know you're being marginalized and either you or your business is not being respected.

Colleagues and senior leaders decline/cancel meetings with you for the fourth time. Or worse, don't decline and then don't show up.

You've been exiled to headquarter your team to a remote location, and there's no parking near the building where a meeting is scheduled. You ride your bike in the rain, balancing one-handed with samples in the other, only to discover that the person you're meeting sent you a cancellation after you left your building, offered no apology, and offered no new meeting date.

When you realize your chain of command operates without decency and you realize they are in serious conflict with your personal values.

Just as it took me time, it may take you some time to figure out where you belong, but you already know where you don't belong. That's a huge step, a huger-than-huge step. And when everything is said and done, you'll come through with a more defined you. Isn't that what each of us seeks? Isn't that the apex of "know-thyself" living, the stuff that's far more enduring and important than paychecks and prestige?

Be clear on what's most important to you. Is it money, power, position—or is it about who you are, your sense of identity, your value system? Life is all about choices and consequences—if not "this," than "that." Standing up for yourself is no different. Either you can be consumed by workplace bullying, allowing it to define who you are, or you can allow your actions to define who you are. There's carnage in whatever choice you make.

One decision might save your job. But you want a decision that saves you.

You set the pace to your life.

Choose wisely.

Unfurled

The Target's Manifesto

You've never read anything like this because I've never written anything
    like this.
I've been hiding under a blanket of shame.
Silence is my enemy, though I've kept her close, like a lover.
Cuddled up with her under the covers when I'm supposed to be working,
    living, friending.
But darkness is my only friend.
The darkness of loss.
Of being lost.
The darkness of sadness.
Of being sad.
The darkness of grief.
Of grieving.
The darkness of anger.
Of being angry.
The darkness of confusion.
Of being confused.
I've been curled up in a ball of nothing.
While upright, I'm first-team-all-everything-is-fine.
Miss Happy-Go-Lucky.
A human Dyson sweeping my problems under the rug.
Next to empty prescription bottles, candy wrappers, and liquid courage.
Yeah, right.

You took my courage, and while you were at it, you shoplifted my
  confidence too.

My. Problem. Is. You.

Or so I thought.

You've had me so tangled up.

I didn't know which way was up.

But here's what's up.

I have values.

I have integrity.

I have love.

I have allies and friends.

I have dignity.

I know who I am.

I have faith.

I have smarts, spirit, and some sage advice.

You better run.

You know that target on my back? The bull's-eye I've been wearing
  around the office?

The one you put there, locked in, bowstring pulled, ready to release?

That's so yesterday's news.

We're done.

I'm done.

The system and org chart may say you've got the power.

But I'm now empowered. And I like it.

That's right. I'm boxing out, throwing elbows, and swinging big.

I'll headbutt you if I feel like it.

You don't like it?

Then, you better get the help you need.

And I'm not talking about finding another target.

Get yourself some professional help.

Because my success shouldn't make you want to harm me.

My ascension shouldn't prompt your condescension.

My competence shouldn't threaten you.

I tried playing nice. I tried being professional. I tried going Michelle Obama high.

You know what that got me?

More bullying from you, a small-minded, incompetent, zero-confidence asshole.

I'm not your friend, your Sherlock Holmes, or your punching bag.

But I just put the gloves on.

So here's how this is gonna go.

I recognize what's happening.

I even understand how it happens, given that I possess greater than average smarts.

What I don't understand is why it keeps happening.

No, we can't control the wind, but we can adjust our sails.

So watch out for that low-swinging boom.

'Cuz I've reclaimed my swagger, my smile, and my sass.

I believe in the magic of connection, counsel, and collaboration.

I believe in happiness, an afternoon run, and walking tall.

I believe in playing big, spreading my wings, and crushing the assignment.

I believe in a bigger table, pulling others up, women supporting women, and people supporting people.

In short, I believe empathy, kindness, and vulnerability are core competencies.

Love is my face paint.

I believe the workplace should be safe.

I believe the workplace should be diverse.

I believe equity, inclusion, and fairness aren't noble causes.

They're the only cause.

I believe my gain is your gain and your gain is mine.

I believe in facts on the table, being open for business, and diving through the portal to the light on the other side.

Remember? I need light to grow. Let everyone see me break through the darkness.

That doesn't mean, Get out of my way.

It means, Join me.
There's no more fight, flight, or freeze.
It's a face-off.
Bullying didn't disappear me. It transformed me.

I am unfurled.

Acknowledgments

Writing this book was a heavy lift—Herculean—made bearable only by the many spotters I had along the way. Channeling author Anne Lamott's three essential prayers—*help, thanks, wow*—and starting with one of my own—*love*—I'd like to share my gratitude.

Thank you for answering my prayer of *love*, giving and receiving unconditionally

To those who shared their stories of workplace bullying, thank you for jumping into the deep end with me. Your courage will allow those who are experiencing workplace bullying to know they are not alone, the first step toward healing.

To the Wing Women cofounders and members, thank you for giving me a safe place to land, a reason for being, and the desire to swing big.

To my siblings—Neil, Jack, Jimmy, Joe, Darrell, Andre, Brian, Nick, and Bryan—first captain, first choose. I choose you. Always.

To my parents—all of you—my mom and dad, Big Dave, Jackie, Marilyn, and Betsey, thank you for being mine.

To Jackie, Spencer, Chris, and Blue, thank you for being my loves at first sight, my loudest cheering section, and my most scrutinizing readers (minus Blue on the reading!). This book, like me, does not happen without you.

Thank you for answering my prayer of *help*, asking for assistance

To my wellness crew Ashley Melin, Brynn Graham, Dr. Colleen Parker, Denni Edlund, Erin Fricke, Ian Wilkinson, Jane Savage, Jeevani Eigen, Laura Salerno Owens, Margaret Gervais, Marjorie Genest, Nathan Mosqueda, Dr. Nicole Levitt, Pam Blair, Paul Loving, Tammie Bennett, Terri Poch, Dr. Stephanie Grootendorst, Stephanie Kjar, and super-sister-guru (SSG) Stephanie Morfitt, thank you for seeing me, for helping me find the meaning, and for providing me with the language I needed to understand what had happened to me as trauma.

To Molly Blakely, thank you for sending me a YouTube video which described "The Dark Triad" with a simple note that read: "Is this what you're experiencing at work?"

To my Adapt Training team Mary, Scott, Andrea, and Eric, thank you for putting Humpty Dumpty back together.

To my go-to Peloton trainers Aditi, Alex, Ally, Chelsea, and Robin, thank you for reintroducing me to my sweat, my swagger, and myself. Yes or yes!

To my Beta readers aunt Jane Sporre, cousin Lynn Jacobs, Ando Nikoghosyan, Courtney Pierce, Deb White, Jacy Whitaker, Jillian Gindin, John Barbour, Kate Delhagen, Konnie Wittman, Linda Barbour, Lisa Rogers, Luisa Molano, Mary Seabright, thank you for asking tough questions and motivating me to continue.

To Ashley Melin, Brian O'Connor, Kate Delhagen, Kelly Hibler, Kirsten Jones, Matt Del Negro, Neil Everett Morfitt, and Phil Cook, thank you for endorsing my proposal and, in doing so, endorsing me.

To Alex Molden, Dr. Gary Namie, Kerri Hoyt-Pack, Dr. Laura Crawshaw, Lauren Morfitt, Naomi McDougall Jones, Reema Zaman, Stephanie Morfitt, Steve Krohn, and Wendy Sweetlove, thank you for the professional scaffolding you provided.

To David Nurse, Em Stroud, Jason Booher, Jana Panfilio, Jillian Gindin, Julian Guthrie, John Paik, Ken Black, Lori Zabel, Luisa Molano, Dr. Mandy Lehto, Marcie Madsen Rowe, Nicki Eyre, and Travia Steward, thank you for giving me reps when I needed them.

To Rhona Marr, Whitney Chapman, Brian O'Connor, and Colleen Quick Thomas, thank you for your creativity and your support.

To Ferrell Dixon and Green Country Marketing Agency, thank you for keeping the work simple, focused, and fun.

To Mia Baricevic, thank you for igniting our efforts with your fresh take and talent.

To Angela Baggetta and Angela Baggetta Communications, thank you for introducing me to your world and for crushing the assignment on the daily.

Thank you for answering my prayer of *thanks*, appreciating the good we witness

To my Gomez sisters Betty (Rene Russo), Anna (Shailene Woodley), and Tori (Maya Rudolph), thank you for inviting me to *dream my dreams with you*.

To MFYC, Eric Sporre, and his wife, Susie, thank you for being so generous with your beach house getaway. It provided me with the solitude I needed to start writing.

To Kirsten Jones, thank you for being my first writing partner as we worked through our projects together at that beach house. And for introducing me to Matt Del Negro.

To Matt Del Negro, thank you for *10,000 NOs*, both the book and the podcast. And for bringing levity, focus, and the Insiders into my life when I most needed all of it.

To Jennifer Pastiloff, thank you for sharing your heart, your Cholula, and your Ojai Dream Team (especially Ellen "BRITH" Bain) with me.

To Amy Dice, Britt McVicar, Bruce Connelly, Jillian Gindin, Kate Delhagen, Katrina Galas, Kristen Falso-Capaldi, Lauren Holden Kilbane, Mandy Magnan, Mel Strong, and Michael Doherty, thank you for pushing, pressing, and pumping me up at all the right times.

Thank you for answering my prayer of *wow*, feeling awe at the world

To Jenn Director Knudsen, thank you for introducing yourself at a 2018 Jesuit High School meet and greet. Who knew that a conversation between two strangers delivering their babies to freshman year would lead me down the path of writing my first book?

To Merridawn Duckler, thank you for being my first-ever writing coach. You nudged and coaxed me along like the beautiful conductor you are.

To Bridget McEachern, thank you for reminding me that slow and steady wins the race, that help is a full sentence, and that ours is a first-team All-Star friendship. LYM.

To Matt Paknis, thank you for writing about workplace bullying in such a way that made me feel as if you were speaking directly to me. For being so generous with your time and for introducing me to Debra Englander.

To Debby Englander, thank you for reading my manuscript, reigniting my hope, and connecting me with the most well-suited agent I could have ever asked for.

To Tim Brandhorst, thank you for being that most well-suited agent, whose opinion I hold dear, and whose friendship even more so.

To the late Jimmy Bartko, thank you for being the definition of courage in sharing your story, *Boy in the Mirror,* which led me to your coauthor, Bob Welch.

To the late Don and Irene Malarkey and to Marianne McNally, thank you for sealing the deal with Bob Welch.

To editor-extraordinaire Bob Welch, thank you for sticking with me on this multiyear siege. We slayed the dragon, wrestled the dinosaur, and forged an unbreakable friendship. Thank you for helping me face my demons and bring my story to life. I would not have been able to live through the solitude of writing if not for you, your feedback, your humor, your faith, and the much-needed "Welch scrub" of my words. In fact, can you scrub this for me?

To Donya Dickerson and the sales team at McGraw Hill, Scott Sewell and the marketing team, Jeff Weeks, Maureen Harper, Pattie Amoroso, Judy Duguid, Maki Wiering, and Patricia Wallenburg, thank you for betting on a first-time writer and for leading with courage, heart, and a willingness to shine a light on "the undiscussable"—workplace bullying.

Appendix

The Playbook

W e've come to the close of the book, and I want to thank you for reading this far. I'm guessing most of you have experienced or witnessed bullying at some point in your career. My hope is that you're now better equipped to identify bullying behaviors, to understand the range of options you have as an individual to deal with bullies, and to appreciate what organizations can do to end bullying and change the cultural norms that nurture bullies.

This Playbook provides a review of the key points in the book and practical steps designed to help you:

- Understand the dynamics of workplace bullying.
- Determine the best response for your situation.
- Make a thoughtful decision on whether to stay or walk away.
- Exit in a way that's best for you if you decide to leave.

Preventing Bullying Is Everyone's Responsibility

Workplace bullying is serious. Recognizing up front that you may end up exiting—whether that's you making the decision to walk away or the

265

organization making that decision for you—is important in determining how you approach what is happening to you, how you process it, how you document it, and how you respond to it. But first things first.

If you're a leader with many direct reports and you're responsible for hiring managers, you have a responsibility to model nonbullying behaviors and to do all you can to build a culture that makes bullying behavior completely unacceptable and punishable by discharge.

But no matter your level, you have an opportunity to lead in your job and in the way you interact with colleagues. Treat everyone with respect, and if you encounter bullying—either directly or as a witness—assess the situation and take appropriate action.

In every organization, it should be a principle that all employees have the right to expect a healthy, safe, and productive workplace. One that values, motivates, and inspires people to do their best and to grow in their careers.

It should also be a principle that all employees must contribute to and participate in a workplace culture that is built on mutual trust, connection, and respect. Stopping bullying behavior is everyone's responsibility. Every day.

But while a healthy culture requires the contribution of everyone, there's no question that it all starts at the top. Every company needs leaders who are committed to building and maintaining a healthy, inclusive culture that prohibits all forms of bullying. Most important, leaders need to talk the talk and walk the walk. Lip service doesn't cut it.

Leaders must reflect their company's core values in all policies, procedures, and decisions. They must display those values in the way they interact with employees—from their colleagues in the executive suite to the most entry-level workers. And they need to make clear that they expect the same behaviors from other leaders and managers all along the line.

As an employee, you need and deserve a company that expresses values you can align with. Your company's success relies on leadership and values coming together in a way that inspires the best in employees. That can only happen when you, your team, your peers, and your colleagues feel recognized and valued. That's the recipe for a healthy workplace. In contrast, a workplace where you (and most others) are undervalued and unheard is a breeding ground for toxicity, hostility, and bullying.

If you're in such a workplace, don't let it *ruin* you. Focus on the following so you can understand the problem better and make the best decisions on how to deal with it for you, others, and the company:

1. Recognize the fundamentals of workplace bullying.
2. Understand the cultural context of workplace bullying.
3. Identify the signs of workplace bullying.
4. Navigate the steps to address workplace bullying.

Recognize the Fundamentals of Workplace Bullying

"I felt so confused by and such shame for being bullied. I tried to avoid it, hide from it, downplay it."

"I felt it was mine to fix. I felt that if I could just work harder, differently, better, the bullying would stop."

"I took complete responsibility for being mistreated, denigrated, and bullied."

What It Is

In the broadest sense, bullying is repeated health-harming mistreatment by one or more coworkers. It can be mental, emotional, and/or physical and can include multiple, repeated, intentional acts of aggression, hostility, social isolation, and/or disrespect. It can take the form of verbal abuse or behaviors perceived as threatening, intimidating, or humiliating. It can also include work sabotage.

What It Isn't

Bullying is not a one-off. It is not healthy/animated debate, creative tension/brainstorming, or a difference of opinion. It is not about being challenged. It is not about the occasional bad day, abrasiveness, or rudeness.

How It Shows Up in the Workplace

A simple way to analyze bullying is to look at the categories that we described in Chapter 1 and are displayed again here in Figure A.1. Bullying can be public or private, or it can be both. And it can be overt or covert, or it can be both.

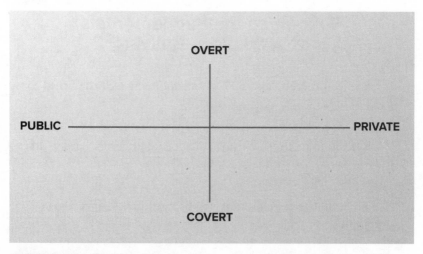

FIGURE A.1 Bullying can be overt or covert and public or private.

As we discussed, overt bullying behavior is obvious. Some examples are yelling, using foul or demeaning language, banging on a table, exhibiting threatening physical behavior or posturing, and committing actual violence.

Covert bullying behavior is hidden, nuanced, subtle. It can be quiet and confusing to the target. Some examples are work sabotage, exclusion, and intimidation.

Public bullying is witnessed by others.

Private bullying is witnessed only by the bully and the target.

How to Identify It

Once we've put language to workplace bullying, it becomes easier to identify the five bullying types and when each is happening. Recall the five bullying types from earlier in the book and shown in Figure A.2.

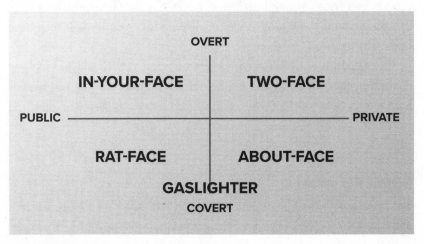

FIGURE A.2 The five bullying types.

The **In-Your-Face (IYF) bully.** IYF bullies like to diminish and insult people in public in order to display their power and show people they can get away with anything. They like to shout, bang their fists, and point fingers at their targets.

The **Rat-Face (RF) bully.** Unlike the IYF bully who insults people in public, the RF bully is sneaky and crafty. RF bullies are disrespectful and like to laugh at other people's expense. They'll sabotage your work, take credit for what you've accomplished, and undermine your effectiveness every chance they get. They're all about bolstering their status in the organization and diminishing everyone else.

The **Two-Face (TF) bully.** Think of the TF as the prototypical back-stabber. TF bullies may support you in meetings, but in private they humiliate and diminish you. Their intention is to wreck your confidence and keep you under their thumb.

The **About-Face (AF) bully.** The AF bully keeps you off balance by abruptly changing course. AF bullies often utilize passive-aggressive behaviors to keep you guessing about their true views and intentions. They might not tell you about a change in a meeting location or time to prevent you from shining in front of others. Or they'll try to trip you up by asking about something you're involved with, even though they have been fully updated by others.

The **Gaslighter.** Within the covert bullying family is a particularly disturbing kind of bully, the Gaslighter. Gaslighters are the ultimate at head games because their whole reason for being is to keep you guessing, confused, and off balance.

Apply the Model

You now know what bullying is and what it isn't. You have a four-quadrant graph to help you plot what you're experiencing or what you're witnessing, or both:

- Can you identify and categorize the type of bullying behavior you're experiencing?
- Which of the five types of bullying is happening? Most likely, it's more than just one.
- Are there patterns to the bullying—location, time of day that you can identify? Are there witnesses to the bullying?
- If you're being publicly humiliated, there are witnesses. Who are they? Can any of them become allies to you? Can any of them provide any kind of support and/or counsel to you?
- Is there anyone higher in the corporate hierarchy whom you trust to provide counsel?
- Are you clear on who your allies are and who the bully's allies are?

Target's Response Options

Once you've recognized you are the target of bullying behavior, you've charted it on your graph, and you've identified the type of bully with whom you're dealing, it's time to decide how to respond. The following options are based on equine therapy, and they work well for targets of workplace bullying:

- **IGNORE.** Refuse to engage or take notice, detach, walk away. Instead, stay connected and self-aware.
- **RESIST.** Hold your ground; set boundaries; withstand the action; exert force in opposition; counteract.
- **COMPLY.** Do as you're told.
- **ENLIST.** Mobilize your allies in the workplace to help you.

More detailed suggestions on how to respond are included in Part III Study: The Xs and Os of Workplace Bullying.

Understand the Company Culture in Which Workplace Bullying Thrives

"It was clear that there was no established policy against workplace bullying and no established referee that I could use to support me. And although I had great HR business partners and dear friends within the HR function, those in positions to help me through my own experience of workplace bullying did not."

"This validation from another woman was exactly what I needed to truly move beyond the effects of being bullied. It didn't stop the bully's behavior, but it helped me to know there was someone else who saw what he was doing to me."

Get the Lay of the Land

To understand bullying, it's important to analyze your company's culture. Is bullying clearly prohibited, or is it passively accepted? The answer will factor into how you respond.

First, find out if there is an established policy against workplace bullying within your organization. What is the HR presence in your organization, and what role does HR play? Is there an established referee and/or intermediary to help you work through workplace bullying?

Values

Objectively evaluate the culture in which you work. Do the values of the organization match your own? Perhaps they did at one time and now they no longer do. This can be tricky because companies can say they stand for certain values and even share those values publicly, but once inside their walls, things are very different. These values are not upheld.

So ask yourself: "Do I still believe in what this place stands for? Does the company still stand for what it once did? Are our values aligned? Is this an aberration, or is this a reflection of the company culture?"

The Lowest Common Denominator

What is the worst behavior being tolerated at your company today that you're aware of? Examples may run the spectrum from the most obvious aggression, to the more subtle exclusion, favoritism, to demeaning texts/emails.

Referees and Procedures

Is there anyone higher within the organization who might be an ally in responding to a bullying situation? Are your friends and trusted advisors likely to support you, or will they tell you to back off from the matter and learn to live with it as best you can?

As you assess the level of support you think you'll receive, keep the people in your support group informed. Use documentation to explain to them what is happening. If your bully has a habit of diminishing you in public settings, follow up afterward with correspondence to others who were in the room and bore witness to the bullying. By doing so, you are gathering additional documentation and facts that will assist your case.

For example, you might send an email like this:

During today's [add the date in parentheses] quarterly business meeting, I was repeatedly humiliated by [name of person] in these ways. It looked like this treatment of me was making you uncomfortable as well and you were ready to say something about it. What was your experience like during that meeting?

Identify How Workplace Bullying Shows Up

"When I shared this with my other manager, his response was, 'That's why we put you there. Do your job.'"

"I started to hear that she was telling people I had gone to HR and that I need a medical leave because I'm 'crazy.'"

"When I reached out to members of the Executive Leadership Team, I always prefaced my message with, 'This is what's happening, but I don't want you to do anything about it,' while quickly diverting to business-related topics to steer the conversation away from my own humiliation."

When and What to Document

After you've developed a deeper understanding of workplace bullying, the types of bullies you might encounter, and the culture in which they operate, it's time to start identifying the specific actions, speech, and behaviors that constitute bullying. Your first step should be detailed documentation.

Commit to creating detailed notes of every instance of workplace bullying. Be as specific as possible. Recount entire conversations verbatim as best you can. Include locations, times, dates, and witnesses in your notes. Do this after every bullying interaction.

Any kind of investigative process requires that you describe the who, what, when, where, and why as best you can. Determining a motive is difficult, so keep that in mind when you're documenting the "why" of your interactions.

Keep these notes in a safe place where you can easily locate them even if you are no longer employed at the company. An easy way to do this is to write an email to yourself using a personal email account—not your company email.

In addition to documenting your experiences of workplace bullying, make it a point to retell your stories to a trusted colleague and ask the colleague to document them as well. Note the dates when the conversations occurred. Again, be as specific as possible and recount the entire conversation verbatim.

Here's a template:

Subj: Interaction at work on 10/14/2021Functional Meeting—Fall 2022

[Specific conference room and number of attendees, including names]

I was presenting my slides when . . . [who, what, when, where, and why].

When Bullying Is Reported to You

When an employee approaches you about being bullied, that should be a trigger that it's your responsibility to do something—regardless of whether you're the person's manager or simply a colleague. That's true even if the person prefaces the conversation with, "I don't want you to do anything about this."

Be sure you understand your company's policies. Many companies have an anti-harassment policy that states that known or suspected issues of harassment and/or a hostile work environment must be reported. So you may have no choice but to report it if someone confides to you they've been a victim of bullying.

In most cases, the person being targeted is looking for some kind of support and ideas about how to proceed. You should be an empathetic sounding board. My hope is that by having read this book, you can help the person understand the situation and explain some of the options for dealing with the bully.

If you're the person's manager or higher up in the organization, you have more responsibility. Again, understand and stay in compliance with your company policies. But even if your company does not have a strict anti-harassment policy, you need to determine a course of action to stop the bullying, protect the targeted person, and make the bully accountable. Anything less is unacceptable.

Rules and Refs

If you've established that there is a policy against workplace bullying and that there is an intermediary to support your situation, you may feel safe enough to meet with the bully in a private, one-on-one meeting. *Don't* do it. In order to provide objective documentation, it's important that you ask the intermediary to join you.

Let the bully know exactly what you've been experiencing, using your documentation. This meeting is not a discussion. You are notifying the bully of the bullying behavior toward you.

You're taking this step because you feel confident in your organization's anti–workplace bullying policy as well as the support you will be provided should the behavior continue. You're putting the bully on notice that he or she or they must change their behavior, or you will pursue the matter further.

Here's an example of what you might say:

> Thank you for meeting with me today. I wanted to make you aware of our company's antibullying policy. It clearly states—I am making you aware of this because your actions toward me on a consistent basis are considered workplace bullying. Here are the examples I want to share with you. At this time, I want to make you aware

that this is bullying and to give you the opportunity to correct the behavior.

In the best-case scenario, perhaps the problem disappears with your identifying the bullying behavior. You've brought it to the person's attention, you've backed it up with facts, and the bully addresses it. Everyone moves on.

If the bullying continues, you should continue to document your interactions with the bully and consider your options for escalating the matter, leaving the organization, and/or enlisting an attorney.

No Rules, No Refs

If you've discovered that there is no established policy and no established intermediary, don't go to the meeting alone. You need a witness. Find a third party who is willing to attend the meeting with you.

Before the meeting with the bully, you and your chosen third party should determine the best approach. Will the intermediary facilitate the meeting or simply be present with you while you do all the talking, using your documentation of what you've experienced as your guide? What are the objectives of the meeting and the next steps in the process? Continue to take these steps if the bullying continues and/or if you sense any sort of danger or potential retaliation.

Always Go Two-Deep

Two-deep leadership means that you always have an ally with you when you anticipate being in front of your bully. If this is not possible, immediately share the outcome of the meeting with someone else and/or record the meeting. In some states, but not all, you can record a conversation on the phone without express consent. But face-to-face, you need consent. Make sure you understand your own state's law on taping surreptitiously. In any event, keep the best record you can of the meeting.

Repeat: Do *not* meet alone with the bully in an organization that does not have established policies and established referees.

While this certainly sounds cumbersome, it's meant to help you deal with an intractable situation. When an organization understands the lengths you'll take because you are not comfortable with a particular employee, the chance the organization will address it will increase. Could it address the problem by removing you from the company? Yes. But by taking these steps, you're drawing attention and declaring that you do not feel comfortable or safe meeting with an employee one-on-one. This should, at the very least, increase the chance that you and your situation will be taken seriously and potentially diminish the chance that you will be removed from the company. You're establishing a new rules-of-engagement protocol as opposed to not being taken seriously. If you do this in a respectful way with documentation, the odds are higher that both you and your concerns will be taken seriously.

Navigate the Steps to Address the Bullying: What's Your Decision?

"As a result of coming forward, my direct-line manager's guidance was for me to ignore the bully and to try and steer clear of future encounters. This was impossible because the bully was my dotted-line manager."

"When I was told that even though all the bullying behaviors that I had reported were 'significantly substantiated,' the bully would remain in role and the organization would try and find me something else to do, I realized that HR was not there to help me."

"When I was trying to determine my options, I had a conversation with an attorney. His response to all the information I shared? 'Unfortunately, it's not illegal to be an asshole.'"

"Once I decided to leave, there would be no Hail Mary. All I had left was my dignity and my professionalism. My grace."

Xs and Os

After each meeting in which the bully is present, meet with your manager, the HR business partner, and the bully's manager to share the facts to ensure these people know what has been happening. Follow up with a written summary of your conversation. This puts those who are making the decisions on notice that you're closely monitoring the situation and their responses.

For example:

> Thank you for meeting with me today and reviewing my summary about my uncomfortable encounter with [name of bully]. I appreciate that you found [his or her] behavior offensive and not in compliance with our values here at work. As a result, do I understand you correctly that your guidance to me is to ignore [his or her] words and behavior and try to steer clear of future encounters?

This example highlights an inappropriate response from a company representative; yet it can often be the recommendation targets receive.

Footprint

Stop commingling your personal digital footprint with your work footprint. Maintain a separate, personal mobile phone and a separate laptop, and keep all personal correspondence, images, and social media visits off your company-supplied electronic tools. Manage social media posts so as not to blur the lines between personal and professional.

Dealing with the HR and Legal Departments

If the bullying behavior continues, notify HR and your organization's legal department, and provide them with your documentation. Ensure you understand what the follow-up actions will be and when. A nonresponse by HR is an indication that you will need to escalate further.

Keep in mind that in some companies HR and the legal team prioritize what's best for the company and for the individuals involved—including the bully. Their first step will most likely be to contact the bully and let him or her know about your allegations. Prepare yourself for things to get worse as the bully is made aware that you've elevated the situation, which will most likely intensify the bullying behavior directed at you. Prepare your allies as your witnesses, and recognize where you are in your preparation process of potentially exiting the company. (See the later Checklist for Walking Away.)

Hiring Your Own Attorney

If the bullying behavior continues, consider seeking legal counsel. You may find helpful and free information online through the Equal Employment Opportunity Commission or a fair employment agency in your state.

If you seek external legal counsel, look for someone experienced in representing professionals in bringing workplace harassment charges against employers. You want to secure an attorney that is seen as a threat to your organization.

Consider what if anything you would want to be made public. The more comfortable you are with your situation being public, the more leverage your attorney may have.

Stay or Go

If you stay, pull your allies/friends/supporters close, and continue to document the bullying behaviors until either you or your bully is moved to another position. This is not a passive wait-it-out period if you've determined you will stay at the company. It's an active hunt for a new role.

What other support will you need if you stay? An employee assistance program, additional wellness help such as working from home, and so on? What are the various factors to consider, and how do you weigh the variables of this decision? Enlist your support system to help you think through the pro-con list of exiting the company. Consider whom you might use as a reference if you decide to exit.

Fast Break

If you make the decision to walk away, this shouldn't come as a complete surprise. You've known this was a possibility from the start, but it can still be a shock to your system. Be professional and prepared should you be walking away on your own accord or if the organization is exiting you. Put yourself in the best possible position. (See the later Checklist for Walking Away.)

Grief

Exiting your workplace can be overwhelming and sad. It will take some time and expert help to be able to evaluate your experience from a professional standpoint instead of an emotional one. Additional resources— physical activity, mental experts, a wellness tribe—can be found in the Further Resources section at the end of the book.

Values

Try to put yourself first and to remind yourself of why you ended up leaving. It most likely had something to do with the misalignment of your values and those of the company. Instead of equating leaving to losing or failing, start discussing it as the best decision you made in your professional career. The knowing is the easy thing; the extracting is the difficult one. It's going to help you in the long haul.

A Checklist for Walking Away

As you assess your future, consider the following:

Professional Reflection
- Is this an opportunity for you to expand your ideas about your career? Don't box yourself in.
- Discreetly update your résumé, LinkedIn profile, and network with contacts and recruiters.
- Consider securing a new job before making your move.

Financial Reflection

- Save. Save. Save. Put as much money away as possible, and use whatever financial tools are available to you to do so (e.g., unemployment benefits, deferred compensation if that applies to you).
- Project your expenses, namely insurance. Do your homework so there are no surprises.
- If applicable, complete all cash-out refinances, home equity line of credit, and home purchases before you depart a W-2 job. It's difficult to get these types of loans once you leave a W-2 job.
- If you have a spouse or partner, plan together to figure out how one income can bridge the gap and/or how soon you'll need to find another job and return to work.
- Achieve and maintain zero debt.
- Nail down a college plan if it applies.
- Secure a financial planner, or seek online resources.
- Diversify your investment portfolio so you're not overinvested in the company's stock.

Work Product

- Secure a digital copy and a hard copy of positive performance reviews, correspondence from superiors regarding exemplary performance, customer reviews, and so on, in an effort to build your personal archives for referrals in later job searches. Oftentimes, companies do not or cannot give referrals for employees who leave. They may only confirm your employment duration.
- Take your work with you. Any work that is considered public domain, that you authored, and that in no way violates confidentiality or nondisclosure agreements should be retained by you. Enlist a witness to what you are removing.
- Have a personal phone, and ensure all personal information/photos are transferred to it.

Benefit Reflection

- Pay attention to major milestones—timing of vesting periods, timing of bonus payouts. Secure all details about options and expiration dates before exiting.
- Verify if you will be paid out for remaining vacation or sick time. Use it if you will not get paid out. Exhaust your sabbatical time (if your organization provides sabbaticals) because there is no financial payout for not taking it.
- Gather intel on company trends for noncompete enforcement, separation packages, and so on.
- Research your own insurance needs, and check benefit start dates. *Example:* Make your effective date the first day of the month, not the last day of the month, to allow yourself at least one more full month of healthcare insurance. If you exit on the last day of the month, the COBRA clock or the uninsured clock starts with the new month.

———

After considering everything, when confronted with workplace bullying, you have to respond to the bully, and to the degree possible, marshal the resources of your organization to provide support to stop the bullying behavior. I hope this playbook provides you with the information and a go-to plan that will help you navigate these very difficult waters. And in the end, walking away must be seen as the courageous, proactive, and positive option that it is for many.

Further Resources

The following resources were suggested by the people who were interviewed for this book.

Organizations

- 988 Suicide and Crisis Lifeline, https://988lifeline.org/
- Conduct Change, https://www.conductchange.co.uk
- The Equal Employment Opportunity Commission, https://www.eeoc.gov
- Inspired Companies, https://inspiredcompanies.global
- The Liberty Collective, https://www.thelibertycollective.com
- Natural Lifemanship, https://naturallifemanship.com
- Workplace Bullying Institute, https://workplacebullying.org

Apps

- Alphy, https://www.alphyco.com
- Insight Timer, https://insighttimer.com/
- Mood Meter, https://moodmeterapp.com
- Peloton, https://www.onepeloton.ca/

Podcasts

- *#Raising Athletes*, with Kirsten Jones and Susie Walton
- *10,000 Nos*, with Matt Del Negro
- *A Bit of Optimism*, with Simon Sinek
- *Bossed Up*, with Emilie Aries
- *Breakthrough*, with Travia Steward
- *Clowning Around*, with Em Stroud
- *Enough*, with Dr. Mandy Lehto
- *Good Life Project*, with Jonathan Fields
- *Huberman Lab*, with Andrew D. Huberman
- *The Kelly Roach Show*, with Kelly Roach
- *My Wakeup Call*, with Dr. Mark Goulston
- *The Plot Thickens*, with Ben Mankiewicz
- *Pivot & Go*, with David Nurse
- *The Show Up Society*, with Tammie Bennett
- *Spaces Between*, with Gina Minardi
- *Tara Brach*, Tara Brach
- *The Tim Ferriss Show*, with Tim Ferriss
- *Unf*ck Your Brain*, with Kara Loewentheil
- *Worklife*, with Adam Grant

Books

- *Alpha Girls*, by Julian Guthrie
- *Atomic Habits*, by James Clear
- *The Beauty of What Remains*, by Steve Leder
- *Becoming*, by Michelle Obama
- *Between the World and Me*, by Ta-Nehisi Coates
- *Cross Purposes*, by Bob Welch
- *The Culture Code*, by Daniel Coyle
- *Extreme You*, by Sarah Robb O'Hagan
- *Finding Me: A Memoir,* by Viola Davis
- *Firing Back*, by Jodie-Beth Galos and Sandy McIntosh
- *The Gifts of Imperfection*, by Brené Brown

- *High on Heart,* by Jessie May Wolfe
- *How to Be an Anti-Racist,* by Ibram X. Kendi
- *Huddle,* by Brooke Baldwin
- *I Am Yours,* by Reema Zaman
- *The Infinite Game,* by Simon Sinek
- *Mastering Civility,* by Christine Porath
- *The Mindful Path to Self-Compassion,* by Christopher K. Germer
- *A New Earth,* by Eckhart Tolle
- *On Being Human,* by Jennifer Pastiloff
- *Radical Acceptance,* by Tara Brach
- *Repacking Your Bags,* by Richard J. Leider and David A. Shapiro
- *Rising Strong,* by Brené Brown
- *Successful Leaders Aren't Bullies,* by Matt Paknis
- *Talking to Strangers,* by Malcolm Gladwell
- *Taming the Abrasive Manager,* by Dr. Laura Crawshaw
- *Thrive,* by Arianna Huffington
- *Untamed,* by Glennon Doyle
- *What Happened to You?,* by Bruce Perry and Oprah Winfrey
- *Wolfpack,* by Abby Wambach
- *The Wrong Kind of Women: Inside Our Revolution to Dismantle the Gods of Hollywood,* by Naomi McDougall Jones
- *Year of YES,* by Shonda Rhimes
- *You Are a Badass,* by Jen Sincero

Index

About
the Author

MEGAN CARLE began her career as a customer service representative at Nike in 1988. Over the next 30 years, she rose steadily through the executive ranks of one of the world's most successful companies and best-known brands. Carle was elevated, multiple times, to roles no woman had ever held before—including stints leading international teams in London and Amsterdam—culminating in the job of vice president/general manager of North America Basketball.

After leaving Nike, she founded Carle Consulting LLC, providing strategic marketing advice to consumer products companies as well as executive coaching to emerging leaders from start-up to C-suite. She speaks frequently about corporate culture, leadership, and workplace bullying to executives and employees of major brands across the United States.

She and her husband live in Portland, Oregon, with their two children and dog.